SPIRIT *of* FIRE

(Fondation Teilhard de Chardin)

SPIRIT *of* FIRE

The Life and Vision of
Pierre Teilhard de Chardin

REVISED EDITION

Ursula King

ORBIS  BOOKS

Maryknoll, New York 10545

Founded in 1970, Orbis Books endeavors to publish works that enlighten the mind, nourish the spirit, and challenge the conscience. The publishing arm of the Maryknoll Fathers and Brothers, Orbis seeks to explore the global dimensions of the Christian faith and mission, to invite dialogue with diverse cultures and religious traditions, and to serve the cause of reconciliation and peace. The books published reflect the views of their authors and do not represent the official position of the Maryknoll Society. To learn more about Maryknoll and Orbis Books, please visit our website at www.maryknollsociety.org.

Manufactured in the United States of America
Design: Roberta Savage

King, Ursula.
Spirit of fire : the life and vision of Pierre Teilhard de Chardin / Ursula King.—Revised edition.
    pages cm
  Includes bibliographical references and index.
  ISBN 978-1-62698-114-0 (pbk.)
  1. Teilhard de Chardin, Pierre. 2. Jesuits—Biography. 3. Paleontologists—Biography. I. Title.
BX4705.T39K56 2015
230'.2092--dc23
[B]

                                                                          2014042094

*This book is dedicated to
my friend, the Swiss Teilhard scholar Richard Brüchsel, S.J.,
in celebration of his ninetieth birthday, and
to my husband, Anthony Douglas King,
in gratitude for more than fifty years' love, companionship,
and continuing encouragement, and also
to our daughters, their partners, and our grandchildren.*

CONTENTS

Pope presents fresh look at creation

The following editorial appeared in the Pittsburgh Post-Gazette:

When Pope Francis said last week that evolution and the Big Bang theory did not conflict with Catholic teaching, it really wasn't news. This pope just has a talent for framing long-held beliefs in a fresh way, as he has done before in taking up the cause of the poor. This news was more a timely reminder.

Despite that unfortunate business with Galileo 400 years ago over his alleged heretical beliefs on the movement of planets, anybody who has been paying attention lately understands that the church has not been at war with scientific knowledge. Other popes have expressed the same ideas, especially on evolution.

Pope Francis, though, has a way of making headlines. In his remarks before the Pontifical Academy of Sciences, he may have raised the eyebrows of everyone from cardinals on down. "When we read about creation in Genesis, we run the risk of imagining God was a magician, with a magic wand able to do everything. But that is not so," the pope said. "He created hu-man beings and let them develop according to the internal laws that he gave to each one, so they would reach their fulfillment."

In other words, the creator God had a process — "a supreme principle" as he called it. "The Big Bang, which today we hold to be the origin of the world, does not contradict the interven-tion of the divine creator but, rather, requires it," Pope Francis said. "Evolution in nature is not inconsistent with the notion of creation, because evolution requires the creation of beings that evolve."

This is a thought that has also occurred to many believers in other branches of Christianity who have wrestled to reconcile their beliefs with the evidence of the workings of evolution in the natural world. What if the Almighty used evolution (and the Big Bang) as His means of creation?

Once again Pope Francis' intellect has clarified an issue, which in the United States at least has brought shadows, not light. The pope's words are also a reminder that those who regard evolution as hostile to Christian belief are actually a minority.

They relate in overlapping and changing networks. Old models of membership become less reliable, something many religious institutions are already struggling with. They need to network with people who think of themselves as religious individuals, offering connection and the rich religious pixels of their tradition while recognizing that they may be only one of many sources in someone's religious identity.

In the emerging digital culture authority is not rooted in position or title. Neither professors nor pastors are granted authority because of their role. Rather religious authority is conversational. It is granted to those whose contribution is engaging, challenging and useful. Success is measured in the quality of the conversation. Successful leaders and institutions will be those that use these fluid digital systems of meaning to engage people in substantive conversations that contribute to their spiritual and social well-being.

▶ *Mahan is the Ralph E. and Norma E. Peck chair in religion and public communication at the Iliff School of Theology in Denver and author of "Media, Religion and Culture."*

You and your sister were among thousands of Hidden Children who survived by hiding your Jewish identify. How did those years in hiding define your life?

Sharing my story has helped me heal inside and become the person I am today. For a long time, I couldn't talk about it, but I have come to understand it better as an adult. When I began to talk about it, things I had repressed came out. Now when I talk to teachers and students, I bring a positive message.

What is it like returning to where you were born, accompanying educators on seminars on the Holocaust and genocide?

It is an amazing journey. For two weeks, we bond as a family. We start in Berlin, at site of the Wannsee Conference where the Final Solution decision was made, travel by bus to the sites of the Theresienstadt concentration camp near Prague, Auschwitz near Krakow and Warsaw. We end in Holland going to the places where I was hidden. We met one of my rescuers, the daughter of the second family that sheltered us. In August she was recognized

Preface

A Great and Splendid Adventure

Pierre Teilhard de Chardin's life was one of passionate intellectual and spiritual adventure. It was a life full of expeditions, travel, and exploration, of relentless questioning and searching for new answers, a life full of extraordinary action accompanied by deep reflection and sustained by a fervent faith. While roaming the earth and working on his scientific tasks in geology and palaeontology, his mind was asking profound questions about the nature and direction of cosmic and human evolution, the meaning and goal of life in the universe. This led him to undertake research into the origins of the human being and all life on earth. Steeped in the evolutionary vision of contemporary science, he produced in his work one of the strongest

The chain of volcanos in the Puy country of Auvregne. (Fondation Teilhard de Chardin)

affirmations of the Christian faith in the incarnation—the presence of God in all things through Christ, a presence strongly felt, passionately believed in, and portrayed with a spiritual power rarely matched by other writers.

The Christian faith was central to his vision and work. Yet he could say that he, like everybody else, walked in the shadows of faith, and that believing is not seeing. With rare insight he diagnosed the pulse of the modern world and asked: Where is its frantic activity going? What is its ultimate goal? He also felt that many people lacked a sense of purpose, meaning, and direction, so that it is imperative to animate and energize to the maximum our zest for life, to discover the value of our work and efforts, to strengthen the bonds of the human community around the world through the powers of love and collaboration, to find new models of holiness and seek a new spirituality, a mysticism of action, commensurate with the world as we know it today.

Teilhard was an ardent seeker, in love with all of life, a modern scientist, a dedicated priest, and a fervent mystic, but also a great friend and spiritual adviser to many, and a great writer. Yet for many he is too complex, too bold a thinker, too difficult a writer, too daring an innovator. He has not been given the appreciation and attention he deserves. The power of his synthesis and vision is not always fully understood; the energizing resources of his life-affirming spirituality are little drawn upon by contemporary spiritual writers. He deserves to be better known, his writings more appreciated and critically studied, his example more followed.

He was in love with the world, the world as a vast, living, tangible organism to which human beings belong as an integral part, and he was in love with God whose creative energy and living spirit pulsate through all that is. He was also a deeply faithful member of the Catholic Church, which opposed and criticized him while alive and has not yet fully recognized the treasures of his spiritual legacy since he died.

Auspicious Light Pagoda, China.

The events of his life and the pattern of his thought are closely intertwined. I shall try to capture the rhythm of their unfolding and growth from cradle to grave in the following pages. Two of the most decisive influences in shaping the overall direction of his thought were the formative experiences of World War I, and the long stay in China (between 1923 and 1946), where he worked closely with Chinese and Western scientists from different countries. He was always a passionate thinker full of fire. The boldness of his ideas singles him out as a man of great originality. The extraordinary intensity of his capacity to love, and be loved, makes him a very special human being, whereas his daring pursuit of all things spiritual, his hope and trust amid all the trials and deep suffering of his life, prove him a man of extraordinary faith blessed by great grace and saintliness.

Acknowledgments

I would like to express my deep thanks to all the people who have helped me in producing this book. My interest in Pierre Teilhard de Chardin was first awakened many years ago by an inspiring teacher, the Belgian Jesuit, Père Paul Henry, S.J. who, in 1962, when the Vatican published a *Monitum* (reprimand) forbidding the teaching of Teilhard de Chardin's ideas in Catholic seminaries, proceeded to give a series of public lectures on Teilhard at the Institut Catholique in Paris, where I was then a student. This first introduction, at a time when few of Teilhard's writings were available in print and mostly only accessible in cyclostyled form, led to many years' research which eventually resulted in my doctorate at King's College, University of London. An extensive reading of Teilhard's writings and correspondence, personal interviews as well as research into Teilhard's French origins and travels in China enabled me to collect material for several books.

The first of these was *Towards a New Mysticism: Teilhard de Chardin and Eastern Religions* (London: Collins, and New York: Seabury Press, 1980) now available in a revised, extended edition as *Teilhard de Chardin and Eastern Religions. Spirituality and Mysticism in an Evolutionary World* (Mahwah, NJ: Paulist Press, 2011). The second consisted of a series of essays, *The Spirit of One Earth: Reflections on Teilhard de Chardin and Global Spirituality* (New York: Paragon House, 1989). It was followed by the first edition of this biography, *Spirit of Fire. The Life and Vision of Teilhard de Chardin* (Maryknoll, NY: Orbis Books, 1996), and also by the Bampton Lectures 1996, delivered at the University of Oxford and published as *Christ in All Things. Exploring Spirituality with Teilhard de Chardin* (Maryknoll, NY: Orbis Books and London: SCM Press, 1997). This book dealt with diverse aspects of contemporary Christian spirituality from a Teilhardian perspective, including spirituality and evolution, interfaith dialogue, the voices of women in Third World theology as well as a discussion of mysticism-in-action.

I would like to acknowledge especially the encouragement given to my earlier work by the late Dr. Joseph Needham, the great scholar of science and civilization of China, and a deeply spiritual person, who knew Teilhard while working for UNESCO in post-war Paris. Dr. Needham always expressed much admiration and respect for Teilhard. He spoke of him as "the greatest prophet of this age" whose importance would become ever clearer as time goes on. Joseph Needham was right in saying this, as Teilhard's ideas seem to attract much new interest, especially during the sixtieth anniversary of his death, celebrated in April 2015.

When Teilhard's works were first published after his death (thirteen volumes in French between 1955 and 1976, and their English translations between 1959 and 1978), they attracted worldwide attention; some became international bestsellers. But since his numerous essays were not published in chronological order, which would have more clearly explained the origin and development of Teilhard's ideas, they are often difficult to understand. They are frequently quoted out of context, since few people know his works in sufficient depth to interpret and communicate Teilhard's thought competently.

While interest in Teilhard's ideas declined after the 1970s, a significant revival of interest is now occurring during the twenty-first century, when some of his bold, anticipatory thinking seems so much more germane to our current concerns.

I hope this biography, which incorporates new research and recent publications on Teilhard, will help to strengthen this renewed interest in Teilhard's ideas among a wide readership, not least the young who would gain most from his all-embracing and dynamic evolutionary vision of hope for all of humanity.

For the chapters dealing with China I found much inspiration through a wonderful journey made in 1994 by rail along the ancient silk road, followed by visits to Shanghai and Beijing, later supplemented by further travels along the Yangtze river, to the province of Shandung, and to the caves of Zhoukoudian where the fossils of Peking Man were found in the 1930s. These travels enabled me to understand many aspects of the context of Teilhard's life in China more fully. Earlier discussions and correspondence with Professor Zhuo Xinping from the Institute of World Religions at the Chinese Academy of Social Sciences in Beijing also helped to clarify further details.

For the help given with the photographic research I owe special thanks to the Fondation Teilhard de Chardin and the Éditions du Seuil in Paris, and to Georgetown University Library Archives in Washington. I was also helped in this work by the personal interest and many kindnesses shown to me by Solange Soulié and Janetta Warre, both now deceased. Last, but not least, I want to thank the University of Bristol for the award of a University Research Fellowship, which initially gave me the time needed to write this book, and the Bristol Arts Faculty Research Fund for providing a travel grant to undertake some of the research for the illustrations. The quotations from Teilhard's works are taken from the existing English translations and follow their conventions. The translations use exclusive language which has been changed where possible, but on the whole has been retained, as have been the idiosyncratic English expressions used by Teilhard in letters written in English to some of his American and English friends. When I have retranslated a passage from Teilhard's essays in French, because of a different meaning of the original text, I have indicated this in the Notes at the end of the book.

I am deeply grateful to Orbis Books for the help given over many years in publishing my books. Special thanks are due the Publisher, Robert Ellsberg, for his great interest and continuous encouragement, and to Maria Angelini for her editorial work on this revised edition.

This book especially wishes to remember the many remarkable women who gave so much of their energy, love, and dedication to Teilhard, providing him with inspiration and support during his lifetime, in particular his cousin Marguerite Teillard-Chambon, Lucile Swan, and Jeanne Mortier, who made such great efforts in getting Teilhard's religious and philosophical essays published, so that others could share in his great vision of the world suffused with the fire of the Spirit.

Last, not least, I would like to acknowledge the helpful interviews given by Teilhard's acquaintances, friends, and relatives between 1973 and 1975: Dr. Claude Cuénot (Paris, March 1973), Mme Béatrice d'Hauteville (Paris, February 1974), Dr. Joanna Kelley (London, March 1974 and June 1975), Fr. Pierre Leroy, SJ (Versailles, March 1973 and February 1974; Chantilly, September 1975), Fr. Henri de Lubac, SJ, (Lyons, September 1973), Mr. Gabriel Marcel (Paris, March 1973), Fr. Gustave Martelet, SJ (Lyons, September 1973; Chantilly, September 1975), Mr. Jacques Masui (Paris, February 1974; Geneva, May 1975), Mlle Jeanne Mortier (Paris, May 1973 and February 1974; Orléans, September 1973; Chantilly, September 1975), Dr. Joseph Needham (Cambridge, May 1973 and May 1975), Fr. René d'Ouince, SJ (Paris, March 1973), Mr. & Mme Joseph Teilhard de Chardin (Paris, March 1973 and February 1974; Les Moulins (Auvergne), September 1973), Mlle Alice Teilhard-Chambon (Paris, March 1973).

Childhood in the Auvergne

Auvergne molded me. . . . Sarcenat in Auvergne gave me my first taste of the joys of discovery. . . . To Auvergne I owe my delight in nature.

The Auvergne is an ancient central province of France. It possesses many extinct volcanoes that give the landscape its characteristic appearance of massive rocks and mountains, of high peaks and endless wooded hills. Its highest summit is the Puy de Dôme. It is not far from there that Marie Joseph Pierre Teilhard de Chardin was born on May 1, 1881, in the old family château of Sarcenat, a few miles outside the provincial capital, Clermont-Ferrand. Among his given names it was the third one, Pierre, by which his family and

"It is a terrifying thing to have been born: I mean, to find oneself, without having willed it, swept irrevocably along on a torrent of fearful energy which seems as though it wished to destroy everything it carries with it."
—"The Mass on the World"

View from the window of Teilhard's childhood home, the Château de Sarcenat. (Fondation Teilhard de Chardin)

1

Church of Notre Dame du Port in Clermont-Ferrand.

"In very truth, it is God, and God alone whose Spirit stirs up the whole mass of the universe in ferment."
—"The Mystical Milieu"

friends always called him. His family's surname is a double one, with the principal part—Teilhard—put first, and it is by this name that he was often referred to in later years.

Besides their country seat the family also had a house in Clermont-Ferrand, where they regularly spent the winter. Many houses in the town were built of volcanic rock, as was the thirteenth-century cathedral whose bells could be heard at Sarcenat when the wind blew in the right direction. At the end of the nineteenth century Clermont-Ferrand was a quiet, rural country town with a proud history going back to the Romans. Its inhabitants had been converted to Christianity in the early centuries of the Christian era. During the Middle Ages this town, situated at the center of much-traveled trade routes, became the seat of an important bishopric. Its wealth is still visible in the beautiful twelfth-century Romanesque church Notre Dame du Port and in the town's Gothic cathedral. The city is famous as the birthplace of the seventeenth-century scientist and religious philosopher Blaise Pascal, an ardent defender of the Christian faith at a time of scientific innovation and change. Teilhard de Chardin was to follow a similar vocation in our own time.

Teilhard's family belonged to an ancient noble lineage of the Auvergne. His father, Emmanuel Teilhard de Chardin, was very much a country gentleman who devoted most of his time to the running of several estates, but this left him free enough to pursue a number of hobbies and intellectual interests. In May 1875 he married Berthe-Adèle de Dompierre d'Hornoy, a young noblewoman from the Picardy in northern France, and a great-grandniece of Voltaire. Both Teilhard's parents were devout Catholics but it was especially his mother who had a strong, unswerving faith of great simplicity, marked by a fervent devotion to the Christian saints and mystics.

Pierre was the fourth of eleven children born to his parents. The eldest was Albéric, followed by Marielle, who died in infancy. The third was Françoise, Pierre's older sister, whom he much admired. After Pierre, seven more children were born: Marguerite-Marie, who later suffered from a permanent illness, his brothers Gabriel, Olivier, and Joseph, his youngest sister, Louise, followed by the two boys, Gonzague and Victor. It was a home full of life and happiness. The family was close-knit and lived a stable rural life punctuated by the rhythm of the seasons, the pattern of daily devotions, and the round of religious festivals.

In the past the enormous mountain mass of the Auvergne had kept the region isolated and remote. The French Revolution had never made much impact on the inhabitants of the Auvergne. It seems almost ironic that in the late nineteenth century Pierre Teilhard de Chardin should have been born there as the sixth direct descendant of Voltaire's sister.

Both Pierre's parents were a strong influence on him. They gave him many lifelong memories of a happy, self-contained, and sheltered family life which extended to the wider family circle, especially to his cousins, the Teillard-Chambons, a differently named branch of the family who lived a few miles away in Clermont-Ferrand.

Teilhard was devoted to his mother, his *sainte maman*, who conveyed to him a deep love of the Christian mystics and a lifelong devotion to the sacred heart of Jesus. His father was highly respected and honored as one of the largest landowners in the province. As a young man he had been trained as an archivist-historian in the École des Chartes in Paris so that, in his spare time, when not busy with his estates or with fishing and hunting, he devoted himself to studying in the archives of the regional capital. He was permanent secretary of the Académie des Sciences, Belles Lettres et Arts of Clermont-Ferrand and in his study at Sarcenat he worked on maps and charts, read books in French and English, and browsed through the English country magazine, *The Field*.

Teilhard's father was a member of all the local learned societies. As something of an amateur natural historian he built up sizeable collections of regional insects, birds, stones, and

Emmanuel Teilhard de Chardin in 1875. (Fondation Teilhard de Chardin)

Bookplate of Emmanuel Teilhard de Chardin. (Fondation Teilhard de Chardin)

Pierre at left, with his brothers and sisters: Olivier, Albéric, Marguerite-Marie, Françoise holding Joseph, and Gabriel. (Fondation Teilhard de Chardin)

plants. It is this love of natural objects, of pebbles and rocks, and an early interest in flora and fauna that the young boy Pierre learned from his father, though without sharing his interest in history.

It was the family custom that the children up to the age of eleven were educated at home with the help of either

English or German governesses. The German *Fräulein* must at least have taught elementary German to the youngsters. Both parents closely supervised and took part in this early education. The father directed the children's reading and supervised their Latin lessons; the mother taught the catechism. All the children followed a strict schedule of regular study and devotional exercises and were surrounded by a well ordered, pious atmosphere, whose somber tone acquaintances sometimes characterized as *la Grande Grille*, the great enclosure.

But it was also a life much lived in the open air, with plenty of games, laughter, and fun. From their earliest years Pierre and his brothers and sisters discovered the freedom of the countryside, the delights of the volcanic hills where they could freely roam about and play to their hearts' content. Family life was simple, with all the bare necessities provided, but rather rigorous and Spartan, especially in winter when the old stone houses were poorly heated.

Spring and summer were spent in the family properties of Sarcenat and Murol, situated by a river and provided with a sprawling farmhouse. When they lived in their townhouse in Clermont-Ferrand during the winter, they met up with their cousins from the Teillard-Chambon branch of the family. It was particularly these childhood contacts with his cousin Marguerite, the eldest daughter of his uncle Cirice, that years later led to a deep permanent relationship for Pierre.

Marguerite's earliest memory of the little boy, at the age of three or four, was of Pierre at a children's fancy dress party that her parents gave at their house in Clermont. She wrote about their games in the old, seventeenth-century mansion:

> These old houses, with their cellar-like entrances, their huge staircases, cold and damp, and their somber, lofty rooms, were a grim setting for our childhood. But they never stopped us from playing—the "terrible quartet" of

"At the age when other children, I imagine, experience their first 'feeling' for a person, or for art, or for religion, I was affectionate, good, and even pious: by that I mean that under the influence of my mother, I was devoted to the Child Jesus."
—*The Heart of Matter*

Berthe-Adèle de Dompierre d'Hormoy, Teilhard's mother, in 1875. (Fondation Teilhard de Chardin)

"However far back I go into my memories (even before the age of ten) I can distinguish in myself the presence of a strictly dominant passion: the passion for the Absolute."
—"My Universe"

5

The church of Orcines, the Teilhard family parish. In the rear is the famous Puy de Dôme. (Fondation Teilhard de Chardin)

Pierre Teilhard de Chardin age five, from a pastel drawing in the Château de Sarcenat. (Fondation Teilhard de Chardin)

boys, Albéric, Pierre, Gabriel and Joseph, wild and noisy, the girls more sedate. . . . If, as sometimes happened, the gang caught one of us by surprise, plaits were pulled and there would be tears. However, the arrival of a nice *goûter* with jam and oranges soon restored peace.[1]

At Sarcenat daily life began with rising at 7:30 a.m. and breakfast in the room of the governess, followed by lessons and later by play. The day ended with the family meal at six o'clock, followed by prayers at eight, when all family members and domestic staff gathered in the dining room to say the evening prayers together. On Sundays everybody went to High Mass in the nearby fourteenth-century village church of Orcines. Later, in the afternoon, the children played charades while the grown-ups drank tea in the drawing-room. It was a life of peaceful regularity which gave the young Pierre a secure outlook. He spent his happy childhood years surrounded by the caring presence of his elders, in the midst of a loving family. Yet it was also a milieu largely cut off from contemporary society and its major events.

Such a life of patriarchal simplicity no longer exists today. Remembering his early experiences in later years, Teilhard wrote,

> I was just like any other child. I was interested specially in mineralogy and biological observation. I used to love to follow the course of the clouds, and I knew the stars by their names. . . . To my father I owe a certain balance, on which all the rest is built, along with a taste for the exact sciences.[2]

Yet in spite of this testimony Teilhard was not simply like any other child. There was a deep passion and natural inclination that, from an early age, attracted him with an almost religious fervor to the mysteries of nature. His young appetite for exploration and discovery gave Teilhard early memorable experiences to which he often referred in later life.

Glow of Matter

The World gradually caught fire for me, burst into flames; . . . this happened all during my life, and as a result of my whole life, until it formed a great luminous mass, lit from within, that surrounded me.

A walk at Sarcenat. (Fondation Teilhard de Chardin)

It was amid the volcanic hills of the Auvergne that the young Pierre first experienced "the crimson glow of matter," "the Divine radiating from the depths of blazing Matter."[3] It was his living contact with the earth, when touching and caressing rocks, stones, and plants, that disclosed to him a deep sense of both the solidity and the fragility of life. He first experienced his vocation here, his calling to chart the history of the cosmos and the rise of human life on earth.

The young boy was always looking for treasures that were incorruptible and would last. As a small child he was much aggrieved by the insecurity of things. His very first memory at the age of five or six was of his mother snipping off a few curls of his hair. Picking them up, he held them close to the fire that burned them in less than a second. "A terrible grief assailed me; I had learned that I was perishable," he lamented.[4]

Decades later, when he described his inner development and the full emergence of his "sense of plenitude," he recalled this strange early attraction to things that were permanent and lasting. He relished the possession of something solid and incorruptible, more permanent than a lock of hair, and found it in different objects he collected as a boy of six or seven.

At first, there were fragments of metal—the lock-pin of a plough, a metal bolt protruding from his nursery floor, the shell splinters from a nearby firing range—which he

"The truth is that even at the peak of my spiritual trajectory I was never to feel at home unless immersed in an Ocean of Matter. . . . "
　　　　　—The Heart of Matter

The Château de Sarcenat. (Fondation Teilhard de Chardin)

"It is a long way . . . from a piece of iron to Omega Point . . . And I was gradually to find, to my cost, to what a degree the Consistence of which I then dreamed is an effect not of 'substance' but of 'convergence.'"
—*The Heart of Matter*

worshiped as his "iron gods." So tangible, they seemed so incorruptible, so utterly solid, indestructible, and consistent. How the child despaired when he realized their vulnerability, discovering that iron can be scratched and can rust. His disappointment was so great that he threw himself on the lawn and shed the bitterest tears of his young life.

He had to look for other things to become objects of his lasting attention and fervent devotion—the flickering flame on the family hearth, the finely colored stone of quartz and amethyst crystals, or, best of all, the glittering fragments of chalcedony he could pick up in the countryside of the Auvergne.

It was this love of stones that would eventually lead him to his passionate study of the "science of stones," to geology. The primacy of material matter so vividly experienced in the minerals and rocks of the Auvergne not only developed his taste for earth sciences; it also nourished in him a growing spiritual vision later so movingly expressed in his ardent "Hymn to Matter," a spirituality rooted in the tangible.

Auvergne, the country of his birth, was the creative matrix for his life's work. Here he developed his "sense of the earth," the great *terra mater* that cradled him like a child, just as his own mother surrounded him with her love and steadfast, simple faith. Her lifelong faithfulness to the deep spiritual values of a strong Christian faith were like a rock to him, giving him a solid foundation and strong sense of consistency for the rest of his life, just as the massive natural rocks around him symbolized to him forever the appeal of matter.

He described this appeal in vivid colors, as an intensive glow of crimson and purple, a vision of fire like that of "the burning bush," which became transformed into the incandescent "gold of the Spirit," "the Diaphany of the Divine at the heart of a glowing Universe."[5] The rich natural environment of the Auvergne was the true birthplace of his strong "cosmic sense," supplemented in years to come by an equally strong "human sense" and "Christic sense."

His attraction to the world of rocks, first discovered in the Auvergne, produced the beginning of what was to become one of the permanent foundations of his interior life. The numerous extinct volcanoes, so much a part of the environment of his childhood, created a love and passion for geology that were to mark the rest of his life. But this initial call from matter led to more than the probing of stones— it made him search for the essence, the "heart" of matter, which revealed to him the heart of God.

The beautiful hills of the Auvergne remained forever home to him. He would regularly return here in years to come in order to rest and recharge his spiritual energies. It was here that he first began to be "drawn by Matter—or, more correctly, by something which 'shone' at the heart of Matter" as he later expressed it in his spiritual autobiography *The Heart of Matter*, written at a desk in his brother's château, Les Moulins, with the striking range of Auvergne mountains in full view.[6]

"Blessed be you, harsh matter, barren soil, stubborn rock: you who yield only to violence, you who force us to work if we would eat.

"Blessed by you, perilous matter, violent sea, untameable passion: you who unless we fetter you will devour us. . . .

"I bless you, matter, and you I acclaim: not as the pontiffs of science or the moralizing preachers depict you, debased, disfigured—a mass of brute forces and base appetites—but as you reveal yourself to me today, in your totality and true nature."
—"The Hymn to Matter"

At Boarding School

*Even if my passion for stones, and even more for antiquities,
has not completely flared up again, I shall rekindle it
during the summer holidays, for the fire is still in me,
more active than ever.*

The École Libre de Notre-Dame
de Mongré, the Jesuit boarding
school in Villefranche-sur-Saône.

Teilhard at twelve. (Fondation
Teilhard de Chardin)

Once the boys in the Teilhard de Chardin family had
reached the age of eleven, it was customary to send
them to a Jesuit boarding school. The girls stayed nearer to
home and attended a school of the Ursuline sisters in Clermont whereas the boys went to the École Libre de Notre-Dame de Mongré in Villefranche-sur-Saône, about eighteen
miles north of Lyons.

This Jesuit-run school set great pride in being one of the
leading French educational institutions in the teaching of
the natural sciences, especially physics. Well-to-do families
sent their sons there from as far away as Paris and Marseilles,
even before there was a railroad connection to nearby Lyons.
The youngsters arrived by horse-drawn carriage and joined
a boarding school where the environment was Spartan, the
discipline strict; learning and devotion were encouraged, and
prizes were regularly awarded to those who did best.

It was a complete, if not traumatic, change in his life
when, shortly before his eleventh birthday, the young Pierre
was taken to Mongré in April 1892. We know little of his reaction to the sober school environment except that he seems
to have been an exemplary, though rather taciturn, and even
self-absorbed pupil. Yet he received many of the coveted prizes at the annual prize-giving ceremony. Among the names of
pupils recorded on the plaques in the school corridor his is
listed several times as the recipient of a first prize.

Henri Bremond, who taught Pierre in Mongré, wrote of
him many years later,

one of my classical pupils was a little fellow from Auvergne, very intelligent, first in every subject, but disconcertingly well behaved. . . . and it was only long afterwards that I learned the secret of his seeming indifference. Transporting his mind far away from us was another, a jealous and absorbing passion—stones.[7]

At home, his mother had nurtured Pierre's love of "the little Jesus" and encouraged his devotion to both the infant Christ and his mother Mary. Even when he was at boarding school, she continued to take much interest in his religious development. She was present when Pierre, shortly after joining the school, made his first communion in the school chapel on Ascension Day, May 26, 1892.

Typical of Jesuit schools, there were several religious societies for pupils to join. As soon as Pierre had made his first communion, he was admitted to the Sodality of St. Aloysius Gonzaga, and he also made an act of personal consecration to the Blessed Virgin on the Feast of the Immaculate Conception. Devotion to Our Lady became deeply rooted in his heart and, in 1895, he joined the Sodality of the Immaculate Conception. Throughout his life Mary was to hold a special place in his meditations and retreats, and he always remained faithful to the recitation of the rosary.

After a year's membership in the sodality he was elected secretary in 1896, then afterward, prefect of the Sodality of the Immaculate Conception. As secretary he had to keep the minutes of their meetings where he faithfully recorded the Jesuits' concern for the interior life of their pupils:

> Father Bonnet, the philosophy teacher . . . showed us how we can attain holiness by the practice of the least showy virtues and by the simple performance of everyday duties just as well as by undergoing martyrdom or by miracles.
>
> Our director, Father Charles Grognier, . . . said the best way to show our love for the Blessed Virgin is to try

"For me the Immaculate Conception is the feast of 'passive action,' the action that functions simply by the transmission through us of divine energy . . . In our Lord, all modes of lower, restless, activity disappear within this single, luminous, function of drawing God to oneself . . . To be active in such a way and such a degree, our Lady must have been brought into existence in the very heart of grace . . . May our Lord give you and me too, a little of her translucence, which is so favorable to God's action."
—Letter to Marguerite, December 5, 1916

11

"Through the workings of faith, Christ appears, Christ is born, without any violation of nature's laws, in the heart of the world."
—"Hymn of the Universe"

to be men with a sense of duty, that is Christians. Then, when we leave school we can really work to bring France back to the road God has mapped out for it and make it Christian again. If we do this we shall give back to Mary one of the brightest jewels in her crown.[8]

In future years, when his adolescent devotion had grown to full maturity, the figure of Mary was central to his understanding of the feminine. He later wrote, "The Virgin is still woman and mother: in that we may read the sign of the new age."[9]

The motto of the Jesuits at Mongré was *Le gré de Dieu mon gré*, "God's will is my will," and the school was run on traditional Jesuit lines. The Jesuits claimed to teach their pupils the sanctification of science by religion and the service of religion by science, a relatively advanced formula at that time, not without its impact on Teilhard. However, the aim of the school was to produce soldiers rather than scientists or administrators.

One of the science teachers took the young boys on brief expeditions to the surrounding countryside of the Beaujolais. Pierre was always keen to be one of the party, but his passion for collecting stones had to be pursued mostly during the long summer vacations, spent at home with his parents and siblings at

Teilhard at fourteen, dressed in the uniform of the Collège de Mongré with his two brothers Gabriel and Olivier. Photograph taken in the courtyard of the family house at Clermont-Ferrand. (Fondation Teilhard de Chardin)

Sarcenat. That is when he "rekindled his fire," the fire of his lifelong passion for rocks and stones.

His school records show that he became an equally proficient pupil in science, Latin, Greek, and German, whereas he gained only one prize for religious knowledge. By all accounts he was a model pupil, with a high sense of duty, exemplary conduct, and great piety, who was clearly well remembered by classmates in later years.

A Young Vocation

When I was seventeen, the desire for the "most perfect"
determined my vocation to the Jesuits.

The Jesuit fathers at Mongré gave the young Pierre more than a formal school education. As he sought moral and spiritual perfection, an absolute that the world of rocks and minerals could not satisfy, the example of his teachers instilled in him the desire to follow a vocation to the religious life. Nothing was more natural than to look to the Society of Jesus itself.

He discussed his thoughts with one of the fathers, who agreed that his vocation was probably genuine. Thus he wrote to his parents in June 1897, at the early age of sixteen,

> It does seem to me as though God is offering me a vocation to leave the world. You can well imagine that once I'm certain that I'm not mistaken, I shall answer the call; and I know, too, that you will be the last to raise any difficulties. All I now need is for our Lord to make me feel unmistakably what he wants of me and to give me the generosity of spirit that is needed.[10]

Yet he did not enter the Jesuit novitiate immediately on leaving school in 1897, after having taken the first and second part of his *baccalauréat*. He was not only still too young, but in a relatively poor state of health at that time. His father insisted that he needed a rest, and also an opportunity to reflect on whether his vocation was genuine or not. Thus Pierre spent a long period at home. He used this to prepare for an additional examination in mathematics, passed in 1898 without difficulty before a local jury. Much of his free time was of course devoted to collecting more rock samples in the neighborhood of Sarcenat.

Teilhard in 1889 as a Jesuit novice at Aix-en-Provence. (Fondation Teilhard de Chardin)

"At the novitiate, he was a model novice, modest and apparently shy, but always ready to oblige others. . . . He was simple and unassuming, anxious not to appear in any way different from others, gay and lively, and a great walker. . . . "
—Quoted in
Teilhard de Chardin Album

Entry to the Old Collège Royal Bourbon, site of the Jesuit novitiate in Aix-en-Provence. (Fondation Teilhard de Chardin)

Pope Leo XIII who consecrated humanity to the Sacred Heart of Jesus. (Library of Congress)

It was a quiet, uneventful, but gloriously happy year at home. Ten years later, when writing to his parents from abroad, Pierre wondered whether it was ever possible to be happier on earth than he had been during that time of rest in the midst of his loving family. It was also a year that strengthened in him the resolve to follow his vocation and become a Jesuit.

Thus a new period of life began on March 20, 1899, when he joined the Jesuits as a young novice in their house in Aix-en-Provence. Not quite eighteen, he left the intimate security of his close family circle at Sarcenat, once described by his brother Albéric as "the security of a glass case," to join what seemed at first an equally closed religious circle devoted to study and prayer. He now was "Brother Pierre," too absorbed with his new religious life to have much time for collecting pebbles and rocks.

The year of his entry into the Jesuit order, 1899, was also the year when Pope Leo XIII consecrated the whole of humanity to the Sacred Heart of Jesus, whose devotion figured so much in Teilhard's life.

As he later admitted, it was primarily his great desire to seek spiritual perfection that made him join a religious community. Given his family and school background, the Jesuit order seemed the most obvious choice.

From March 1899 to September 1900 Pierre was a Jesuit novice at Aix-en-Provence. After completing his novitiate, he was transferred to another Jesuit house in Laval where he began his juniorate. He took his first religious vows on March 25, 1901. During these early years of his Jesuit formation two other novices, Auguste Valensin and Pierre Charles, became his closest friends. They later grew into well-known theologians in their own right, but they always remained friends and confidants for Teilhard with whom he stayed in touch for most of his life.

The Jesuit juniorate included the study of language and literature. Pierre excelled as a classical scholar, composing

Latin and Greek verses. He even wrote a short Greek play for the entertainment of his community. His literary studies eventually led to his first academic degree, a Licence in letters, awarded by the University of Caen in northern France. Teilhard's vivid interest in contemporary literature is evident from his journal entries and essays. Many of his later writings contain references to French authors and novels, and also to English ones.

The fervor of his religious devotion is apparent from a letter written to his parents shortly after his first vows. He expressed his deep satisfaction that he was

> at last entirely at the disposition of the Blessed Virgin . . . completely attached, forever, to the Society at the very moment when it is being so severely persecuted. . . . I shall never forget all you have done to assist my vocation. But keep on praying that I may continue to be equal to whatever God asks of me.[11]

Little could he know then what trials and tribulations he would have to face throughout the coming years of his life.

The most immediate one was an unexpected move from France to England. During 1901 the French government, in a phase of heightened anticlericalism, passed laws restricting the activities of religious orders. Thus life became very difficult for the Jesuits, and the communities from Laval and other French Jesuit houses left for England and the Channel Islands in some haste. The Jesuit fathers and brothers traveled in secrecy, discreetly dressed as laymen in an assortment of clothes provided by their families, an experience that in retrospect seemed rather amusing. These political developments were the reason for Teilhard to find himself completing his studies as a junior on the island of Jersey, which provided his new home environment for the next four years.

"The more I think about it, the more clearly I see that I would be psychologically incapable of making the least effort if I were unable to believe in the absolute value of something in that effort."

—"My Universe"

The Maison St. Louis in Jersey where Teilhard spent three years (1902-1905) as a Jesuit scholastic. (Fondation Teilhard de Chardin)

"I know, Lord, that you will send me—at what moments only you know—deprivations, disappointments, sorrow."

—"Hymn of the Universe"

15

Jesuit in Jersey

Teilhard around 1902 in Jersey.
(Fondation Teilhard de Chardin)

"God is at work within life. He helps it, raises it up, gives it the impulse that drives it along, the appetite that attracts it, the growth that transforms it. I can feel God, touch Him, 'live' Him in the deep biological current that runs through my soul and carries it with it."
—"Cosmic Life"

There was the dawning attraction of the nature of plants and animals; and, underlying everything, one day . . . there came my initiation into the less tangible (but how exciting!) grandeur brought to light by the researches of physics. On both sides I saw matter, life and energy: the three pillars on which my inner vision and happiness rested.

Teilhard arrived in Jersey in October 1901 and stayed there until the summer of 1905—four important years that contributed much to the future direction of his life. Although he lived in a French-speaking community, he was surrounded by speakers of English. He now became more fully acquainted with Anglo-Saxon ways of life, first discovered at home through reading the English country magazines his father used to keep at Sarcenat.

The Jesuits had acquired the Maison St. Louis in St. Helier, the island's capital. This former hotel was transformed into a college for training Jesuits, so used until well into the middle of the twentieth century. The house was to become an important center for teaching and research in geology, and later also in archaeology; it even had its own observatory. For the young novices the strict intellectual discipline of studying scholastic philosophy and theology went hand in hand with instruction in the sciences, especially in geology and zoology.

More important still was the natural beauty of the island and its physical features. The terrain lent itself to geological work, and Teilhard felt encouraged to revive his interests in that field. Soon he was spellbound by the magic appeal of the wide, open sea, the wind and waves, the lonely, rock-strewn shores. These captured his senses and imagination.

Here was nature in the raw, untamed and wild, full of grandeur and overwhelmingly powerful forces.

Any time he could spare from his philosophical studies, and all his holidays, he devoted to scientific excursions on the island. His inner attraction to the great forces of nature, so deeply rooted in earlier childhood experiences, became so immensely strong that it awakened in him a vibrant cosmic consciousness—an experience of such intensity that he felt divine vibrations running through all things.

Teilhard in 1905 with some of his fellow philosophy students in Jersey. (Fondation Teilhard de Chardin)

At the same time his involvement with the world, the powerful "initiation into the cosmos," made him feel like being carried along so that he "relaxed in a sort of sensual abandonment" that flung him into a "godless crisis." Nature was a temptress bringing dissolution in her train; the alluring face of her divinity "masked a lack of thought and an empty heart." But when surrendering himself "to the embrace of the visible and tangible universe," he learned to feel the hand of God. And then he saw, "as *though in ecstasy, that through all of nature I was immersed in God*."[12]

He now became fully aware of a deeply pantheistic and mystical inclination in him. This vibrant sense of a strong nature mysticism was to remain with him all his life. The exhilaration, the unforgettable joy of seeing and feeling something so powerful, captivating, and attractive beneath and beyond the familiar levels of ordinary day-to-day existence

"Every encounter that brings me a caress, that spurs me on, that comes as a shock to me, that bruises or breaks me, is a contact with the hand of God."
—"Cosmic Life"

Postage stamp issued by the Jersey Post Office in 1982 to commemorate Teilhard.

"Human suffering, the sum total of suffering poured out at each moment over the whole earth, is like an immeasurable ocean. But what makes up this immensity? Is it blackness; emptiness, barren wastes? No, indeed: it is potential energy."
—"Hymn of the Universe"

shaped in him an inner vision he would never lose. Reflecting on these experiences more than ten years later, he wrote in his journal: "All I shall ever write will only be a feeble part of what I feel."[13]

Yet he expressed his emotions strongly, and they echoed through him for years. It is no coincidence that his powerful essay "The Spiritual Power of Matter," which ends on a stirring "Hymn to Matter," was written in Jersey when, after his participation in the First World War, he returned there for a holiday in August 1919. It opens with the lines:

> Blessed be you, harsh matter, barren soil, stubborn rock. . . .
> Blessed be you, perilous matter, violent sea, untameable passion. . . . [14]

Rocks and sea surrounded him, conveying majestic solidity and consistence. They made him inquire into their nature, search more deeply into the stuff of matter. He delighted in his science courses, especially in physics, where he could discover a demonstrable physical basis for the fundamental sense of unity he so strongly experienced in nature.

This passion for scientific studies was shared by some of his fellow students. From 1904 onward he collaborated with Father Felix Pelletier, a graduate in chemistry and mineralogy, with whom he later produced his first note on the geological and mineralogical features of Jersey. At this time Teilhard was still an amateur, but it was during this period that his preliminary investigations of the earth really began; it was his "honeymoon" with geology.

His geology teacher was Father Charles Noury, the "Father of Jersey geology," who provided the first full geological survey of the island. Teilhard himself wrote three scientific papers dealing with Jersey, two on geology and mineralogy, the other on the tectonics of the island. Father Pelletier and Teilhard also assembled an important mineral collection. In its essentials at least, Teilhard's monograph *Sur la structure de l'Ile de Jersey* (1920) still forms part of the currently accepted view of the island's structure. The islanders remember him for this and, in 1982, the Jersey Post Office commemorated Teilhard by issuing a set of postage stamps accompanied by a brief account of his life.

The study of rocks was such an absorbing passion for Teilhard that some colleagues referred to him in later years as primarily a hard-rock geologist. The rocks of Jersey left such a lasting impression that even thirty years later he

"Death surrenders us completely to God; it makes us pass into God. In return we have to surrender ourselves to it, in love and in the abandon of love, since, when death comes to us, there is nothing further for us to do but let ourselves be entirely dominated and led onwards by God,"
—"Hymn of the Universe"

compared the geology of North China to that of the Channel island, writing to a fellow geologist that he used to characterize his Chinese rocks by Jerseyan names.

But this passionate commitment was not without its problems. Already at school the young Pierre had experienced the deep tension between his attraction to nature and the spiritual perfection of the gospel. Now, as a junior in Jersey, he suddenly faced a deep personal crisis in his vocation, accentuated by the suffering brought about through

Rocks on the Jersey shore.
(Fondation Teilhard de Chardin)

"I remembered some things that Françoise once said to me— when she was already a Little Sister—about the unique and beatifying importance that the reality of God had assumed in her life—and I felt that I understood that we were fundamentally much more like one another than I had thought before. The only thing was that she was following a road where the realities of the world were much more obscured or left behind than happens with me."

—Letter to Marguerite, February 28, 1919

the sudden death of his eldest brother, Albéric, in September 1902, through tuberculosis, and the onset of an incurable illness in his younger sister, Marguerite-Marie, called Guigite by the family.

Should he now abandon his scientific studies and devote himself to a less active, more contemplative life, entirely oriented to "supernatural" activities? Should he completely leave the world, as a vocation to the religious life seemed to demand, and concentrate on seeking spiritual perfection?

With his eldest brother gone, his sister Françoise planning to enter a convent of the Little Sisters of the Poor, another sister ill, his brother Olivier leaving for Mexico to see the world, all the old family certainties suddenly seemed shattered. In his own mind he was far from sure what his vocation really was.

Pierre took his troubling problems to his former novice master, Père Troussard, who encouraged him to continue with his scientific studies and combine them with his religious life, rather than abandon one for an exclusive commitment to the other.

> I seriously considered the possibility of completely giving up the "Science of Rocks" which I then found so exciting. . . . And if I did not at that time "run off the rails," it is to the robust common sense of Père T . . . that I owe it. In the event, Père T. confined himself to assuring me that what the God of the Cross was looking for in me was the "natural" expansion of my being as well as its sanctification—without explaining how or why. What he said, however, was enough to leave me with a firm grasp of both ends of the line. And so I emerged from that trial unscathed. Gradually, through the synthesis which is effected by experience, detachment and attachment, renunciation and development, automatically came together as one within me.[15]

Thus he decided to continue with his excursions, searching for geological specimens on the island while pursuing his scientific studies along with those of philosophy and theology.

Intellectually, it was a difficult time for the church. The modernist crisis was about to erupt as theological and biblical studies began to be challenged by critical modern inquiries. This led to much tension and confusion, and to an authoritarian enforcement of traditional conservative views in the Catholic Church.

Studying theology in this climate was not easy, but Teilhard was lucky in being part of a small circle of lively young minds keenly interested in philosophy and theology and in the place of the church in the contemporary world. As they dreamed of their future tasks in the church, Pierre was cast by his fellow students as the "Apostle to the Gentiles" who would defend the Christian faith to his contemporaries in the world at large. As it turned out, much of his future work was indeed to be concerned with this.

The years of study in Jersey were a time of happy companionship and lively exchange, but also a time of parting, loss, and sorrow. In April 1903 his sister Françoise joined the Little Sisters of the Poor and soon left France to become a missionary in China. In August 1904 his sister Marie Louise, affectionately known as Loulou, died of meningitis at the age of thirteen, the second of his siblings to die so young. Death and grieving loomed large in his family during these years, and Teilhard experienced his share of suffering.

Soon he was to depart, too, and leave his circle of close friends when in September 1905 he was sent to the College of the Holy Family, a high school run by the Jesuits in Cairo, to teach physics and chemistry and look after the "museum," the jumble of collections assembled by the fathers of the school.

Albéric Teilhard de Chardin, a naval officer, in 1900. He died on November 27, 1902. (Fondation Teilhard de Chardin)

Marguerite-Marie Teilhard de Chardin in 1900. (Fondation Teilhard de Chardin)

The Wonder of Egypt

I . . . experienced such sense of wonder in Egypt.

"A sheet of steel-blue, almost gray, water, that the yellow cliffs of the desert suddenly confront. In the shallows, fishermen push their flat boats; they beat the water with great blows of their poles, to drive into their nets a species of carp. . . . In the distance the pelicans, standing in a row to fish, look like a white line traced on the surface of the lake. The sun disappears and we glide on opalescent waters ringed by deep violet mountains."

—"Relations d'Orient," December 1907

It was customary for Jesuit novices to devote themselves to a period of teaching between their years of philosophy and the beginning of their theological studies. The Jesuit province of Lyons, to which Teilhard belonged, had in its charge the Catholic mission work in the Middle East, especially in Armenia, Syria, and Egypt. This included educational responsibilities of which the College of the Holy Family in Cairo formed an important part.

It must have been exciting and adventurous to travel to Cairo in 1905. The cargo boat that Teilhard and his colleagues took from Marseilles slowly made its way through the Mediterranean, along Corsica, Sardinia, the coast of Italy, Sicily, and Crete to the ancient city of Alexandria. They spent a few days taking in the unfamiliar sights and then moved on by train, crossing the Nile delta to reach their final destination, Cairo.

On arriving there in early September 1905, Teilhard wrote to his parents that it was too hot to do much walking. That was something he was hoping for during the winter. But he had to think of his classes too, "tidy up the physics room and laboratory, which need it badly."[16] The official school records list his duties as teacher of physics and chemistry, curator of the school museum, and sacristan for the school chapel.

Teilhard was an enthusiastic teacher who loved his pupils and was much loved by them. His lessons were stimulating, though perhaps rather above the heads of some of his pupils. He commented on how difficult it was to make himself understood by the younger boys, but it was a challenge that helped him clarify his own ideas. As always, his main interests remained focused on research, so that the young geologist and budding paleontologist was hunting for fossils whenever his duties allowed.

He soon worked out a routine and was able to undertake regular scientific excursions with one or the other of his colleagues. Sometimes they were lucky and came home with "fantastic fossils,"[17] which he carefully examined and then wrote about and published his findings. He made a special study of sea fossils during his time in Egypt, and he was thrilled when one of the specimens found by him was named *Teilhardi* by the Geological Society in France.

He made many visits to the countryside around Cairo, but also to other parts of Egypt. Some of these are vividly described in his *Letters from Egypt*, addressed to his *Cher papa and chère maman* in France. They reveal his sharp powers of observation, his enthusiasm for flora, fauna, and fossils, and his thirst for greater knowledge and understanding. Describing his latest finds to a friend, he affirmed,

> These results show what one can do in between classroom duties and the various school chores, if you take the trouble to find a companion who doesn't mind spending the only free day in the week turning over stones right out in the desert, or detaching some big fossil from a rocky wall, in heat like a furnace.[18]

Primarily a collection of observations on natural history, on sites visited and fossils collected, his letters express a far greater interest in nature than in society. Addressed to his parents, they remain formal and descriptive. Distant in tone, they reveal little of the tremendous emotional impact that these years in Egypt made on him. Only his essays, written years later, give strong expression to his memorable experiences and reflect something of the haunting and lasting appeal that a large Eastern country had on the life of his mind.

To visit the East had been one of Teilhard's dreams ever since he had listened to the earlier travelogues of Albéric.

"I have been possessed by a great yearning to go and find, far from men and far from toil, the place where dwell the vast forces that cradle and possess us, where my over-tense activity might indefinitely become ever more relaxed."
—"Cosmic Life"

Beside an oasis, Teilhard and a fellow Jesuit with a group of children. (Fondation Teilhard de Chardin)

His eldest brother had roamed widely in the Middle and Far East and had been to China, where he collected many souvenirs for his family at home. The discovery of the East, so much hoped and wished for, was now for Teilhard to become forever connected with "the lonesome waste of the desert whose purple plains rose and fell one after another to a vanishing point on the wildly exotic horizon."[19]

The unforgettable experience of magnificent sunsets, the vast spatial expanses of the desert whose immensity, tranquil calm, and entrancing beauty he later missed so much in Paris, echoed in him for the rest of his life:

> The East flowed over me in a first wave of exoticism. I gazed at it and drank it eagerly—the country itself, not its peoples or its history (which as yet held no interest for me), but its light, its vegetation, its fauna, its deserts.[20]

Teilhard wandered the colorful, thronging streets of old Cairo and Alexandria, where he spent three summer vacations. The atmosphere was exhilarating and exciting, the people colorful and very different. He went home to the families of his Muslim students, whose warm hospitality he much appreciated, made excursions on the Nile, and visited the pyramids, Upper Egypt, Heliopolis, Memphis, Luxor, and Karnak.

He searched out the beautiful mosques and the bustling Arab markets, regretting more than once that he had not enough time to learn Arabic. If only he had had an Arab governess from whom he might have picked up the language in his childhood! His knowledge of Egyptian art and antiquities developed through regular visits to the archaeological and art museums, and he also attended the scholarly meetings of the Institute of Egyptology in whose bulletin he published some notes about his excursions and studies in the desert.

This stay in Egypt provided him in addition with an opportunity to discover as yet unknown aspects of Chris-

Oasis of El Faiyum. (Library of Congress)

tianity, represented in Egypt through its Orthodox, Coptic, Maronite, and Roman Catholic forms. Teilhard experienced different Christian liturgies, visited early Christian remains such as the shrine to the Holy Family not far from Cairo, and met dignitaries from different churches. This encounter with the rich, ancient forms of Christianity, enhanced by reading on the legacy of Byzantium, an interest also stimulated by his brother Albéric, provided him with a lasting knowledge about Eastern Christianity.

But the high point of it all was the experience of the desert, which may well have reminded him of the life of the desert fathers in the early centuries of Christianity when asceticism, monasticism, and Christian mysticism first began to flourish in the desert regions of North Africa.

Most important was an eight days' excursion in early April 1907 to the desert area of El Faiyum, southwest of Cairo. Teilhard, the fervent geologist, and another Jesuit, a specialist in Egyptian hieroglyphs, as well as five helpers, traveled with a little caravan of donkeys to the Faiyum oasis, visiting a large lake nearby, and exploring the surrounding desert region for fossils and archaeological sites. Many of the scenes they saw reminded them of biblical descriptions. The city of Faiyum, located about 100 kilometres southwest of Cairo, is now a modern administrative capital within a wider desert area. It occupies part of an ancient site, founded around 4000 BCE,

In El Faiyum he collected "fantastic fossils, said to be a symbiosis of hermit crabs and polyp colonies. . . . Alas, above the wall are marine deposits with the remains of whales. . . . But, for research here, a full-scale expedition would be required."
—Quoted in Claude Cuénot, *Teilhard de Chardin*

25

"There lay matter, and matter was calling me. To me in my turn, as to all the sons of man, it was speaking as every generation hears
it speak; it was begging me to surrender myself unreservedly to it, and to worship it."
—"Cosmic Life"

and is said to be the oldest city in Egypt and one of the oldest cities in Africa. This expedition was a welcome opportunity to explore the Faiyum fossil deposits of Upper Egypt, about which Teilhard later published a note in the *Bulletin scientifique du Cairo.*

The two explorers felt a real sense of adventure when they came across ancient Greek remains and old Coptic monasteries situated in isolated places, barely accessible. They knew that long ago this area had been populated by thousands of Christian ascetics and monastics. Even in the eighth century there had still existed thirty-three monasteries in the area. It was a region rich in memories, though rather poor in monuments now.

This first real expedition left an indelible impression on Teilhard's mind. Was it here under the harsh conditions of the sun and the desolate loneliness of the desert that he ex-

The Sphinx. (Library of Congress)

perienced again deep doubt and danger? Was it here that he met his greatest temptation, greater than in Jersey, of dissolving himself in nature, of becoming one with the All, of seeking pantheistic fusion with the cosmos, as he later described and repudiated it in his essay "Cosmic Life"?

His cosmic sense, his sense of the All, so vividly experienced since childhood and youth, certainly vastly expanded and grew through his prolonged stay in Egypt. Here he experienced another decisive desire to escape from the world, from the round of activities, and from social relations with other people. But once again he overcame this crisis and was transformed by it.

In future years, when he took to writing, he referred back to this again and again. The solitude, the vastness, the call of the desert symbolically came to stand for the experience of pantheism, for a particular stage of the religious quest that, he felt, must be overcome by integrating and transforming it into something else.

Teilhard with philosophy students at the Collège de la Sainte-Famille in Cairo, around 1906. (Fondation Teilhard de Chardin)

Teilhard would encounter the desert again and again in other parts of the world. How often did it remind him of those memorable years in Egypt!

Never again would he live for three years in a predominantly Islamic country, and even in Egypt his contacts with Islam remained largely confined to his Muslim pupils and their families. The wider social world of his order was limited too, for most of it extended only to the expatriate colonial milieu of French scientists, businessmen, and administrators who lived in Egypt at the turn of the century. Thus the life of the Jesuit community was relatively removed from that of the indigenous population, although some of Teilhard's colleagues specialized in the study of Islam and later became well-known experts in it.

It was with these specialists that Teilhard had an opportunity to explore the old Arab quarters of Cairo, experience the fast of Ramadan, meet Muslim pilgrims returning from Mecca, and learn something about the beliefs and practices of the Muslim faith. When meeting local people, he felt they enjoyed discussing moral and religious matters. But whatever acquaintance he made, whatever knowledge he gained—far more than what most Christians would have acquired at that time—remained incidental and was gathered at random.

Street scene in Old Cairo. (Library of Congress)

He mentions the reading of a thirteenth-century Arab poet whose description of ancient Cairo he compares with his own impressions; he is touched by the great dignity and respect shown to Muslim religious figures; but his first and foremost interests always belonged to fossils and their scientific study, pursued with more fervor than anything else.

In 1908 it was time to return to Europe to begin the customary four years' study of theology. Like other French Jesuits from the province of Lyons, he went for this to the Jesuit house at Ore Place, Hastings, in the South of England.

But Egypt was so difficult to forget. However beautiful the countryside and coast of Sussex, they were incomparable to what he had experienced in Egypt. He maintained contact with his friends and former colleagues in Cairo, corresponded with past pupils, kept in touch with research and expeditions in Egypt, and received the occasional visitor from Cairo. Even after a year in England he still felt that part of his heart had been left in the mountains near the Red Sea.

He told his sister Françoise that, once ordained, his whole ambition was to return to Egypt. She agreed wholeheartedly, saying she wanted him to go back there for his own happiness, so that he could once again be "among his intellectual contacts, his fossils and all the old memories of the pharaohs."[21]

Hastings

. . . buried in a forest whose life-laden shadows seemed to seek
to absorb me in their deep, warm, folds . . .

In 1906 the French Jesuits from the province of Lyons and Paris had moved their theological house of study, their "scholasticate," to Hastings in the South of England. They had acquired "Ore Place," an imposing building, almost new, which they retained until 1926. The young Jesuit Teilhard spent the years 1908-1912 there, studying for his degree in theology and preparing for the priesthood.

Hastings, in the county of Sussex, is a picturesque town. Famous as the site of the Norman invasion of England in 1066, and also one of the medieval English Channel ports, it is now a seaside resort, surrounded by sandstone cliffs overlooking the ancient fishing settlement and a harbor at the mouth of a steep valley. Not far away is the Sussex Weald, a large forest area with an ancient Saxon name, heavily wooded, with alternating sands, clays, and rocks dating from several geological eras. Well known for its fossil finds, especially for the abundant remains of dinosaurs, it was an ideal terrain for a young geologist and paleontologist.

After leaving Cairo and on his way to Hastings, Teilhard stopped in France to visit his family in Sarcenat. It was a happy reunion after so many years of separation. Yet when writing to his parents after the visit, he wondered whether it would have been better not to see each other again. Was he disappointed to see the disintegration of his family, with three of his brothers and sisters having died, one permanently ill, and the others gone away?

His older sister, Françoise, had become a nun; his younger brothers were away at boarding school. His father and mother, with their quite different temperaments, were now

"Ore Place," the Jesuit scholasticate in Hastings, England.

"You the Center at which all things meet and which stretches out over all things so as to draw them back into itself: I love you for the extensions of your body and soul to the farthest corners of creation through grace, through life, and through matter."
—"Cosmic Life"

Teilhard in Hastings in 1911.
(Fondation Teilhard de Chardin)

*"Lord Jesus, who are as gentle
as the human heart, as fiery as
the forces of nature, as intimate
as life itself, you in whom I can
melt away and with whom I
must have mastery and freedom:
I love you as a world, as this
world which has captivated my
heart; and it is you, I now
realize, that my brother-men,
even those who do not believe,
sense and seek through the magic
immensities of the cosmos."*
　　　　　　　　—"Cosmic Life"

on their own, without their children. It was no longer the lively family circle he remembered where he had been the beloved "Pierrot" of his brothers and sisters.

Painful as it was, Teilhard had grown beyond his family. His main interests, his overall focus, the center of his being, were no longer found among them nor among the cherished memories of the past. He had to look ahead to find a focus in the future and see where his vision would lead him. His theological studies were a help in finding such a center of integration, providing him with plenty of stimulation and challenges to work out a very personal synthesis of all that he read, studied, experienced, and felt.

At that time, Jesuit theological training was thoroughly grounded in scholasticism, especially the thought of Thomas Aquinas. But Teilhard was never very comfortable with static forms of thought; he soon left Thomist categories and methods behind. Yet Thomism provides much of the background of his early thinking. Even as late as 1955 he could say that he felt like being "mounted 'on the shoulders' of Plato, Aristotle and St. Thomas."[22]

By inclination and temperament Teilhard was not particularly interested in biblical studies or exegesis. But the theology students had to take a scripture course in their first year. Learning Hebrew at this stage was a mere formality, but his excellent knowledge of Greek helped him to study the New Testament. Teilhard took the opportunity to make detailed summaries of all passages speaking of Christ and creation, particularly in St. John's Gospel and St. Paul's letters, which affirmed the primacy of Christ, in whom all things have their being.

In these texts he found his own experience of the oneness, the ultimate unity of the whole of creation confirmed. The cosmic hymns of St. Paul resonated in him when he felt the density of life stretching out from its fossil forms in the distant past through present life and nature toward some future point of maturation. It was as if all of creation consisted of a continuous stream of living matter, energy, and spirit, a cosmic web animated by divine life itself.

This divine life revealed itself as a presence, the presence of a person that took for him the figure and face of Jesus. There slowly emerged as the center of all things what he later named the cosmic Christ, whose elements stretch across all matter, all life, all creation.

In his regular letters home to parents, brothers, and sisters, he described his experiences, reported on his studies, and regularly remembered the death anniversaries of family members, especially of his brother Albéric. Speaking about their lost loved ones, he wrote to his father: "When we see each other, I hardly dare mention them to you. I can see that you are suffering, and I am afraid to hurt you even more. But you know that I don't forget them either."[23]

He also wrote enthusiastically about the fragrant beauty of spring. Even forty years later he could still recall

the extraordinary solidity and intensity I found then in the English countryside, particularly at sunset when the Sussex woods were charged with all that "fossil" Life which I was then hunting for, from cliff to quarry, in the Wealden clay. There were moments, indeed, when it seemed to me that a sort of universal being was about to take shape suddenly in Nature before my very eyes.[24]

While Teilhard was studying theology in Hastings, his sister Françoise was delighted to learn that her religious congregation had decided to send her to work in the Christian missions in China. She left on August 1, 1909, by boat, arriving a month later in Shanghai where she lived and worked among the urban poor. Brother and sister were very close because they both shared the ideal of dedicating their whole life to God. Like Teilhard, Françoise prayed with similar ardor to the Sacred Heart, and in her letters to her brother and parents she also expressed her strong dedication and love for China.

"Heart of Jesus, give me a heart that is filled with ardor and generosity, that thrills with joy when sacrifices have to be made; a heart whose zeal knows neither fatigue nor obstacles; a heart whose only love is your heart, and whose only knowledge is your name."
—Prayer of Françoise Teilhard de Chardin

Françoise Teilhard de Chardin around 1910. She died in 1911. (Fondation Teilhard de Chardin)

31

Teilhard with his family on the day of his ordination in England.
(Fondation Teilhard de Chardin)

"As far as my strength will allow me, because I am a priest, I would henceforth be the first to become aware of what the world loves, pursues, suffers. I would be the first to seek, to sympathize, to toil: the first in self-fulfillment, the first in self-denial—I would be more widely human and more nobly terrestrial in my ambitions than any of the world's servants."

—"The Priest"

But she was not to live for long in the convent of the Little Sisters of the Poor in Shanghai. In 1911 she caught smallpox and died at the age of thirty-two, just a few months before her brother's ordination as a priest and a year after she had been made mother superior of her community. What a blow to her family her death was! Yet another beloved family member had passed away at such a young age.

Teilhard was experiencing yet more deep pain and facing another family crisis. Now he was the oldest living descendant of his parents. Yet in some way he was lost to them, too, because he had offered up his life to God and dedicated himself to the church and his order. Though deeply aggrieved, he could help his mother and father only through his faith: "Our greatest consolation, surely, is that it is difficult to imagine a holier or more beautiful end," he wrote about his sister's death.

Françoise had, indeed, found just the death she wished for above all: in China and for China. Our Lord is giving her her reward before its time has come: we have no right, even, to regret the good she would have done had her life been longer. The fine life is the life that fulfils God's plans.[25]

When Teilhard's parents together with four of his younger brothers—Gabriel and Joseph, Gonzague, and Victor—went to Hastings for his ordination on August 24, 1911, they all wore black as sign of their mourning. It must have been a meeting tinged with mixed feelings of sorrow and joy. They remembered the loss of a dearly loved sister while celebrating their eldest son's and brother's new stage of life as an ordained priest, consecrated to serve God and his fellow human beings.

Was Teilhard thinking of that moment when he wrote some years later in his war essay "The Priest":

I shall tell those who suffer and mourn that the most direct way of using our lives is to allow God, when it pleases him so to do, to grow within us, and, through death, to replace us by himself.[26]

Now that he was ordained, he could assist with pastoral work in parishes and convents. He wrote to his parents about retreats he gave in Malvern near Worcester and in a convent near Brighton, a visit to Oxford, and pastoral work in Ashford in Kent. A visit to the coast, to Reculver where the Thames enters the North Sea, haunted him with the beauty of a sunset over misty waters. Here he felt drawn again to the magic appeal of nature, to "cosmic life."

When visiting a local monastery, he felt equally impressed by the powerful affirmation of something supernatural in the lives of the monks. In one of the convents, the unusual personality of a certain "Sister Mary Agnes," a convert to the Catholic faith, much impressed him. She drew his attention to the writings of Robert Hugh Benson whose book *Christ in the Church* Teilhard had already read the previous year.

Benson was the youngest son of a former archbishop of Canterbury who had joined the Roman Catholic Church and written some remarkable novels that speak with much fervor about the Christian faith. Teilhard was fascinated to read *The Light Invisible, The Lord of the World,* and other titles that so much inspired him that a few years later, when he began to write himself, he composed "Three Stories in the Style of Benson" which bear the overall title "Christ in the World of Matter" and form part of his *Writings in Time of War.*

His considerable theological study program did not prevent Teilhard from pursuing his scientific interests in Hastings and deepening his understanding of evolution.

"The man who is filled with an impassioned love of Jesus hidden in the forces which bring increase to the earth, him the earth will lift up, like a mother, in the immensity of her arms, and will enable him to contemplate the face of God.

—"The Mass on the World"

Reculver

Discovery of Evolution

*To have become conscious of evolution means . . . that we
have become alive to a new dimension. The idea of evolution:
not . . . a mere hypothesis, but a
condition of all experience.*

*"Lord, it is you who, through
the imperceptible goadings of
sense-beauty, penetrated my
heart in order to make its life
flow out into yourself. You came
down into me by means of a
tiny scrap of created reality; and
then, suddenly, you unfurled
your immensity before my eyes
and displayed yourself to me as
Universal Being."*
—"The Mystical Milieu"

Teilhard around 1912. (Fondation
Teilhard de Chardin)

The Rector of Ore Place, the Jesuit house of theological
study in Hastings, allowed Teilhard to pursue his scientific interests as much as he could and go fossil hunting
in the bone beds of the Sussex Weald whenever theological
studies left enough time. There was so much to be found
and examined. Teilhard could now follow up his interests
in vertebrate fossils and early human origins much more
systematically. The specimens collected on his scientific
excursions to the surrounding countryside, the Hastings
Beds and Weald Clay, were offered to the local museum
in Hastings, and eventually also to the British Museum in
London.

He also followed some of the debates about the modernist crisis by reading the Jesuit journal *Études*, where he himself published a traditional theological article in early 1909.
He could not be studying contemporary science without
encountering current theories of evolution. Combining
these with the static worldview of theology posed considerable problems. In a contribution to an article on "Man" in a
Catholic apologetic dictionary published in 1911, Teilhard
still took a predictably traditional, rather dualistic stance
against evolution. But that was soon to change.

During the summer of 1909 he revisited all the coastal
sites in Jersey, which always seemed so beautiful to him, and
in 1910 he spent a month in Holland and Belgium where
he met up with his friend Père Charles and got acquainted
with Père Joseph Maréchal in Louvain. Unclear himself

how theology and science could fit together, Teilhard was enthusiastic to meet Maréchal and other Jesuits working in the physical and natural sciences. Here were role models he could emulate, older, more experienced men with whom he could discuss his own uncertainties with regard to interpreting scientific data adequately while yet remaining a totally committed Christian.

Maréchal taught biology and experimental psychology at Louvain, but from 1908 onward he also published comparative studies on the psychology of mystics, which Teilhard read and was influenced by. Teilhard consulted Maréchal more than once and always took much note of his advice.

Eventually, however, he was to find his own synthesis between the understanding of his scientific studies and the doctrines of his faith. While studying theology at Hastings and going on scientific excursions in the Sussex Weald, the transformation of his thinking gradually happened until it was suddenly all brought together through reading Henri Bergson's book *Creative Evolution* which, he later remembered very clearly, he read avidly at that time.

Published in France in 1907 and translated into English in 1911, this book, still in print today, became very popular in the early decades of the twentieth century since it provided an alternative explanation to Darwin's theory of the mechanism of evolution. Reading it made Teilhard discover the dynamic pattern and rhythm running through the whole universe—a universe fully alive and unfinished. But he rejected Bergson's idea of a vital impulse, of a cosmos originating from a central source developing in divergent directions. Instead, he saw the cosmos in a process of evolutionary creation, of convergent cosmogenesis unfolding in space-time. As he wrote years later:

> I can now see quite clearly that the only effect that brilliant book had upon me was to provide fuel at just the

"Life can be seen to move. Not only does it move but it advances in a definite direction. And not only does it advance, but in observing its progress we can discern the process . . . whereby it does so."
—*The Future of Man*

"Is the world not in the process of becoming more vast, more close, more dazzling . . . ? Will it not burst our religion asunder? Eclipse our God?"
— *The Divine Milieu*

right moment, and very briefly, for a fire that was already consuming my heart and mind. And that fire had been kindled, I imagine, simply by the coincidence in me, under "monist" high tension, of the three inflammable elements that had slowly piled up in the depths of my soul over a period of thirty years. These were the cult of Matter, the cult of Life, and the cult of Energy. All three found a potential outlet and synthesis in a World which had suddenly acquired a new dimension and had thereby moved from the fragmented state of static Cosmos to the organic state and dignity of Cosmogenesis.[27]

It was a change of tremendous importance, of much consequence for all his future thinking. The magic word "evolution" haunted his thoughts "like a tune"; it was to him "like an unsatisfied hunger, like a promise held out to me, like a summons to be answered."[28] Evolution was vital. It was the necessary condition of all further scientific thought. But evolution was also psychic and spiritual. It was sacred.

The attraction of "matter" and "cosmic life" was still powerful, but he now perceived the oneness of nature on a much vaster scale. Spirit and matter were no longer two separate realities but two *states* or "two aspects of one and the same cosmic Stuff, according to whether it was looked at or carried further in the direction in which . . . it is becoming itself or in the direction in which it is disintegrating."[29] Spirit was itself a unity achieved by synthesis. The insights of his faith and the dynamic understanding of the process of evolution and life were fused into one single certainty, one awareness. The dualism of matter and spirit, of body and soul, dissolved before him "like fog before the rising sun."

Matter and spirit were two aspects of one single reality. Spirit slowly emerges from matter. It eventually takes precedence over the physical and chemical, and it is ultimately in spirit, the highly complex, that all consistency resides. The unity of the world was of a dynamic, evolutive character pointing to spirit, experienced by him as the feeling of God's presence everywhere. The world was reverberating with divine life. Thus he could speak of "sacred evolution."

This overwhelming realization led him on the path to his future work. It took of course several more years before all these insights acquired a precise meaning in his mind, but from then on he was confirmed in an attitude that was henceforth to govern the whole of his inner development, and that he defined in the simple words of "the primacy of the Spirit or, which comes to the same thing, the primacy of the Future."[30]

Teilhard's "cosmic sense" became now more all-embracing. As he later remembered,

> It was during the years when I was studying theology at Hastings . . . that there gradually grew in me, as a presence much more than as an abstract notion, the consciousness of a deep-running, ontological, total Current which embraced the whole Universe in which I moved; and this consciousness continued to grow until it filled the whole horizon of my inner being.[31]

St. Mary Star of the Sea, Hastings, UK

Many passages in Teilhard's later works express this strong sense of the interdependent unity and organicity of all living things. Studying the history of the cosmos and all forms of life,

> we have gradually come to understand that no elemental thread in the Universe is wholly independent in its growth of its neighboring threads. Each forms part of a sheaf; and the sheaf in turn represents a higher order of thread in a still larger sheaf—and so on indefinitely. . . .
>
> This is the organic whole of which today we find ourselves to be a part, without being able to escape from it . . . In countless subtle ways, the concept of Evolution has been weaving its web around us.

Henri Bergson. (Library of Congress)

"The bigger the world becomes and the more organic become its internal connections, the more will the perspectives of the Incarnation triumph. . . . Through frightened for a moment by evolution, the Christian now perceives that what it offers him is nothing but a magnificent means of feeling more at one with God and giving himself more to him."
—*The Human Phenomenon*

While initially believing that we do not change, he could now see that our knowledge and beliefs have been radically transformed by being endowed "with a new structure and a new direction." It is important to understand that Teilhard's full evolutionary awakening occurred at Hastings, after he had read Henri Bergson's *Creative Evolution*; the impact of this key experience led to a radical transformation of his own understanding and vision which affected all his future thinking and writing.[32]

Through his work on fossils Teilhard soon established a reputation as a serious researcher. During the years he spent studying at the Jesuit house at Ore Place in Hastings he collected some 150 plant and animal fossils which he gave to the Hastings Museum. They can still be found there today in the original cigar-boxes and French medicine-boxes in which they were handed over in 1912. Teilhard also made contact with scientists at the Kensington Science Museum in London. Moreover, he became friendly with Charles Dawson, a solicitor and amateur scientist living near Hastings. In the summer of 1909 the two ran into each other when digging for fossils in a local quarry. Through Dawson Teilhard became acquainted with yet more English scientists, and they went out together on excursions searching for fossils.

He was thrilled when, in 1913, one of the British scientists published a description of the fossil plants Teilhard had collected in Hastings. The article appeared in the journal of the Geological Society in London and included among others a genus *Teilhardia* and a species *Teilhardi*. It was very gratifying to him that his scientific work was taken note of by others.

Meanwhile his theological studies were soon completed. He passed his final examination with flying colors, obtaining a qualification equivalent to a doctorate in theology. But it was by no means clear what definite direction his future life and work should take. He was awaiting a decision from his superiors but suspected that his wish to go East again soon was not to be granted. Given his scientific interests and inclination, and his early successful research results, he was instead sent to Paris to take up advanced scientific studies.

"To say that Christ is the term and motive force of evolution, to say that he manifests himself as 'evolver,' is implicitly to recognize that he becomes attainable in and through the whole process of evolution"

—*Science and Christ*

Paris and Piltdown

. . . attaining Heaven, by fulfilling Earth.

Cathedral of Notre Dame, Paris.

Teilhard was thirty-one when he went to live in Paris, a city that delighted him and greatly expanded his outlook. After he had lived and traveled in different parts of France, Egypt, and England without being rooted anywhere but in the Auvergne, Paris now became the true home of his adulthood. The future globe-trotter would always return here, whether with delight or a heavy heart. Here he could see his friends, seek help and advice, find new inspiration, and replenish his energies.

Life in Paris was like a whirlwind where he could never get everything done that needed his attention. He arrived in the middle of 1912 to begin his new life as a research student. Happy to make new friends, he worked and wrote, but greatly missed the wide, open spaces—the countryside, the sea, and the far-from-forgotten desert.

Without losing contact with England or Jersey he enrolled himself in several geology and paleontology classes at the Institut Catholique, the Collège de France, and the Museum of Natural History. Here the great authority was the formidable Marcellin Boule, well-known professor of paleontology, also an Auvergnat, described by Claude Cuénot as

> short, sturdy, with something of the bulldog in him, . . .
> dictatorial in manner, choleric, impatient of contradiction, with a biting tongue, but he was a man, too, of rare intelligence, a fine geologist (particularly brilliant in comparative paleontology) and one of the great specialists on Neanderthal man.[33]

Teilhard first went to see him in July 1912. This decisive meeting was to launch him "into what has been my whole life ever since: research and adventure in the field of paleontology."[34] Teilhard found his mind stretched. But his sharp intelligence and scientific ardor soon marked him out as an outstanding student. He responded avidly to the intellectual and spiritual ferment around him. A progressive and forward-looking scholar, he wanted to be in the vanguard of the movements of his time.

Ten years later Boule was to assess Teilhard's development with great praise when he awarded him a distinguished scientific prize for his doctoral research:

> He . . . possesses every quality required of a first-rate naturalist; an aptitude for work, penetrating observation, a combination—valuable as it is rare—of keenness for minute analysis and a gift of wide synthesis, and great independence of mind. His career, though just begun, already gives promise of being among the most brilliant.[35]

This was an outstanding, yet objective assessment of Teilhard's abilities as a scientist. Boule was best placed to make it, for he had taught Teilhard and was his mentor and research adviser. He soon gave his new student the task of examining the carnivores and primates found in the phosphorites from the region of Quercy, a district in southwestern France. Teilhard carefully analyzed the fossil data in the museum collection by tracing their links with past and future forms. Studying the primates of the tarsier group, he realized that the only one of the past lines to have survived into the present was "the one which developed the largest brain." This was to become one of his great future themes when reflecting on the place of human beings in the natural world: that the development of a larger brain marks

"Since my childhood . . . I have always loved and sought to read the face of Nature; but, even so, I can say that my approach has not been that of the 'scientist' but that of the 'votary.' It seems to me that every effort I have made, even when directed to a purely natural object, has always been a religious effort."
—"My Universe"

Marcellin Boule, professor of paleontology at the Museum of Natural History in Paris. (Fondation Teilhard de Chardin)

The Museum of Natural History in Paris. (Photograph by Ursula King)

the transition from simple consciousness to more complex forms, and eventually to a higher, self-reflective consciousness.

He avidly pursued his paleontological studies and made new friends with other scientists, especially with the prehistorian Abbé Breuil, whom he first met through Boule, and with whom he remained in contact throughout his life.

Another decisive encounter occurred in October 1912 when he visited his uncle's family in Paris. He met up again with his childhood cousins and playmates, not seen for years. His cousin Marguerite Teillard-Chambon, close to him in age, was now in her early thirties. A fine and independent woman who had taken her *Agrégation* in 1904, she became a writer publishing under the name of Claude Aragonnès. She also was headmistress of a well-known Catholic girls school, the Institut de Notre-Dame-des-Champs. Attractive and lively, she shared many intellectual and artistic interests with Teilhard.

Studying in Paris also provided Teilhard with new opportunities for travel. During the summer of 1912 he stayed in Louvain, in Belgium, where he attended a week's conference on "religious ethnology." Missionaries, ethnologists, and anthropologists met to discuss the latest theories about the origin and development of religion among different human groups, tracing the outline of primal worldviews, perhaps bound to disappear in the modern world.

In a published account of this conference Teilhard already points to some of the questions that later so much shaped what he called his "vision of the past." All these huge efforts of so many geologists, paleontologists, archaeologists, and historians to uncover the life of our ancestors, to find the traces of a lost or hidden world, to what purpose are they undertaken? Why are we so keen to rediscover the past? And for what? What does all this knowledge we are so proud of eventually lead to? What meaning has it got for us? These questions were to reappear again and again.

In June 1913, Abbé Breuil with a group of friends, Teilhard among them, traveled to northwest Spain to visit the prehistoric caves around Altamira, but also to search for fossils. Teilhard shared some of their experiences with his parents:

> What I've really been doing is to shift a great deal of earth and of stones, or watch them being shifted. In the morning, about 8 o'clock, that is, we go up to the cave, in our outlandish rig-out, and stay there till six in the evening, in the open air and wonderful sunshine, with a magnificent view in front of us. We haven't made any sensational find; . . . but even so I find it extremely interesting, since this is the finest collection of Quaternary dwelling places known at present.[36]

Reflecting on their work, he wrote:

> I can assure you, seeing these remains of a mankind earlier than any known civilization really gives you something to think about; I love staying alone there, looking at them in absolute silence, broken only by the sound of water dripping from the stalactites.[37]

"*The Universe stimulates the 'zest for being,' and provides the nourishment which are transformed into love of God. To my mind, at least, this process is extremely clear: Heaven cannot dispense with Earth.*"
—"My Universe"

Teilhard with group on expedition to Spain, 1913. (Fondation Teilhard de Chardin)

He was amazed to see the paintings in the Altamira caves:

> I found a marvellous sight in one section where the roof
> is covered with magnificent bison, painted in three colors
> (red, yellow, and black) and with an extraordinary degree
> of clarity and expression. . . . When you think that these
> were drawn during an age when Egyptian culture was
> still non-existent, you are completely amazed.[38]

This memorable Spanish expedition whetted Teilhard's
appetite for prehistory and early human fossils. He had
kept in touch with the English amateur archaeologist and
geologist Dawson, whom he had first met during his studies
at Hastings. Much discussed then were the human fossils
found at Trinil, Java, in 1891, and at Heidelberg, Germany,
in 1907. Yet they were disappointing because they showed
no evidence of the early development of a large brain, so
important in human evolution. Scientists were looking for
a "missing link" between apes and humans to support their
arguments about evolution. Thus it was a great thrill when
Dawson, who had been digging for bones since 1910, found
some thick fragments of human cranial bone, chocolate-
brown in color, together with some hippopotamus teeth,
elephant fossils, and flint tools in the gravel deposits of a
long-vanished river bed at Piltdown in Sussex.

Dawson subsequently took the fossils to Arthur Smith-
Woodward, Keeper of Geology at the Natural History Museum in South Kensington, London. Stimulated by the find,
they pursued systematic excavations secretly together. They
soon found more fragments, including fossilized animal
bones, stone tools, and an apelike lower jaw, all stained with
the same brown color of the gravels. Soon they were to announce with great excitement their new find to a packed
session of the London Geological Society. Here was a new
kind of early man, *Eoanthropus dawsoni* ("Dawson's Dawn
man"), different from the apeman found in Java or from
Neanderthal man in Germany.

Further finds were made on the site until 1915. Teilhard worked with both Dawson and Smith-Woodward at Piltdown, without being present when any of the major fossils were found. However, when he accompanied the two during another visit to Piltdown in the summer of 1913, he had the remarkable "luck" of finding a canine tooth that closely fitted Woodward's reconstruction of the Piltdown skull.

At that time he had full confidence in the expertise of the eminent Smith-Woodward, but later, when more fully trained and competent in paleontology, he always felt uneasy about this "puzzling Dawn man." With the help of more advanced research techniques, including radiocarbon dating, the *Eoanthropus* fossil was in 1953 unmasked as a hoax on the basis of work undertaken in the research laboratory of the Oxford scientist ET 'Teddy' Hall (1924-2001) and studies pursued by the geologist and palaeontologist Kenneth Oakley (1911-1981), then on the staff of the Natural History Museum in London. But the details of this clever fraud and the identity of the Piltdown forger have never been fully unraveled and are still a matter for speculation. Many different theories have been proposed without a satisfactory answer being found. Some have argued it may have been an inside job, and that Arthur Smith-Woodward (1864-1944) at the Natural History Museum may himself have been the culprit.

From 1912 to 1953 Piltdown man existed in the London Natural History Museum as a candidate for human origins

Teilhard on Spanish expedition, 1913. (Fondation Teilhard de Chardin)

"The man who is filled with an impassioned love for Jesus hidden in the forces which bring death to the earth, him the earth will clasp in the immensity of her arms as her strength fails, and with her he will awaken in the bosom of God."

—*Hymn of the Universe*

until this fossil was exposed as a crude forgery of human and orangutan remains. Teddy Hall established that the bones had been stained with potassium dichromate to make them look fossilized; they were contaminated with microscopic bits of iron filings, indicating that someone had filed down the teeth. This later turned out to be part of the jawbone of an orangutan that had been connected to a human cranium. Suspicion fell on a number of people, including occasionally Teilhard, whose innocence is without doubt, although he fell for the deception. Some think that the most likely perpetrator of this hoax may have been the writer Sir Arthur Conan Doyle, creator of the fictitious Sherlock Holmes. Doyle had lived close to Piltdown when the fossils were found and belonged to the same archaeological society as the amateur archaeologist Dawson, who had befriended the young Teilhard.

When Teilhard learned about the unraveling of this fraud in 1953, he wrote to Oakley:

Excavation at Piltdown.

I congratulate you most sincerely on your solution of the Piltdown problem. Anatomically speaking, *"Eoanthropus"* was a kind of monster. And, from a paleontological point of view, it was equally shocking that a "dawn man" could occur in England. Therefore I am fundamentally pleased by your conclusions, in spite of the fact that, sentimentally speaking, it spoilt one of my brightest and earliest paleontological memories.[39]

Piltdown man certainly attracted much attention and controversy, not least between the different interpretations given to the finds by Smith-Woodward and Marcellin Boule. For Teilhard, who studied under Boule, to be associated with such a famous find at so early a stage in his scientific career was certainly of some importance.

His own studies of the carnivores in the phosphorites of Le Quercy resulted in a monograph of almost a hundred pages, published in the *French Annales de Paléontologie* during 1914-1915.

Meanwhile Teilhard was to go to Canterbury in England to start his Jesuit tertianship. He had spent the early summer of 1914 in the French Alps "amid magnificent landscapes" where again the beauty and grandeur of the cosmos beckoned and enthralled him. But the radiance of nature was soon to be replaced by the darkest shadows of a terrible Great War.

At first he was not called up for war service but remained free to pursue his scientific studies. He even began the final stage of his training as a Jesuit in Canterbury. But this lasted for only three months. Then a French medical review board declared him "fit for service," and in December 1914 he joined the military as a medical orderly. He was first posted to Vichy, then to Clermont, but at his own request he was soon sent as a stretcher-bearer to the front.

One wonders why he asked for this. Was it to prove something to himself or to make another sacrifice soon after his younger brother Gonzague had died at the front during the preceding month? What were his feelings? What was his share in the grief of his parents who had lost yet another of their offspring?

We will never know, but it must have been a silent, painful parting from his beloved and yet further diminished family.

Phosphorites from Le Quercy, the subject of one of Teilhard's first scientific papers. (Fondation Teilhard de Chardin)

At the Front

I think one could show that the front isn't simply the firing-
line, the exposed area corroded by the conflict of nations, but
the "front of the wave" carrying
the world . . . toward its new destiny.

By the time the war began, Teilhard had spent more than ten years as student, teacher, and researcher—enriching years full of exciting discoveries, new friends, and real growth. They were also years marked by memorable spiritual experiences and a restless quest leading to more definite certainties.

Now at the front, he found himself cut off from his customary, stable environment with its predictable pattern. He was hurled into an entirely new and different world, a world of battle and collision, a colorful world of different groups of people, with soldiers drawn from all parts of the French colonial empire. He experienced a new sense of camaraderie and fellow-feeling, and discovered more than ever before the sense and meaning of human realities. In the face of imminent danger, bloodshed, and frequent loss of life, in the terrible fight of the trenches, he discovered a powerful new vision not seen before.

Teilhard had never done any military service nor had he received any physical or spiritual training to prepare him for a soldier's life, although he enjoyed robust health and loved walking and an open-air life. He certainly had not met with anything equivalent to the hardships of life at the front, nor the physical effort and sufferings that awaited him there. The call to war was an inconvenient interruption of his studies but, like many others at the time, Teilhard hoped that this would be a short war.

Although ordained a priest in 1911, Teilhard chose to be enlisted as an ordinary soldier working among the ranks

rather than enjoying the official status and privileges of an army chaplain. After being called up in December 1914, he was sent to his regiment on January 22, 1915 where he worked throughout the war as a stretcher-bearer, one of the humblest positions in the army, often looked down upon by the combatant troops. He was attached to a Moroccan ambulance unit that became part of the 4th Mixed Regiment of Zouaves and Tirailleurs (light infantry) which combined Tunisians, Moroccans and European settlers in North Africa. It is difficult to know how far Teilhard had a say in being with these troops, but they certainly reminded him of his earlier years in North Africa.

He served with a specially chosen regiment of assault troops, one of the last to be formed, but it soon gained recognition for distinguished service and came to be counted among the best. On arrival Teilhard made himself look more like an Arab by exchanging his field-service blue for the khaki colors of the African troops, and his French military cap for a red fez.

On joining, he described his situation as being partly among non-believers, "but there's no lack of Christians, and I'm the only *priest* in the regiment."[40] Looking after the wounded, he sometimes felt helpless "when it comes to dealing with the native troops, because of the difference in language and the gulf that separates the two mentalities." He was very much a "soldier-priest" and out of regard for "Corporal Teilhard" the men used to improvise an altar and decorate

left to right:
Fort Douaumont at Verdun.
Zouaves—French Colonial Forces.
Aftermath of battle of Ypres.

"When I am in the front-line, I am frightened of the shelling, just as everyone else is. Like everyone else, I count the days until our relief, and I watch carefully for the signs that announce its arrival. When we go 'go down the line,' no one is more delighted than I am. Every time this happens I feel that this time I have at last had enough, and more than enough, of the trenches and war."
— "Nostalgia for the Front"

it for Sunday Mass, sometimes "with two or three inopportune shells to take the place of the bell." He also performed, quite spontaneously, another type of ministry at the front by assisting in parish work that had fallen to pieces in the fighting areas. There might be an abandoned or damaged church but no priest, yet there would still be people living in the area with no form of public worship. So Teilhard would go there when possible, say Mass and hold services. As his cousin records, during his four years at the front, Teilhard "carried on his ministry whenever circumstances made it possible, for he was, as he would be all his life, a priest first and foremost.[41]

Periods of battle alternated with those of rest when he could write and reflect. After the end of the second battle of Ypres he wrote to his cousin on May 28, 1915:

Breakfast in the trenches: Verdun, 1916. (Fondation Teilhard de Chardin)

> It's a long time I had a pen in my hand, and now that I have, I am writing on a packing-case in a field of beet. . . . I must humbly admit that we began to blossom out again as we left the area of shelling and became people who could look at the crops untouched and towns full of life, without any burden of danger to weigh down our spirits. In a week's time, if they leave us idle for so long, I shall no doubt feel a nostalgia for the firing line. . . . On the whole, the last part of our time at Ypres was quieter than the beginning, but then one found that the spacing out of deaths and hazards enabled one to "savor" all the bitterness more fully.[42]

Sometimes he felt weary, but at other times he described

the great diversity of people around him with considerable delight. After seeing a lively, colorful performance of the troops, he exclaimed:

> One would have to have lost the capacity to be astonished by anything not to be moved by such a scene . . . an audience of Senegalese, Martiniquans, Somalis, Annamites, Tunisians and French. . . . I brought back from it the very definite conviction that, among other results of the war, will be that of mixing and welding together the peoples of the earth in a way that nothing else, perhaps, could have done.[43]

Like so many other letters, this one was also addressed to his cousin Marguerite, with whom he corresponded regularly from December 1914 onwards. She was his major friend and confidante throughout the war years, and for many years after that. On his brief leave from duty he always went to see her to enjoy a good conversation about his thought and work.

She was the only person who really understood his ideas at this time. To her he could open himself completely. His creative essays resonated with her own work, so that they could act as mutual critics of each other's writings. She was the first to read all the essays Teilhard wrote during the war, and his fourth one, "The Struggle against the Multitude," was originally dedicated to her with the words, "An affectionate token of union in thought and Christ, Pierre, 25 March 1917."[44]

In future years, after Teilhard's death and shortly before her own, Marguerite prepared these letters for publication. Entitled *The Making of a Mind*, they reveal Teilhard's thought on death and doubt, but also his utter dedication and faithfulness to God. There are many questions, moments of suffering, sadness, and grief, but never any despair—only a deep trust in the ever-sustaining presence of God and a fervent, passionate love of life in all its forms.

His regiment was constantly on the move and was sent from one end of the front to the other. It took part in the

Marguerite Teillard-Chambon, Teilhard's cousin and close friend (1915). The war saw the beginning of their correspondence. (Fondation Teilhard de Chardin)

"I would rather like to be able to analyze and account for, briefly, this feeling of a plenitude of being and of something more than human that I've often experienced at the front and that I fear I'll miss after the war."
—Letter, September 23, 1917

"Fundamentally, I'm glad to have been at Ypres. I hope I shall have emerged more of a man and more of a priest. And more than ever I believe that life is beautiful, in the grimmest circumstances—when you can see God, ever-present, in them."

—Letter, May 28, 1915

main battles of the First World War, at Ypres, Arras, Dunkirk, Verdun, and the Marne. It was a bloody, dirty war, with many wounded and killed. Almost daily Teilhard felt at the brink of death, uncertain whether there would still be life tomorrow.

The extremes of this situation were a crucible of fire, a "baptism of the real" that forced him to give of his best, to test the strength of his faith, and to focus his inner vision by welding it to the concrete struggles of suffering humanity.

Ten days before the bloody, muddy battle for the recapture of Fort Douaumont, the most formidable of forts guarding the walled city of Verdun which the Germans had captured in February 1916, Teilhard wrote on October 14, 1916, at the end of his essay "Christ in the World of Matter":

I tell you this: I shall go into this engagement in a religious spirit, with all my soul, borne on by a single great impetus in which I am unable to distinguish where human emotions end and adoration begins.

And if I am destined not to return from those heights I would like my body to remain there, molded into the clay of the fortifications, like a living cement thrown by God into the stone-work of the New City.[45]

Teilhard on home leave, 1917, in Sarcenat. (Fondation Teilhard de Chardin)

He threw himself so fully into serving the needs of others that he became known as a man to be relied upon in dangerous situations. He was popular with both the officers and the ordinary soldiers, who were mostly Muslims. They were deprived of a chaplain of their own, and Teilhard assisted the dying and consoled the suffering men as far as he could.

The soldiers greatly appreciated his presence and help; they also recognized his power and strength of faith. Indifferent to the perils of life in the trenches, Teilhard emerged unscathed from all the battles he experienced. Working as an active stretcher-bearer under the savage conditions of the World War I battlefields, looking after the wounded, the dying, and the dead, it seems almost miraculous that he never experienced as much as a single wound himself nor a single day of illness. The soldiers of his regiment came to believe that he was specially protected by *baraka*, by divine power and grace. They called their "Monsieur Teilhard" affectionately *Sidi Marabout*, a title of great esteem and honor. *Sidi* refers to a North African settled in France—so they must have seen him as one of theirs—whereas *Marabout* comes from the Arabic *murābit*, which means a man closely bound to God, a saint and ascetic blessed with divine favor.

Teilhard discharged his daily duties as stretcher-bearer under constant enemy fire without fear. He hated the work he had to do, but he carried it out with calm courage and sovereign peace of mind, although not without fatigue and exhaustion. He was soon promoted to corporal but refused further promotion and turned down amenities his superiors would have been willing to obtain for him, since he did not want to accept anything that would distinguish him from his comrades. His efforts attracted praise and public comment. Each year he was cited in army dispatches that described him as a "model of bravery, self-sacrifice, and coolness," a man with "contempt for danger" whose "sterling character" won him the confidence and respect of all.

He was given several war decorations, and after the war, at the request of his old regiment, he was made Chevalier de la Légion d'Honneur. The award of this honor was accompanied by a laudatory description that summed up his war efforts for the outside world:

> An outstanding stretcher-bearer who, during four years of active service, was in every battle and engagement the regiment took part in, applying to remain in the ranks in order that he might be with the men, whose dangers and hardships he constantly shared.[46]

"Men who have suffered, even to the verge of death, from thirst or cold, can never again forget the deserts or the pack-ice where they enjoyed the intoxication of being the first and only men."
—"Nostalgia for the Front"

The Légion d'Honneur, awarded to Teilhard.

Crucible of Fire

There is a communion with God, and a communion with earth, and a communion with God through earth.

French soldiers at Verdun.

The war meant much more than battles, dangers, and hardship to Teilhard. It was a decisive and truly unforgettable step in his inner development.

It is astonishing what a surprising amount of work he got done between all the exhaustion of battle. With heightened sensibility and, some might say, extraordinary detachment, he went for lonely walks, reflected in solitude, and sensed the urgent need to clarify his ideas so that he could put them down on paper.

What was the meaning of all life, and of his own? Where was God on these fields of death and battle? What was humanity aiming for? And what is the role of the Christian faith in the immense cosmic process that is the evolution of life?

He started a war journal, made notes, wrote letters to relatives and friends, and composed a series of stirring essays. He wrote them for himself, but he also wrote them for the world, for he wanted to make others see what he felt, saw, and believed.

And so I started to think again, and to jot down in an exercise-book some notes about a subject that has always been for me the real problem of my interior life. . . . It is how to reconcile progress and detachment, a passionate and legitimate love of the earth's highest development and the exclusive quest for the kingdom of heaven. How can one be as much a Christian as any other man, and yet more a man than anyone?[47]

His journal, in which he noted down ideas almost daily, contains the seeds of his thought, the initial plans of his essays, later written out with a meticulous hand in full length between the spells of battle.

The turmoil of the war clarified his inner vision. It made him realize in a new way that matter was charged with life and with spirit. He felt so deeply, so vividly a love of matter, of life, that he later often used to urge his friends to trust and choose life. Even during the war he could affirm his deep-felt conviction "that *life is never mistaken*, either about its road or its destination," and proclaim that "The true summons of the cosmos is a call consciously to share in the great work that goes on within it," a vision taken up and widened many years afterwards in Thomas Berry's *The Great Work*.[48]

During the war years his own life was existentially immersed in crowds of humanity, bound up with the daily lives of many other people. He was convinced that each of us is connected by all fibers of our being—material, organic, psychic, or mental—with everything else around us. The human being, like every other being, is essentially cosmic. But all human beings together are in the process of forming a new unity, higher than merely that of a collection of individuals.

The war experience gave him a new and larger horizon. Strangely enough, it also gave him a new sense of freedom and opened the door to literary creativity. Living on the battlefield under extreme conditions, on the boundary between life and death, compelled him to articulate his thought and communicate what he had experienced. But circumstances were difficult and little conducive to writing. There were inner constraints, too, as he felt uncertain that he could really fully express what he so ardently felt.

But he had a deep desire to leave his "intellectual testament" in case he did not return from the front. Thus in the early months of 1916 he wrote with a great sense of urgency the first of his war essays, "Cosmic Life," soon to be followed by many others. Strongly autobiographical, as many of his writings are, its lyricism powerfully recaptures the bewitching, magical appeal of nature, the enchanting life of the cosmos.

"My war papers may be interesting psychologically for studying theontogenesis of an idea, but there is nothing in them that I have not expressed more clearly at a later date."
—Letter to Marguerite, 1952

Teilhard de Chardin in 1918.
(Fondation Teilhard de Chardin)

55

"To live the cosmic life is to live dominated by the consciousness that one is an atom in the body of the mystical and cosmic Christ. The man who so lives dismisses as irrelevant the host of preoccupations that absorb the interest of other men: his life is projected further, and his heart more widely receptive. There you have my intellectual testament."
—"Cosmic Life"

He describes the intoxication of the seeker with the "temptation of matter," experienced through the haunting beauty of the desert, the sea, the woods charged with life—as he had awakened to their enticing attraction when living in Egypt, Jersey, and Sussex. Should one abandon oneself to this appeal, surrender to nature, to matter? Become a pantheist, a monist?

That would mean to take the wrong road, a road of fusion and abandonment. He was searching for something greater, more universal and transcendent, a reality that could incorporate all these experiences, and he then made the ecstatic discovery that the whole of nature was filled with life that led to God.

"Cosmic Life" is preceded by the motto "To *Terra Mater,* and through her, above all, to Christ Jesus." It is in and through mother earth, through the life of nature and the world, that incarnate, divine life is encountered and felt in its full dimension. That is why the essay is preceded by the affirmation "There is a communion with God, and a communion with earth, and a communion with God through earth."

The sense of feeling is strongly present, too. Another motto, later crossed out, was penned on the first sheet of the essay: "To those passionate about the largest space;—To those who feel;—To those who will understand me."[49]

The essay is signed Dunkirk, Easter week, April 1916. In the midst of terrible battles, surrounded by the experience of death, Teilhard opens with the great affirmation:

I am writing these lines from an exuberance of life and a yearning to live; it is written to express an impassioned vision of the earth, and in an attempt to find a solution for the doubts that beset my action—because I love the universe, its energies, its secrets, and its hopes, and because at the same time I am dedicated to God, the only Origin, the only Outcome, and the only End. I want to express my love of matter and life, and to reconcile it, if possible, with the unique adoration of the only absolute and definitive Godhead.

"Cosmic Life" describes the awakening to the cosmos, the vision of its unity and structure, that he had experienced as a "temptation of matter," as a "communion with earth." This "communion" refers to a realization of cosmic consciousness, an experience of nature mysticism and pantheism. In future years Teilhard understood this "communion with earth" also as political and social engagement, as passionate struggle and effort to develop all human and natural resources and build a world of peace and justice.

But such communion, so important and necessary, was nonetheless a stage that had to lead to more. It had to be transformed and grow into a fuller vision of "communion with God through earth."

He remembered his earlier initiation into the cosmos as a temptation and crisis that his faith and the discovery of evolution had helped him to overcome. In the evolutionary process of life he discovered the rhythm and breath of spirit, the lineaments of the face and hands of God, the taking shape of what he called "the cosmic Christ." The essay culminates in a long, deeply moving, mystical prayer to Christ including the following lines:

> Lord Jesus Christ, you truly contain within your gentleness, within your humanity, all the unyielding immensity and grandeur of the world . . .
>
> I love you, Lord Jesus, because of the multitude who shelter within you and whom, if one clings closely to you, one can hear with all the other beings murmuring, praying, weeping . . .
>
> Lord Jesus, you who are as gentle as the human heart, as fiery as the forces of nature, as intimate as life itself, you in whom I can melt away and with whom I must have mastery and freedom. I love you as a world, as this world which has captivated my heart. . . . [50]

Wounded soldiers at Verdun.

"In the first world war the great citadel of Verdun became the anvil upon which French manhood was to be hammered to death."

—Winston Churchill

*"The world must have a God:
but our concept of God must be
extended as the dimensions of
our world are extended."*
—Letters from a Traveller

After a battle.

The war was like a crucible of fire wherein all his previous experiences became fused together into one great mystical vision that compelled him to write, and write ever more, in order to pass on his vision and communicate what he had experienced and seen. His childhood passion for consistence and coherence, for an Absolute, had first led him to the discovery of the immensity of the cosmos. His scientific studies and expeditions had in turn brought about the discovery of evolution, the realization that the world was alive and that it revealed the presence of some universal being. Teilhard then recognized this living being as God incarnate, present in the stream of becoming as a "Christic" element in all things, as Christ in the cosmos, whom he later named the "God-of-evolution," the universal Christ and "Christ-Omega."

His vision consumed his heart with a fire from within. As he was soon to write, he was one of those "whom the Lord had drawn to follow the road of fire,"[51] a calling that led him away from the road of fusion and abandonment to the life of matter into a world of people and action, a world that needed kindling anew with fire, the transforming fire of love and union. He was a passionate thinker, with a depth and intensity of feeling that are rare, a man full of a consuming fire burning in his heart and mind.

The symbolism of fire, and that of the road, were to recur in his writings again and again in years to come. This fire was fueled by his real, living contact with an immense world—a world of fossils, bones, stones, rocks, plants, animals, places, people, friendships, and ideas—they all provided him with the concrete, tangible "stuff of the universe." He spoke of fire as a spark, a glow, a blaze, as flames that illuminate, set alight, and consume. Nowhere is this vision more radiant and empowering than in the description of his mystical experiences. They truly express a vision of fire that filled him with wonder and amazement, ecstasy and joy, and made him see the world burst into flames. It is this fire that he wanted to pass on and kindle in others.

Mystic and Seer

Where do we seek the secret? In the desert? In the faraway past?
In secret matter? It is to be found in the future and its increase.

All his life Teilhard felt he had seen something new. Seeing God as Christ in all things brought together the cosmic, the human, the Christic. This was a powerful vision linked to experiences of a deeply mystical, or what might be called a panentheistic character, although he often simply called them "pantheistic." These experiences had occurred over many years. But he was able to describe this "vision," or what he sometimes called "his gospel," only in the intensity and heightened experience of the war.

During these years he often reflected on the nature of the mystic, the "voyant" or seer, and compared his experience with that of others. His cousin Marguerite lent him many books and reading them helped him to clarify his own ideas. He read avidly, not only contemporary novels by H. G. Wells, Maurice Maeterlinck, and other writers, but also Ralph Waldo Emerson and William James, on whom he made detailed notes.

A favorite text was Edouard Schuré's *Les grands initiés,* a popular history of Western and Eastern mysticism that he read enthusiastically, though not uncritically. He found many of his own experiences confirmed by the long row of "initiates" described by Schuré who appeared as a like-minded soul "from whom I've had a great . . . pleasure":

> the joy of finding a mind extremely sympathetic to my own,—the spiritual excitement of making contact with a soul full of enthusiasm for the world,—the satisfaction of realizing that the questions I'm concerned with are indeed those that have animated the deep-rooted life of

"I speak to you, my fellow-priests, . . . if there be any among you who are at a loss in so unforeseen a situation—with your mass unsaid and your ministry unaccomplished —remember that over and above the administration of the sacraments, as a higher duty than the care of individual souls, you have a universal function to fulfil: the offering to God of the entire world.

—"The Priest"

Christ, architect of the world.

"Never again, please God, may we be able to say of religion that its influence has made men more indolent, more unenterprising, less human; never again may its attitude lie open to the damning suspicion that it seeks to replace science by theology, effort by prayer, battle by resignation, and that its dogmas may well debase the value of the world by limiting in advance the scope of inquiry and the sphere of energy. Never again, I pray, may anyone dare to complain of Rome that it is afraid of anything that moves and thinks."

—"Mastery of the World and the Kingdom of God"

Monstrance

humanity,—the pleasure of seeing that my attempts at a solution agree perfectly, on the whole, with those of the "great initiates" without doing any violence to dogma, and (because of the integration of the Christian idea) have at the same time their own very special and original slant.[52]

He wrote two more essays during 1916. The second one, "The Mastery of the World and the Kingdom of God," returns to his earlier question of how to harmonize "service of the Earth" with "life in heaven." Their apparent clash can be resolved by pursuing both together, by showing "that religious faith is not hostile to progress but represents, rather, an additional force to be used by Christians, in the name of what they hold most sacred, to forward the common task of evolution,"[53] and what he later was to call "the building of the earth."

His third essay, "Christ in the World of Matter," bears the subtitle "Three Stories in the Style of Benson." Inspired by the mystical novels and account of Robert Hugh Benson's conversion, Teilhard writes here at his most personal and intimate, describing a vision of Christ in a picture, a monstrance, and a pyx, vessels in which the sacred host is kept. This vision was put into words when the German battle around Verdun was going on, and he himself was soon to be engaged in that battle. Amid all the fray and danger of war he sees, and is lifted up by, the face and figure of Christ whose lines are melting away into the universe, toward infinity. The entire world is vibrant with movement, with life emanating from Christ's heart, the dazzling center of matter. Here he first describes the radiant power, majesty, and beauty of Christ to which he returned in later years again and again.

The concreteness of the vision is expressed in Christ's garments, in his eyes that reflect "everything that has power to charm us, everything that has life"[54]: eyes "so gentle and filled with pity that I thought my mother stood before me"; eyes "like those of a woman, passionate and filled with the power to subdue, yet at the same time so imperiously pure that under their domination it would have been physically impossible for the emotions to go astray"; eyes "filled with a noble, virile majesty, similar to that which one sees in the eyes of men of great courage or refinement or strength."[55]

Ardently gazing into the pupils of Christ's eyes, he describes himself as dumbfounded before these "abysses of fiery, fascinating life." He could not decide whether their powerful final expression denoted "an indescribable agony or a superabundance of triumphant joy." But he knew he caught a glimpse of these absorbing eyes once again "in the glance of a dying soldier."[56] And his own eyes were dimmed with tears.

French troops advancing into battle.

There is the same experience of fusion and expansion when holding the consecrated host. It is such an overwhelming experience of unity, of the intimate connections between this divine center and the whole world, including his entire life, the years still remaining to him "to be lived and to be divinized."[57] The host in his hands, he felt he was not holding the host at all, "but one or other of the thousand entities which make up our lives: a suffering, a joy, a task, a friend to love or to console."[58]

God is at the heart of everything. That is why even the war could not disconcert him and why he could still maintain equanimity when faced with the most tremendous, terrible battles of the First World War. He was endowed with the strength of

"It is impossible for me, Lord . . . to look on your face without seeing in it the radiance of every reality and every goodness. In the mystery of your mystical body—your cosmic body—you sought to feel the echo of every joy and every fear that moves each single one of all the countless cells that make up mankind."

—"The Mystical Milieu"

an extraordinary faith and the power of a deeply discerning spirituality, a gift of grace that enabled him to transform even the suffering and violent loss of life on the battlefield into an experience where he could sense the presence of God.

Less personal, but more reflective on mystical experience is "The Mystical Milieu" (1917), written a year after "Cosmic Life." Here Teilhard describes the progress of the mystic in a series of expanding circles, not unlike the different mansions in St. Teresa's *Interior Castle*. The experience of the fundamental oneness of the universe is captured in the three successive circles of presence, consistence, and energy. The "seer" or mystic is "immersed in a *universal Milieu*, higher than that which contains the restlessness of ordinary, sensibly apprehended life: a Milieu *that knows no change*, immune to the surge of superficial vicissitudes—a *homogenous* Milieu in which contrasts and differences are toned down." But on its own, this experience means nothing less than to "be lost in naturalistic mysticism" or "godless pantheism."[59] Yet the ecstatic experience of ultimate unity makes the mystic cry out "*the world is filled* and filled with the Absolute. To see this is to be made free."[60]

The mystic's vision must lead higher still, to a communion with the essence of the universe that is creative action, pulsating energy: "The mystic was looking for the devouring fire which he could identify with the Divine that summons him from all sides: science points it out to him. *See, the universe is ablaze!*"[61] Now the mystic is plunged into an "ocean of energy" from which he draws "undiluted joy":

> In very truth, it is God, and God alone whose Spirit stirs up the whole mass of the universe in ferment. . . . The fact is that creation has never stopped. The creative act is one huge continual gesture, drawn out over the totality of time. It is still going on.[62]

The "circle of energy" leads on to the "circle of the spirit" at whose summit there is the "circle of the person." Now the seer turns from his own experience of interiority to the multitude of other beings surrounding him who, at first, had seemed "an infliction hard to bear."[63] The Divine is experienced as both transcendent to the cosmos and yet interwoven with it at all levels. The seer now realizes that action and communion are situated in neither the divine nor the created sphere alone,

but in a special reality born of their mutual interaction. The mystical milieu *is not a completed zone* in which beings, once they have succeeded in entering it, remain immobilized. It is a complex element, made up of *divinized created being*. We cannot give it precisely the name of God; it is his Kingdom. Nor can we say that it *is*: it is in the process of *becoming*.[64]

French troops in the trenches at the Marne.

How extraordinary that Teilhard could experience this process of becoming in the midst of war! That he could feel the presence of God amid so much strife, see the human and divine intermingle and take shape in the person of Jesus who in truth "*must be loved as a world*"! Kathleen Duffy offers an inspiring, new interpretation of "The Mystical Milieu" in her book *Teilhard's Mysticism. Seeing the Inner Face of Evolution* (2014), revealing how his spiritual development and mystical experience unfolded in close interdependence with his scientific understanding of the world. By drawing on contemporary scientific knowledge, musical analogies, and striking, little known passages from Teilhard's writings, she shows how the discovery of the inner face of evolution led him to the heart of God at the center of an evolutionary world. Her close reading of Teilhard's mystical experience catches the fire and radiance of what Teilhard saw and ex-

"The zest for life, which is the source of all passion and all insight, even divine, does not come to us from ourselves. . . . It is God who has to give us the impulse of wanting him."
—"The Mystical Milieu"

"Would not the reconciliation of our age with God be effected, if men were to see in themselves and in one another a part of the fullness of Christ? If they were to understand that the universe, with all its natural opulence and all its exciting reality, does not reach its full development save in Christ? And that Christ, for his part, does not reach full stature save through a universe pushed to the very limits of its potentialities?"

—"The Priest"

perienced during the Great War, and throughout his life. It conveys much of the audacity, originality, and powerful attraction of his new mysticism, steeped in a synthesis of faith and science that many are longing for today. [65]

Toward the end of "The Mystical Milieu" each paragraph finishes with an evocative invocation of the name of Jesus, almost a Jesus prayer. At the same time Teilhard points to the mystery of Christ's mystical body—his cosmic body. Here we have a vision of the cosmic and universal Christ in whom all beings converge, a powerful, unitive experience that reminds us of Gerard Manley Hopkins's lines: "The world is charged with the grandeur of God" and "Christ plays in ten thousand places, lovely in limbs, and lovely in eyes not his to the Father through the features of men's faces."[66] Teilhard later understood his own experience as a "pan-Christic" mysticism.

It was a mystical vision of great power, a vision of fire whose blaze and radiant glow were alive in him to the very end of his life. He took to writing because he wanted to pass on this vision of fire to others. He felt that those who possess the fire will inflame the world.

No sooner had he set down his powerful mystical vision than he proceeded to work out a "philosophical synthesis" of his thought, which he called "creative union." It was his own personal answer to the philosophical problem of the One and the many. Creative union was understood as a deeply coherent vision of a union between God and the world, God and the universe, and of all spiritual and material realities within it.

For Teilhard, union always implies a simultaneous process of unification as well as differentiation. Coming together in closer union always means that differences are enhanced and heightened through being combined in a new synthesis. This is where the creative moment lies, a moment he perceived in all realities, in personal relationships, in everything that is in process, everything that is truly alive.

Cry of Hope from an Abyss

. . . submerged in the tears and blood of a generation. . . . I thank you, my God, in that you have made me a priest—and a priest ordained for War.

The alluring, magical appeal of the beauty of nature resonates through every one of Teilhard's war writings. This is all the more remarkable because it is an appeal largely based on his own memory and creative imagination, for there was little beauty to be found in the trenches of the First World War except perhaps during the lull of battle, in rare moments of rest in the surrounding woods of the countryside before they were destroyed.

His sense of beauty was primarily shaped by the indelible imprint of his earlier nature experiences, the mountains, the woods, the rocks, the sea, and the desert charged with the mysteries of their hidden life. As a scientist he had analyzed the minute details of all their visible, concrete manifestations, all that he could touch, weigh up, and dissect. But his glancing eyes pierced deeper, the fibers of his soul felt and touched the inner aspects of things as much as their outer appearances.

This intensity of feeling, the celebration of exuberant life and sensuous beauty, the palpable concreteness as well as spiritual depth of his vision vibrate through all his early essays, especially "The Mystical Milieu" (1917), "The Soul of the World" (1918), "The Great Monad" (1918), "My Universe" (1918), "The Universal Element" (1919), and "The Spiritual Power of Matter" (1919). They are full of lyrical poetry that makes Teilhard's works "rank with the finest of the world's religious poetry."[67] Many passages are preludes to his later works "The Mass on the World" and the *Milieu Divin*.

Teilhard calls the experiences described in "The Mystical

"Sometimes I feel that my heart is full of things that should be said about 'mighty Nature,' about the meaning and reality of her appeal and magic, about the complete and unexpected realization . . . which Christianity grants to the pantheistic aspirations (properly understood) that will always arise with increasing intensity in man's heart."
—Letter, January 22, 1916

"The inspiration of Teilhard's poetry was threefold: mystical, derived from the cosmic Christ revealed by St. Paul; epic, derived from a paleontologist's familiarity with the vast story of man, his origins, and the origin of the universe in which he lives; and finally eschatological, derived from his semi-prophetic view of man's future."
—Claude Cuénot

Milieu" as only "*an introduction to mysticism*,"[68] but this essay points already to the rich vision of the divine "milieu" as both a radiant center and an environment in which we live and breathe. It is the fullness of life animated by and permeated with tangible and palpable signs of the divine. He also mentions the important *goût de vivre*, the zest for life, which he cherished and considered as central to human life and its future on the planet.

Yet this celebration of life and its exuberance was expressed in the midst of the horrors of war. No wonder François Mauriac praised these essays:

> The most optimistic view a Christian thinker has ever held of this criminal world was conceived at Verdun; this frantic cry of hope has been uttered from an abyss. . . . The same sort of courage that was necessary to hold out in the trenches of Verdun was also necessary for conceiving thoughts as joyful as these, so permeated by hope.[69]

Between 1916 and 1919 Teilhard wrote eighteen essays, but had little success in getting them published. Only two were accepted for publication. He asked himself quite rightly whether he would ever be understood. Aware of the originality and newness of his ideas, he realized early on how difficult it would be for his ideas to become known "except in conversation or manuscript form, passed surreptitiously from hand to hand."[70]

This remark made at the end of 1916 in a letter to his cousin was truly prophetic. This is exactly what happened to his works over the next forty years. Almost none were to be published during his lifetime. The war essays, together with some others written shortly after the end of the war, appeared eventually under the title *Écrits du temps de la guerre*, but not before 1965.[71]

They contain the germs of all his later ideas. Here we find already his urgent concern for the reinterpretation of Christianity, the need for a new image of God, the quest for a practically engaged spirituality appropriate to the needs of the contemporary world—all themes not merely worked out intellectually, but experientially rooted and developed through daily pastoral contact with men from very different religious, cultural, and social backgrounds.

Many passages of the war essays speak directly in his own voice. They are some of the most personal, most poetic passages he wrote until much later, toward the end of his life, when he returned to the same immediate form of expression in his spiritual autobiography *The Heart of Matter.* There he gathers up once again the most significant moments of his life, the most memorable and formative experiences.

Looking back at his early writings at the end of his life, Teilhard recognized them as absolutely foundational and continued to quote from them. However, they also contained nothing that was not expressed again, though differently, in years to come. Some of the early ideas eventually found their final shape in his book *The Human Phenomenon,* completed in 1940 but not published until after his death. The war experience was for him the culmination of a long, drawn-out, inner development whereby all his earlier impressions came together into one, fused into a large, universal perspective that henceforth was to carry him through the changing tides of life.

The impressions of the Great War were so overwhelming, and so essential to his inner growth, that he later felt that neither the attractions of Egypt nor the intellectual stimulations of Paris were worth as much as the dreadful horror of the war. Here, amid blood, death, and terror the soldier-priest offered up the life of the world, and his own and that of his comrades, to the transforming power and presence of God. Here he ex-

> *"The effect of the war was to break through the crust of t he commonplace and convential. . . . When peace comes, everything will once more be overlaid by the veil of the former melancholy and trivialities."*
> —"Nostalgia for the Front"

Armistice Day in Paris.

ercised his pastoral and priestly ministry for the first time to the full. And here, among all the painful suffering and loss of life, his great vision of humankind as truly one first emerged, of humanity sharing a common origin and destiny in spite of all its diversity and divisions.

The war had immersed him in an ocean of humanity where he had discovered yet another dimension of life—the sense of the human in all its organic complexity. This strengthened and further enhanced his sense of the cosmic and Christic. The powerful combination of these three senses nourished and sustained all his future work in a single vision. It is a compelling and attractive vision of great coherence, although our contemporary experience of many more horrific wars since then makes one wish that Teilhard had voiced more directly the cries of pain, the utter sense of loss and immense destruction, especially of precious human life, during those tragic battles of the First World War. His cry from the abyss of the trenches was transformed into such a strong message of hope that it is sometimes difficult to remember the powerful presence of horror and evil in this terrible war.

It was still wartime when he made his solemn vows. A few days' leave enabled him to go to Lyons, where the French Jesuits had now installed their novitiate house after returning from exile in England. His experience of the war was recognized as replacing the customary Jesuit tertianship and, with the permission of his superiors, he was allowed to take his vows on May 26, 1918, in the chapel of Sainte-Foy-lès-Lyon.

This was an occasion for joy. But a little earlier the same month another grief had been inflicted on the family. His younger brother Olivier, affectionately called Yégé, had been killed at the front on May 3. Of his brothers only Gabriel, Joseph, and Victor were still alive. First his ordination and then his solemn vows were intertwined with family deaths. It was to be a pattern of his life to have joy and suffering, growth and diminishment so closely together, like two sides of the same reality.

"After all, was it not your dearest wish that your sons should serve and that their lives should 'mount to something'— much more than that they should grow old? You see, there are lives that you could not bear to see bent or become shut in or constricted, and yet you cannot see how they could just continue to grow. It was like that, I think, with Olivier."

—Letter to his parents
May 16, 1918

Geological excursion in May 1920. Destruction from the war is plainly evident.
(Fondation Teilhard de Chardin)

During the war, Teilhard was not only a pastor, stretcher-bearer, and writer. He also remained a scientist. Wherever he went, science was never far from his mind. Whenever war activities temporarily ceased, he grasped the chance to collect minerals and small fossils. During a lengthy posting in Champagne, he was able to collect a number of valuable specimens of prehistoric fauna sufficient to provide him with the necessary material for his doctoral thesis after the war.

Following the armistice in November 1918, he was demobilized on March 10, 1919. It had been a "Great War" like none before, with more countries and people involved than in any previous war in history. The human cost had been immense, with ten million dead, killed in fights on the battlefields, by gunfire, gas, and shelling.

Somewhat disoriented at first, he even felt nostalgic about the front and its heightened sense of awareness and action. There he had felt like an "explorer" and an "extrovert," immersed in "the discharge of energy, carried to the point of self-exhaustion."[72] There he had been part of a soul greater than his own, for "the man who has passed through the fire is another species of man."[73] Survivors from the front, he felt, "will always have a void in their heart, so large that nothing we can see will ever be able to fill it." The superhuman reality that had been disclosed to them "in the

"Even in this century, men are still living as chance circumstances decide for them, with no aim but their daily bread or a quiet old age. You can count the few who fall under the spell of a task that far exceeds the dimensions of their individual lives. . . . After having for so long done no more than allow itself to live, Mankind will one day understand that the time has come to undertake its own development and to mark its one road."
—"The Great Monad"

"I should wish, Lord, in my very humble way, to be the apostle and, if I may ask so much, the evangelist of your Christ in the Universe."

—"The Priest"

shell-holes and barbed wire will never completely withdraw from the pacified world."[74]

But he was soon ready to take up his previous life again and return to the scientific studies begun before the war. As he devoted himself once more to the tasks of everyday existence, not in a spirit of selfishness, as before, but religiously, this meant for him "the consciousness of forwarding, in God and for God, the great task of creating and sanctifying a Mankind that is born above all in hours of crisis but can reach its fulfilment only in peace."[75]

Two months after his final vows, he expressed the fervor of his dedication and complete commitment in the essay "The Priest." Here traditional spirituality is interwoven with a vision of the new:

> I want, by practicing the counsels of perfection, to salvage through self-denial all the heavenly fire imprisoned within the threefold concupiscence of the flesh, of avarice, of pride: in other words, to hallow, through chastity, poverty and obedience, the power enclosed in love, in gold, in independence.
>
> That is why I have taken on my vows and my priesthood (and it is this that gives me my strength and my happiness), in a determination to accept and divinize the powers of the earth.[76]

"The Priest" introduces important themes of sacramental, Eucharistic spirituality repeated in future writings. The whole cosmos, bursting forth with teeming life, is consecrated to God and becomes an immense sacrament:

> Since today, Lord, I your Priest have neither bread nor wine nor altar, I shall spread my hands over the whole universe and take its immensity as the matter of my sacrifice. . . .
>
> The seething cauldron in which the activities of all living and cosmic substance are brewed together—is not that the bitter cup that you seek to sanctify? . . .

You, my God, have given me the gift of discerning, beneath this surface incoherence, the living and deep-rooted unity that your grace has mercifully imposed on—instilled beneath—our hopeless plurality, . . . Let creation repeat to itself again today, and tomorrow, and until the end of time, so long as the transformation has not run its full course, the divine saying: "This is my body."[77]

The essay celebrates the priestly acts of consecration, adoration, and communion. After communion Teilhard prays: "And now, my God, that in and through all things you have made me one with you, I no longer belong to myself." He considers it his vocation, his apostolate to "spread abroad the fire you have imparted to me"; he wishes "to be the apostle—and, if I dare be so bold—the evangelist—*of your Christ in the universe.*"[78]

It was a fire kindled by the vision of God's power and presence in all parts of cosmic and human life, a vision centered on a cosmic Christ of infinite extension. The consistence and coherence of this vision, its unbreakable strength, were tested to the utmost in the crucible of fire that was the war. The vision held, and would hold for a lifetime.

It was also a vision fired by the power of love: love of the world, love of God and, above all, a love of God through all the currents of life that animate the world and its myriad of faces that he sensed so strongly, desired so passionately, and embraced so totally with all his inner and outer senses. It was like being in an ocean, like bathing in the "fiery waters" of matter, in touch with the source of all life and youthfulness.[79] Nowhere was the warmth of fire greater, the attraction stronger, the love richer than in the realm of the human where it found its most intense expression in the feminine. The discovery of different faces of the feminine before, during, and after the war years fused together the cosmic, human, and Christic dimensions of Teilhard's vision into an intimate union fueled by the fires of human and divine love.

"The questions I'm concerned with are indeed those that have animated the deep-rooted life of humanity."
—Letter, December 13, 1918

Faces of the Feminine

The tender compassion, the hallowed charm, that
radiate from woman—so naturally that it is only in her that
you look for them, and yet so mysteriously that you cannot say
whence they come—are the presence of
God making itself felt and setting you ablaze.

"Everything in the universe is made by union and generation—by the coming together of elements that seek out one another, melt together two by two, and are born again in a third."
—*"The Eternal Feminine"*

A few months before completing "The Priest" Teilhard had written another essay that praises the all-pervading presence and power of love, love experienced "in the raptures of contact with God," in "the surface of divine fire,"[80] presented as a prose poem under the title of "The Eternal Feminine." He celebrates here in lyrical terms the role of love in the universe as a fundamental reality of mutual attraction and union, whether among the forces of the atom, between human beings, or between the human and divine. The feminine was to symbolize for him something universal, the unitive element in the cosmos, expressed in this essay in largely idealized, spiritual form, whether seen as wisdom, the handmaid of God's creation, as mother nature, or as the figure of Mary and the church.

He used the well-known expression "the eternal feminine" from Goethe's *Faust*, but this eternal, universal reality also expressed itself in many individual faces and forms, through the presence and friendship of particular women without whom Teilhard's personal spiritual growth would not have occurred the way it did. Such female individuality is important; it is distinct, personal, and tangible, so that it can be related to and described. It is always in a particular person that human love finds its embodiment and attraction, that it experiences the focus of its desire and passion. Perhaps it is no mere coincidence that the essay is dedicated "To Béatrix," the blessed and happy one who recalls Dante's

Beatrice, but probably points in veiled form to the person of his cousin. Had he not written to her some months before composing his essay, in the context of reflecting on Dante, "that there are few better examples than Beatrice to make one understand what is meant by the expansion (to the level of the universe) of the feeling nourished by a particular object (and of the object itself)"?[81]

Many years later, when he came to tell the story of his inner vision, Teilhard admitted that one of its essential elements would have been left out if he did not add that

> from the critical moment when I rejected many of the old moulds in which my family life and my religion had formed me and began to wake up and express myself in terms that were really my own, I have experienced no form of self-development without some feminine eye turned on me, some feminine influence at work.

He meant by this simply

> that general, half-worshipping, homage which sprang from the depths of my being and was paid to those women whose warmth and charm have been absorbed, drop by drop, into the life-blood of my most cherished ideas.[82]

As his younger brother Joseph later used to say, Teilhard was always much attracted by feminine charm. His sensibilities responded strongly to all forms of beauty, whether in nature, people, or art.

The warmth and comforting intimacy of loving feminine faces had initially been experienced through the deep family bonds that linked him to his mother and sisters, especially the older Françoise, with whom he shared a deep spiritual affinity and religious vocation, and the younger Marguerite-Marie, whose acceptance of her illness of many years embodied for him a spiritually empowering and transforming attitude toward suffering that he found deeply inspiring and energizing.

"Following up the ideas which you and I have begun turning over recently, I also asked our Lord . . . that woman may become among us that which she should be, for the perfecting and salvation of the human soul."
—Letter to Marguerite, September 8, 1916

73

Marguerite Teillard-Chambon around 1935. (Fondation Teilhard de Chardin)

But it was above all his mother with her quiet religious fervor and committed devotion who had lit the first spark of an ardent love of God in his heart that "illuminated and inflamed" his childish soul.[83] He always knew that he owed her all that was best in him. In his writings he recalls the light in her eyes, "the maternal shadow leaning over the cradle—and the radiant forms assumed by youth's dreams,"[84] but he discovered the full power of "the ideal Feminine" and its "unfading beauty"[85] only when he encountered his cousin Marguerite as an adult woman, a woman of a cultivated, fine mind, great grace, and loveliness, as well as deep faith and devotion. When meeting on the eve of the war, they fell deeply in love with each other. She became the first listener to his ideas, his first audience and reader, his first critic. Theirs was an intellectual and spiritual collaboration, but Marguerite was also the first woman who loved him as a man, and it is through her that he fully found himself.

This was a powerful experience, a new and different fire, which gave him ecstasy and joy but was not without difficulties and dangers. As he described it, it was inevitable that sooner or later he should come "face to face with the feminine."[86] The only strange thing about it was that it did not happen until he was thirty when he went to study in Paris. His cosmic and human senses were then emerging more fully, but his spiritual aspirations were still lacking in human warmth. The discovery of his love for Marguerite and her loving response changed all that. It was just the energy he needed for his ideas "to ferment and become completely organized."[87]

Yet "the feminine" is not simply identical with a particular, individual woman. It is "eternal" in that it stands for a universal principle seeking unity everywhere; it brings into being, nurtures and renews, draws into itself and makes whole. It is the unitive movement at the heart of creation, unfolding in the vast process of life. As in the Old Testament, the figure of wisdom speaks in Teilhard's poetic prose poem on "The Eternal Feminine":

Follow with your eye the vast tremor that runs, from horizon to horizon, through city and forest.

Observe, throughout all life, the human effervescence that works like leaven in the world—the song of the birds and their plumage—the wild hum of the insects—the tireless blooming of the flowers—the unremitting work of the cells—the endless labors of the seeds germinating in the soil.

I am the single radiance by which all this is aroused and within which it is vibrant.

Man, nature's synthesis, does many things with the fire that burns in his heart. He gathers power, pursues glory, creates beauty, devotes himself to science. And often he does not realize that, under so many different forms, it is always the same passion that inspires him— purified, transformed, but alive—the attraction of the Feminine.[88]

Reflecting on this attraction Teilhard realized that the living heart of the tangible is the flesh, and for a man this is encountered through the love of a woman. It dawned on him that no man, however devoted to a cause or to God, can find a road

> to spiritual maturity or plenitude except through some "emotional" influence, whose function is to sensitize his understanding and stimulate, at least initially, his capacity for love. Every day supplies more irrefutable evidence that no man at all can dispense with the Feminine, any more than he can dispense with light, or oxygen, or vitamins.[89]

It became clear to Teilhard that the powers of sexual attraction and human love not only have deep cosmic roots, but that the human propensity toward loving union—the attraction of person to person set off by a spark and bursting into flame—is part of an immense universal process of unification that he sees at work everywhere in the universe. As to

"When a man loves a woman with a strong and noble passion that exalts his being above its common level, that man's life, his powers of feeling and creation, his whole universe, are definitely held and at the same time sublimated by his love of that woman. But however necessary the woman may be to that man, to reflect, reveal, transmit and 'personalize' the world for him, she is still not the center of the world."
—"Human Energy"

"The time has perhaps come when, in conformity with the inflexible laws of evolution, man and woman—on whom life has laid the charge of advancing to the highest possible degree the spiritualization of the earth— will have to abandon that way of possessing one another which has hitherto been the only rule for living beings."
—"The Evolution of Chastity"

the relationship between men and women, he reflected on the possibilities of revolutionary transformation. His own position was determined by an utter loyalty to his faith and his vow of chastity, evident throughout his life, but his deep spiritual friendship with several women over the years made him often reflect on the relationship between the sexes and on that between sexuality and spirituality.

In 1950 he wrote that

however primordial in human psychism the plenifying encounter of the sexes may be, and however essential to its structure, there is nothing to prove . . . that we yet have an exact idea of the functioning of this fundamental complementarity or of the best forms in which it can be effected. We have a marriage that is always polarized, socially, toward reproduction, and a religious perfection that is always represented, theologically, in terms of separation.

He was looking for a third, higher road where spirit is reached through synthesis rather than dematerialization:

It is no longer a matter of retreating (by abstinence) from the unfathomable spiritual powers that still lie dormant under the mutual attraction of the sexes, but of conquering them by sublimation.[90]

He practiced such sublimation, though a harmonious balance was not always achieved without effort. Perhaps it was easiest with his cousin with whom he shared close family ties, happy childhood memories, and a deep love of the Auvergne countryside, but also much that could be taken for granted in terms of expected behavior, decorum, and respect. It was perhaps not too difficult to maintain the right kind of distance while sharing the most intimate thoughts of their souls.

The power of this love was a tremendous energy that fed his larger vision of God and the universe. Though not personally named, it is hinted at in his war essays. Right at the beginning of "The Mystical Milieu," when describing "the Circle of Presence," he speaks of a light that "glows for a moment in the depths of the eyes I love." God has initiated him through "three things, tiny, fugitive: a song, a sunbeam, a glance," resonating in all his affections:

> It drew me out of myself, into a wider harmony than that which delights the senses, into an ever richer and more spiritual rhythm that was imperceptibly and endlessly becoming the measure of all growth and all beauty.

He felt his body, soul, and spirit in a new way for

> under the glance that fell upon me, the shell in which my heart slumbered, burst open. With pure and generous love, a new energy penetrated me—or emerged from me, which, I cannot say—that made me feel that I was as vast and as loaded with richness as the universe.[91]

This love is mystically transformed. It binds him even more strongly to God so that he can exclaim:

> Lord, it is you who, through the imperceptible goadings of sense-beauty, penetrated my heart in order to make its life flow out into yourself. You came down into me by means of a tiny scrap of created reality; and then, suddenly, you unfurled your immensity before my eyes, and displayed yourself to me as a Universal Being.[92]

His heart and senses were passionately set ablaze, but his vocation was never in doubt. Marguerite became the close friend and confidante of his soul, the midwife attendant at the birth of his work while she soon emerged as a writer herself. It is difficult to say who needed the other most in these

Marguerite reading. (Fondation Teilhard de Chardin)

early years of their friendship. Initially drawn together by kinship ties, Marguerite and Teilhard discovered that they shared a deep intellectual affinity and close spiritual sympathies.

In many ways Marguerite was a pioneer who showed much courage, but also much self-effacement. Only half a year older than Teilhard, she had studied philosophy and literature at the Sorbonne and after passing the prestigious competition of the Agrégation in 1904, at the young age of twenty-four, she had been appointed headmistress of a well-placed Catholic girls school in Paris, a position of considerable responsibility where she could fully put into practice her double dedication to the education of girls and the ideals of Christian service.

A family reunion had brought them together when Teilhard went for his graduate studies to Paris before the war. Marguerite had an important position and an active social life. She could introduce her newly arrived cousin, who had spent all the years of his youth in religious houses outside France, to the literary and intellectual activities of the French capital. She could invite him to give talks about evolution and science at her school; she could turn to him when she needed sympathetic help and advice.

When he soon went off to the front, she sent him many much appreciated parcels full of necessities, but also books he requested, and book reviews, and all the things that might interest him. They wrote many letters to each other sharing their ideas, and when Teilhard had a few days' leave, they would meet and talk and talk, full of joy of being together, with the conversation continuing into their letters. There were so many ideas they wanted to discuss and explore. Thus their friendship was "precious," like a "musical note" that "gives 'tone' to our whole life." And Teilhard prayed to the Lord to help them "to make it such that it is wholly transformed into a force that leads us to him, with nothing wasted in fruitless mutual gratification (which would be a waste of energy and love)."[93]

Coming out of the war wholly unscathed, without any wound nor a single day's illness, Teilhard could see that the war had given him much, a "life of adventure and freedom from care," many open-hearted friendships with his comrades, but most of all that very special, deep friendship between him and Marguerite that they both needed so much and that he hoped would continue to grow and sustain them. He wrote to her:

> It's quite true: you were given to me for the war. But what we both gained during those five years should still be put to good use. . . . I'm sure to need you very much, to tell you what I'm feeling and doing. . . . I pray that the shadows that surround you and enter into your soul . . . may soon disappear. Never let these periods of darkness dishearten you. . . . Is there any better way of understanding and enjoying intimacy with the divine than the knowledge that our Lord is at the heart of all that moves us? Have unbounded trust, and may all your thoughts and searchings end in a feeling of complete abandonment to the infallible and loving guidance of God.[94]

Marguerite drew great strength from Teilhard's spiritual direction and advice. At one stage she wondered whether she should enter the religious life, but she did not really have a vocation and Teilhard felt that she should wait to see where God would lead her through natural development and circumstances, to practice action and sanctification together hand in hand.

Her ideals found expression in her total dedication to the education of women and their professional advancement, later actively supported through her work for a union of Catholic women teachers. The spiritual significance of this, and of her closeness to Teilhard, were expressed through a solemn promise to God to devote herself wholly to education, made some months after Teilhard himself had taken his final vows as a Jesuit.

"However fundamental woman's maternity may be, it is almost nothing in comparison with her spiritual fertility. Woman brings fullness of being, sensibility, and self-revelation to the man who has loved her."
—"The Evolution of Chastity"

Teilhard acknowledged the importance of Marguerite's promise, writing to her:

> how deeply I shared your joy and how much at the same time I feel that our union was being made closer "*in Christo Jesu*," in whom union never stands still, but progresses indefinitely, in intimacy and fruitfulness and beauty.[95]

At the same time he assured her that while marching with his regiment he continued to think of her and all that made up their common interest. He knew how much he owed to her. His profound indebtedness was expressed at the moment of the armistice:

> Pray that I may take the right road in these opening hours of the new life that is soon to begin for me. And pray still more that the passion for living and spiritualizing, which is my only strength and which you help me so much to keep burning, may never cease to glow.[96]

Teilhard's passion for "living and spiritualizing" was always kept alive. Other women friends, besides his cousin, helped to keep it burning in the years to come. It cannot always have been easy for Marguerite, who remained deeply loyal to Teilhard. She outlived him by a few years but, like other women, she stands in the shadow of a great man so that we know relatively little about her except that she edited the letters written during Teilhard's travels, and, before her death, she also prepared the edition of his war correspondence addressed to her, preceded by a fine essay on "the Great War" and Teilhard's experience in it.

However, we have none of Marguerite's letters, and all personal references in Teilhard's letters have been cut; some of his letters are also missing. Not all the emotional turmoil, searching questions, and uncertainties of two people at a decisive stage in their lives are given expression in the texts we have. What are the dark shadows surrounding her? Marguerite may well have fallen ill with depression, for she gave up her headship in 1922 and took a year's rest in Italy to recover from illness. Afterward she returned to her school, but simply as a teacher, no longer the head. For the next thirty years of her life and more, her energy went into teaching, and into her historical novels, one of which was on President Lincoln and another attracted a distinguished literary prize. Some dialogues between men and women in her novels reflect perhaps some of her own thoughts and experiences, but one would have to do detective work to unravel their emotional threads.

It is beyond doubt that Marguerite was the first great love of Teilhard's life. The deep bond between them lasted to the end of his days. But she was not his only woman friend. Many other remarkable women were to give him warmth, love, energy, and inspiration, contributing to the development of his ideas, his well-being, his happiness. In 1918, during one of his brief leaves from the trenches, Marguerite herself introduced him to one of her closest women friends, Léontine Zanta, whose student she once had been. Teilhard developed an important friendship with Léontine Zanta who soon became another of his regular correspondents.

Born in 1872, this remarkable woman intellectual from Alsace stands out through her writing, lecturing, and numerous social activities. Her salon brought together distinguished philosophical, literary, and ecclesiastical figures who regularly met in her home. Taught Latin and Greek as a young girl by her father, she had insisted on studying philosophy in Paris and was only the second woman to obtain a philosophy degree, in 1898, followed by the first doctorate in the same subject, in 1914. Her thesis had been on "The Revival of Stoicism in the Sixteenth Century," but she was also much drawn to Plato and other ancient philosophers, and to different ideas of religion and mysticism.

Her passion, however, was the advancement of women and their right to take up professional careers, a right she

Teilhard on a walk in Chambon in the company of his cousins and Lèontine Zanta, around 1924. (Fondation Teilhard de Chardin)

Lèontine Zanta in 1923.
(Fondation Teilhard de Chardin)

vigorously defended in public speeches and newspaper articles. Thus she came to play a leading part in French feminism during the early decades of the twentieth century. Some of her friends called her by the name of "Hypatia," after the ancient woman philosopher, and others called her "the lamp." While she never held a position in higher education, she did become a journalist and writer, publishing several novels. Simone de Beauvoir later remembered being inspired by Léontine Zanta's example as a woman philosopher. She was not only well known for her ideas but also for her outstanding beauty and elegance, much commented upon by her contemporaries, who compared her appearance to that of a Renaissance princess.

Teilhard was introduced to her circle of friends, whom he met regularly at her house. After the war, when he was living in Paris again, they had many long discussions on philosophy, but also on social and feminist issues, such as the role of women in contemporary society, Léontine Zanta's great theme. She opened up yet another large horizon and helped to develop his ideas about the importance of women and the feminine as the unitive element in the unfolding of a new and greater world.

He wrote to her regularly between 1923 and 1938, intimate, personal letters in which he freely described his experiences, and spoke of his crises, doubts, and reflections, but also addressed lines of spiritual direction to her.[97] It is almost as if this correspondence carries on from the earlier letters exchanged with Marguerite in telling us about his significant inner development between the two world wars. Mademoiselle Zanta, as she was often called, was almost ten years older than Teilhard. A committed Catholic with quite an exceptional mind, she now became his wise woman friend whom he truly trusted, who "commented, questioned, clarified—in fact played her part in the building of the magnificent edifice" of his work.[98] But he was never passionately drawn and committed to her with his whole being in the way he had been "set on fire" by his cousin.

Teilhard was to encounter many more women friends in his life, and we'll meet several of them later in this book. Several corresponded with him for many years. His letters to Léontine Zanta were written between May 1923 and February 1939; his friend then died on June 14, 1942. In the mid-1920s an American, Ida Treat, had also come into his life, opening yet other new horizons with her ardent views on Marxism and her active engagement as a communist. A decade later, it was Rhoda de Terra, the wife of a paleontological colleague, and in the early 1930s he formed a lasting bond of deepest love with an American sculptress, Lucile Swan, who loved him with a radiant warmth and passion he had not met before. Lucile, "the light," sparked off a fire of great intensity that burnt throughout the mature years of his manhood. His family, friends, and future admirers were not to know of the power of this mutual love, its intimacy and commitment, its separations, disappointments, and pain, until many years after the death of both Teilhard and Lucile, when the publication of their letters broke the long maintained silence over the nature of their relationship.

But this love between Teilhard and Lucile emerged only when he later worked in China, whereas the years immediately after the First World War were spent in metropolitan Paris.

Post-War Years in Paris

*All around us, tangibly and materially, the thinking envelope
of the earth—the noosphere. . . .*

*"Already, in the silence of the
night, I can hear through this
world of tumult a confused
rustling as of crystalline needles
forming themselves into a
pattern or of birds huddling
closer together in their nest—
a deep murmur of distress, of
discomfort, of well-being, of
triumph, rising up from the
Unity which is reaching its
fulfilment. My heart was
trembling with an emotion that
embraced everything in
the world. . . ."*
            —"The Great Monad"

Teilhard spent Easter 1919 in Paris. After some rest
following the exhaustion of war, he was soon back at
work completing his studies for a natural science degree at
the Sorbonne. He installed himself in a house in the Rue du
Vieux Colombier, which he described as his "dovecot" where
he could study, think, and write. In July 1919 he passed his
certificate in geology, and that in botany in October 1919
and zoology in March 1920. As he already had experience of
advanced research, he was encouraged to return to Marcellin
Boule at the Museum in order to work for a doctorate.

Thus, after Easter 1920, he immersed himself in research
work for his dissertation. This was concerned with the study
of the mammals of the Lower Eocene in France. It was his
third major scientific research project after his earlier examination of first the carnivores and then the primates of the
phosphorite beds of Le Quercy.

He made more new friends, too. From a professional
point of view it was important that the prehistorian Abbé
Breuil introduced him to the mineralogist Abbé Gaudefroy,
recently appointed to a chair at the Institut Catholique.
Through his recommendation Teilhard secured a teaching
position in geology at the same institute, where he gave
courses from 1920 onward. He was happy that he now had
a platform from which to expound his ideas and also the
opportunity to give talks to student groups in other colleges.
But being honest with himself, he confided to his friend
Father Auguste Valensin that although he had made every
effort to obtain this teaching appointment, he would "naturally have preferred a post as 'prospector' at Beirut, Shang-

hai, or Trichinopoly, where I could get away from crowds."[99]
There was still the lure of the East and the attraction of being a lone researcher.

Abbé Breuil also introduced him to Édouard Le Roy (1870-1954), the distinguished philosopher of science, ethics, and religion, and successor of Henri Bergson at the Collège de France. Teilhard found him congenial and shared his philosophical views on pragmatism. Not unlike William James, Le Roy held that the truth and full significance of beliefs is found in acting them out, for this will truly show whether they work.

Teilhard visited Le Roy regularly on Wednesday evenings when the two discussed their ideas, and during the years 1921-1946 they also corresponded with each other. Le Roy was a thinker of great originality who stimulated Teilhard's own thinking and in turn drew on Teilhard's views on the philosophy of biology and the biosphere, which greatly influenced his lectures and publications. The two worked so closely together that Le Roy could later say of his own book *L'exigence idéaliste et le fait d'évolution* (1928), "I have so often and for so long talked over with Père Teilhard the views expressed here that neither of us can any longer pick out his own contribution."[100] But the importance of Le Roy's thought for Teilhard cannot be overestimated either.

While undertaking detailed scientific work for his doctoral research, Teilhard simultaneously continued to pursue his philosophical and religious questions. In the spring of 1922 he gave a brilliant defense of his doctorate before an unusually distinguished gathering in Paris. One of the examiners noted:

> The oral examination amply confirmed the excellent impression produced by reading the manuscript. The way in which the questions making up the second thesis were treated brought out the candidate's teaching ability and clarity of mind. He is certainly marked out for a fine fu-

No. 13, Rue du Vieux Columbier in Paris, where Teilhard lived for several years. (Photograph by Ursula King)

"What we now propose is to regard the thinking envelope of the biosphere as of the same order of zoological . . . magnitude as the biosphere itself. . . . And this amounts to imagining, in one way or another, above the animal biosphere a human sphere, the sphere of reflection, of conscious invention, of the conscious unity of souls (the Noosphere, if you will) and to conceiving at the origin of this new entity, a phenomenon of special transformation affecting preexistent life: hominization."

—"Hominization"

ture in science. The board of examiners had no hesitation in conferring on him the title of doctor, with distinction.[101]

His success was crowned by being elected president of the Société Géologique de France and promoted to an adjunct professorship in geology at the Institut Catholique. He was now an acknowledged master of his profession, recognized and consulted by his peers. His network of international contacts widened; he counted Maurice Blondel, Auguste Valensin, Abbé Breuil, Marcellin Boule, and others among his friends. It was a period of intense intellectual activity leading to new creativity and more writing in the scientific and religious fields.

If one thinks of the later French "worker-priests," we could say that he was one of them, but in the sense of a "researcher-priest," who wrote in one of his essays: "Christ requires for his body the full development of man, and that mankind, therefore, has a duty to the created world and to truth—namely, the ineluctable duty of *research*."[102]

During 1922 he attended conferences in Basle and Brussels. There he met for the first time Dr. Wong, the co-director of the Chinese Geological Service. Little did he know then that he himself would be later associated with the scientific work of this service. He also kept up his pre-war connections and friendships. During the summer of 1919, soon after his return from the army, he went back to Jersey to study and see his friends, but also to write. It was here that his monistic experience of the presence of spirit in matter found its strongest expression in the stirring essay "The Spiritual Power of Matter," culminating in a rhapsodic "Hymn to Matter":

I bless you, matter, and you I acclaim: not as the pontiffs of science or the moralizing preachers depict you, debased, disfigured—a mass of brute forces and base appetites—but as you reveal yourself to me today, *in your totality and your true nature.*

He addresses matter directly, blesses and praises its beauty, its pain, its potential as crucible of spirit:

Blessed be you, impenetrable matter: you who, interposed between our minds and the world of essences, cause us to languish with the desire to pierce through the seamless veil of phenomena. . . .

You who batter us and then dress our wounds, you who resist us and yield to us, you who wreck and build, you who shackle and liberate, the sap of our souls, the hand of God, the flesh of Christ; it is you, matter, that I bless. . . .

I acclaim you as the divine *milieu*, charged with creative power, as the ocean stirred by the Spirit, as the clay molded and infused with the life by the incarnate Word. . . .

If we are ever to possess you, having taken you rapturously in our arms, we must then go on to sublimate you through sorrow.

Your realm comprises those serene heights where saints think to avoid you—but where your flesh is so transparent and so agile as to be no longer distinguishable from spirit.

Raise me up then, matter, to those heights, through struggle and separation and death; raise me up until, at long last, it becomes possible for me in perfect chastity to embrace the universe.[103]

He showed this essay to his friend Valensin, who was writing a survey article on pantheism for a Catholic encyclopedia at that time. Teilhard was convinced of the power of "living pantheism" and argued that it needs to be integrated into the Christian faith. In his view, Valensin didn't see this and was simply interested in criticizing an unacceptable philosophical system without taking into account the human need "to revere an omnipresence" in the universe. Teilhard, on the contrary, wanted to emphasize "the Christian

"The least one may say is that many people have believed that they have experienced 'cosmic consciousness.'"
—"Pantheism and Christianity"

The Institut Catholique in Paris.

> *"In the present teaching of theology and asceticism, the most prominent tendency is to give the word 'mystical' (in mystical body, mystical union) a minimum of organic or physical meaning . . . it may be because to build up a theology it is much simpler and safer to deal with juridical relationships . . . than with physical relationships and organic connections."*
> —"Pantheism and Christianity"

Teilhard and Paul Jodot on a geological excursion in 1921. (Fondation Teilhard de Chardin)

soul of pantheism or the pantheist aspect of Christianity."[104] True Christianity must embrace the whole of creation, the whole of the cosmos, it must take up the "spellbinding grandeur" of nature and assimilate it in order to respond to the deepest human yearnings.

He similarly countered Blondel's criticisms of "The Spiritual Power of Matter" and concluded from their exchange of letters that Blondel perhaps lacked a certain "cosmic sense." Blondel, as others after him, was probably shocked by the realism, the very concreteness of Teilhard's love of the universe. His pantheism and mysticism combined in a new way the love of God with love of the world. Wanting to distinguish between true and false pantheisms, he was groping to express what is best called "panentheism," a feeling of the presence and action of God in all things.

For most religious people the mystical has little organic or physical meaning, but exists only on an abstract, spiritualized level. But for Teilhard every reality, every experience is rooted in the texture of the living cosmos from which it draws its life and nourishment. The spiritual is not "an attenuation of the material, . . . it is in fact the material carried beyond itself: it is super-material."[105] The unifying experience of the cosmos represents a "natural mysticism of which Christian mysticism can only be the sublimation and crowning peak."[106]

He already perceived a religious crisis among his contemporaries because of the antagonism between the traditional understanding of God and new attitudes to the natural world. The human need for worship is seeking new forms of expression that he recognized after the First World War in "the present proliferation of neo-Buddhisms, of theosophies, of spiritualist doctrines."[107]

This often repeated insight was not unlike another idea he developed during these years. Since the war he had realized that humankind formed a single whole, a large, cosmic reality that far transcended individuals and groups. This human reality could be studied and was like a dynamic, living organism that covered the entire globe, a network whose threads stretched over the face of the whole earth.

At first, in the trenches, he had likened this vision to the rise of an immense Thing, the rise of a unified, new earth, which he compared to the rising of the pale moon over a sleeping world. In January 1918 he had written:

> I have just been watching the moon rise over the crest of the nearby trenches. The timid slim crescent of earlier evenings has gradually grown to a full and shining disc. Solitary and majestic, the moon, which a fortnight before had been invisible, disengaged itself from the ridges of black soil, and seemed to glide across the barbed wire. In this shining body that hangs in the heavens I greet a new symbol. . . . Is it the moon that rises over the dark trenches this evening, or is it the earth, a unified earth, a new earth?[108]

After the war he referred to the thinking earth as the "Anthroposphere," but eventually, in 1925, this reality was given a new name, "noosphere." This was to become one of his key ideas, an absolutely central element of his vision. Just as the zone of life—the total mass of living organisms—was the biosphere, a living layer above the non-living world of the geosphere, so there was yet another, thinking layer, a sphere of mind and spirit surrounding the globe. It is like a thinking envelope of the earth of which all humans are part. All contribute to it through their thinking, feeling, connecting, and interacting with each other, and above all, through their powers of love. The emergence of the noosphere is an important step forward in becoming human, in the process of transformation he called "hominization."

Teilhard first described the noosphere in a long essay titled "Hominization," written in 1925. It bears the subtitle "Introduction to a Scientific Study of the Phenomenon of Man" and is a remarkable pointer to his major book on this

Teilhard in 1923. (Fondation Teilhard de Chardin)

"We now understand that when Christ descends sacramentally into each one of his faithful it is not simply in order to commune with him; it is in order to join him, physically, a little more closely to himself and to all the rest of the faithful in the growing unity of the world."
—"Pantheism and Christianity"

"All around us, tangibly and materially, the thinking envelope of the Earth—the Noosphere—is multiplying its internal fibers and tightening its network; and simultaneously its internal temperature is rising, and with this its psychic potential."

—"The Planetization of Mankind"

subject, not begun until the late 1930s. The human being is the key to the understanding of evolution; it is also pointing beyond itself, to "a higher pole or center that directs, sustains and assembles the whole sheaf of our efforts."[109]

After Teilhard had coined the word "noosphere," the philosopher Édouard Le Roy and the Russian geologist Vladimir I. Vernadsky soon adopted the term and helped to make it better known. Teilhard was especially close to Le Roy between 1920 and 1930, but their interests developed in different directions after that. But even in the 1940s Le Roy could still say that his own work consisted in little more than reproducing the results of their joint thinking. On learning about Le Roy's death in December 1954, Teilhard wrote to Le Roy's wife that the philosopher had helped him "to see," just as his friends Pére Valensin and Pére Charles had done, and they had all passed away within one year of each other. Teilhard had now lost three of his oldest and most precious friends. He summed up his relationship to Édouard Le Roy, about ten years his senior, in a letter to Claude Cuénot:

Sacré-Coeur, the Basilica of the Sacred Heart in Paris.

I loved him like a father, and owed him a very great debt. It was not exactly that I owed any particular idea to him, but . . . he gave me confidence, enlarged my mind (and my feeling of loyalty to the Church), and also served (at the Collège de France) as spokesman for my ideas, then taking shape, on "hominization" and the "noosphere." I believe, so far as one can ever tell, that the word "noosphere" was my invention; but it was he who launched it.[110]

Discovery of China

What better opportunity to initiate . . . and associate myself with the building-up of the future could I hope for than to go and lose myself for weeks on end in the fermenting mass of the peoples of Asia?

Teilhard's work in Paris was going well. His career as a brilliant research scientist and much sought-after lecturer might simply have continued in the same way for years, had he not received an invitation to go to China. It came from one of his Jesuit confrères, Father Émile Licent, who had explored the Yellow River Basin and assembled a substantial natural history collection in the port city of Tianjin (formerly known as Tientsin), not far from Beijing. During the late nineteenth century the ancient city of Tianjin, situated on the Hai river and Grand Canal close to the sea, was opened to foreign trade, thus developing into a major seaport and gateway to the capital. The Treaty of Tianjin (1856) gave Europeans the right to establish "concessions" for trade on the mainland. As a result British, French, German, Russian and also Japanese concessionary bases were developed as separate settlements along the Hai river, forming a colonial expatriate milieu which Teilhard came to know well in the 1920s and '30s. Today Teilhard would not recognize the modern metropolis that Tianjin has become, the fourth largest city in China with a population of over 10 million.

An explorer rather than a paleontologist, Émile Licent was not able to analyze by himself all the fossil finds he had collected during his travels in China. He sent the most significant specimens to Marcellin Boule at the Paris Museum, where Teilhard was entrusted with studying them.

The two Jesuits began to correspond in 1921. They had already met briefly in 1914 when Licent had visited the

"In the life of the Far East his mind found a new freedom. The grandeur of nature in a vast new continent, the multiplicity of human types he met on his travels and in the cosmopolitan society of Peking, gave depth and richness to his thought. . . . The trenches of the 1914 war had been for him what the cell is to the monk or what his 'stove' was to Descartes. Père Teilhard now became the wandering hermit of the Asian deserts, a background that facilitated the ascent of his powerful spirit, and gave full scope to an outstanding personality and outstanding destiny."
—Marguerite Teilhard-Chambon

Church in Tianjin.

Father Émile Licent in 1927.
(Fondation Teilhard de Chardin)

Paris Museum of Natural History and felt they could collaborate. Though very different personalities, Teilhard and Licent were near contemporaries and for years shared each other's work. However, to assess the scientific value of Licent's Chinese finds in full, Teilhard needed more information. He had to go to China himself. A French paleontological mission was set up under Licent's direction, supported by grants from the French Ministry of Education, the Paris Academy of Sciences, the French Natural History Museum, and the Jesuit fathers of North China. As Teilhard could get a leave of absence from his teaching post at the Institut Catholique, he was sent by the Museum to join Father Licent in a newly planned expedition along the Yellow River.

What good fortune! At long last his dream to go farther East would come true. But the trip would also provide an opportunity to distance himself from some of the personal connections with his cousin and the close emotional attachment they had formed. On April 6, 1923, he sailed from Marseilles, fully knowing that without Father Licent's invitation he might never have set foot in the Far East. Apart from the great scientific opportunities this visit offered, it also answered his desire to see for himself the distant country his brother Albéric had visited more than twenty years earlier and the place where his beloved sister Françoise had lived and died.

Teilhard's approach to the East was slow. The outward journey included brief stops in Port Said, Colombo, Penang, Malacca, Saigon, and Hong Kong. Multiple new impressions increased the fascination and confusion created by the East. New people and places, different landscapes and cultures, attracted his reflective attention and were carefully recorded in the letters sent home, later published as *Letters from a Traveller*, edited by his cousin Marguerite and mainly addressed to her, but also to some other friends. He wrote with enthusiasm: "I came to China to follow my star, and to steep myself in the raw regions of the universe."[111]

After landing in Shanghai, Teilhard took the train to the treaty-port of Tianjin, then already a large city and important trade center. By 1920 Tianjin had a foreign population of over 11,000, mainly Europeans,

The University of Tianjin in 1923. (Fondation Teilhard de Chardin)

Americans, Japanese, and Russians, settled in concession districts next to the indigenous city with a Chinese population of 837,000. Thus the newcomer Teilhard joined a well-established expatriate colonial milieu, living in a Jesuit house located in the British concession.

The Jesuits had built a small museum to house Father Licent's natural history collection. In 1923 they had also opened the High Institute of Commercial and Industrial Arts "to give young men of China a serious training in technical subjects which the economic development of the country renders necessary."[112] Little did Teilhard realize on arrival that this particular place in China was soon to be his own base and "milieu" for many years to come. Shortly after his arrival toward the end of May, he wrote to his friend Abbé Breuil:

> My strongest impression at the moment is a confused one that the human world (to look no further than that) is a huge and disparate thing, just about as coherent, at the moment, as the surface of a rough sea. I still believe, for reasons imbued with mysticism and metaphysics, that this incoherence is the prelude to a unification. . . . The multiplicity of human elements and human points of view revealed by a journey in the Far East is so "*overwhelming*" that one cannot conceive of a religious life,

"I am persuaded that at all costs we must cling to a faith in some direction and in some destination assignable to all this restless human activity."
—Letter, May 27, 1923

93

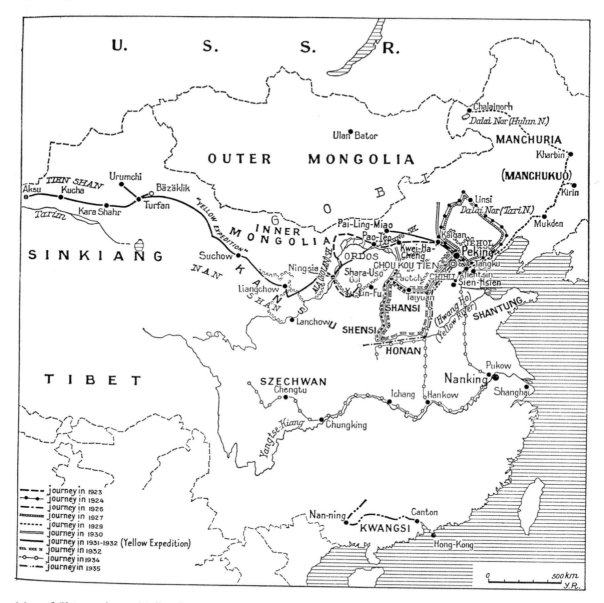

Map of China indicates Teilhard's journeys. (Fondation Teilhard de Chardin)

a religious organism, assimilating such a mass without being profoundly modified and enriched by it.[113]

While he expressed the wish to become a stronger Christian, he also referred to "the spiritual unity of humanity"[114] and looked for "new currents of thought and mysticism" from the East that might help "to rejuvenate and fertilize our European world."[115] This need for renewal is also expressed in another letter of the same period where he writes:

> I feel, more strongly than ever, the need of freeing our religion from everything about it that is specifically Mediterranean. . . . The majority of oriental thought-patterns are . . . outmoded and obsolescent, fated to disappear. . . . But . . . by taking these forms, decayed though they be, into account, we discover such a wealth of potentialities in philosophy, in mysticism, and in the study of human conduct that it becomes scarcely possible to be satisfied with an image of a mankind entirely and definitely enveloped in the narrow network of precepts and dogmas in which some people think they have displayed the whole amplitude of Christianity.[116]

Yet there was little time to pursue these ideas in depth. He was soon to set out for his first expedition to western Mongolia. Sailing up the Yellow River, Licent and Teilhard pitched their camp on the banks of the Shara-ousso-gol, "a strange little river which runs at the bottom of a canyon over two hundred and fifty feet deep," near a Mongol settlement.[117] The river's Mongolian name means "yellow waters" as its channel is always loaded with silt. Another name for it is Red Willows River, for its banks were once lined with such trees. This site was at the edge of the Ordos Desert, where they set to work digging for fossils, wandering for weeks on mule-back across mountains and deserts. They were lucky in gathering numerous remains from the Upper Paleolithic era. In about ten days they collected five hundred kilos of worked stones several hundred thousand

"The Mongol women . . . look you frankly in the eyes from beneath their coral-beaded diadems, and they ride on horseback like the men. . . . I remember running into a traveling family . . . Well, it was the woman who led the way, like a queen. I told myself that you would have liked to see it."
—Letter to Léontine Zanta, August 7, 1923

years old. They also found many perfectly preserved animal fossils—rhinoceros, elephant, bison, deer—so that Teilhard could take some fifty cases of stones and fossils with him back to the Museum in Paris. It was an abundant harvest, for seldom do fossils occur in such a well-preserved state as they did at this site.

The four months' expedition was so successful that he decided to extend his stay until the next year. This allowed him to undertake another expedition with Father Licent in the following spring, when they traveled to the high Mongolian plateau and along the edge of the Gobi desert, enlivened by caravans of Mongol carts, between a hundred and two hundred at a time traveling nose to tail, carrying or coming back from carting salt to China.

Between the two expeditions, during the winter of 1923-1924, he was busy studying the materials in the museum in Tientsin. He also had opportunities to visit Beijing several times and make contact with the Christian communities served by the Jesuit missions in North China. Moved by their very simple living conditions, he felt impressed by the good effect of their work on the people around them. Yet on his travels he often had reason to be critical of Christian missionaries, just as he was critical of the Buddhist lamas he encountered in Mongolia.

During his visits to Beijing he met American anthropologists, paleontologists, and geologists, but also Chinese, French, English, Swedish, and Russian scientists who came to attend scientific meetings. Teilhard felt enthusiastic about

> tackling the study of the earth in a more radical and comprehensive fashion . . . looking at it as a whole, endowed with specifically terrestrial, mechanical, physical, and chemical properties. . . . If I had to start again I should go in for geodynamics or geochemistry.

At the same time he was enchanted with discovering the charms of Beijing:

"I have not found in China (so far as I have seen it) the ferment whence I hoped we might draw the generous wine that would reinvigorate our West."
—August 15, 1923

Great Wall of China.

What I like, at Peking [now called Beijing], is the feeling of being at the heart of old China. My finest memories of the place may be recollections of coming home at night sometimes in a rickshaw through dark and twisting little streets under magnificently starred skies, against which there loom, just like "Chinese" shadow-pictures, the little curved roofs, and the gnarled and ancient trees covered with ravens' nests.[118]

The Gobi Desert. (Photograph by Ursula King)

The encounter with China was a momentous experience for him. It affected him as deeply as, though very differently from, the war. The discovery of the heart of this vast continent, at a time when only the simplest forms of travel were possible, revealed to him the immensity of the earth, but also the rich diversity of its people.

On their expeditions, when not camping in tents, the two Jesuits stayed in simple Chinese country inns or farm houses, in Buddhist lamaseries, and occasionally at Christian mission houses. They met very different people, whether from Mongolian, Tibetan, and Chinese Muslim backgrounds. Their scientific excursions led them away from the centers of habitation into very isolated, ancient regions where the slow pace of travel left plenty of time for reflection.

Mongolia struck Teilhard "as a 'museum' of antique specimens . . . a slice of the past" that seemed like "an empty reservoir."[119] Yet this period in isolated Mongolia was like a retreat for him, almost like the war, in that it led him "to the heart of the unique greatness of God."[120] Surrendering himself to an "active feeling of communion with God through the Universe" he felt the power of the heart of Christ as "a fire with the power to penetrate all things." He felt "more and more intensely that this 'great Christ' alone can animate my life."[121] Many years later he was to say that his "pan-Christic" mysticism emerged in full and found its mature form through the experience of "the two sweeping winds of Asia and the War."[122]

In the great deserts and steppes of China he discovered a new sense of life, a sense of its meaning and direction. Aware of the vastness of Outer Mongolia, with Turkestan and Tibet not far away, and with its mixture of races and cultures, he savored the beauty of the seasons and recalled his favorite memories. Toward the end of his first expedition, in late September 1923, he wrote:

> The season is remarkably mild this year, and autumn is at its most alluring. This past fortnight the steppe has been piercingly beautiful. The sun—gold, and not so fierce—has cast a gentle glow over the great grey undulations. . . . No sound but the calls of little red-beaked crows, or the strange cry of camels at pasture, or the tinkle of some caravan. All my memories of autumn (my favorite season) came crowding in on me: autumns on the high plateaux of Auvergne . . . autumns in Egypt when evening is almost cool as it falls over the violet desert; autumns at Hastings with the golden beeches and the sea wind over the rounded "downs" or the wide saltings. I feel it all as I never have before; but also in a rather different way: with a certain melancholy, for autumn is upon my life, too, and yet with much greater clarity and peace, for now I am better able to discern what it was that vaguely called to me across the deep and enigmatic charm of those hours in which one feels nearer to, more enveloped in, the world.

At the same time he realized that "historical and geographical research is, in itself, empty and deceptive, the true science being that of the future as gradually disclosed by life itself."[123]

Writing down his impressions of Mongolia after his first

expedition, he expressed his disappointment in not finding elements of renewal in this ancient region, among its very different people. It was a remote world where the Mongols still lived in their yurts as they had lived a thousand years ago. He could find nothing really new there but had to look for that in another direction. Thus his expedition made him conclude: "I am a pilgrim of the future on my way back from a journey made entirely in the past," a remark often quoted to characterize Teilhard's future-oriented vision.[124]

The relative isolation of the Ordos expedition was a kind of retreat that stood in stark contrast to his intensive war experience when he had been immersed among people, surrounded by continuous movement and action. In China he experienced the opposite—solitariness, lack of life, absence of vigorous activity. Halfway through the first expedition he commented:

> Though I have less leisure than during the war, and perhaps less freshness too . . . , in the last two months I have found myself in similar isolation and confronted with realities equally vast. And both these conditions are eminently favorable for meditating on the great All. Now, in the vast solitudes of Mongolia (which, from the human point of view, are a static and dead region), I see the same thing as I saw long ago at the "front" (which from the human point of view, was the most alive region that existed): one single operation is in process of happening in the world, and it alone can justify our action: the emergence of some spiritual reality, through and across the efforts of life.[125]

How this reality revealed itself across the sustained efforts of his own daily life is movingly expressed in what he wrote during this first visit to China. The intensity of his spiritual experience and vision are gathered up in a short literary work that eventually came to be known as "The Mass on the World."

"I only came to China in the hope of being better able to speak about the 'great Christ' in Paris. I feel more and more intensely that this 'great Christ' alone can animate my life."
—September 12, 1923

Mass on the World

In a sense the true substance to be consecrated each day is the world's development during that day—the bread symbolizing appropriately what creation succeeds in producing, the wine (blood) what creation causes to be lost in exhaustion and suffering in the course of its effort.

"Instinctively. . . . I would rather set up my tent here below on some hill-top of my own choosing. I am afraid, too, like all my fellow-men, of the future too heavy with mystery and too wholly new, towards which time is driving me. Then like these men I wonder anxiously where life is leading me. . . ."

—*"The Mass on the World"*

Communion with Christ through all things was Teilhard's particular vocation. As a dedicated priest, also passionately devoted to the science of the earth, its life, and that of human beings, he wanted to offer up the whole of creation to God. He first began this particular kind of offering when he lived in the trenches. Often with no place or time to say his daily Mass, he thought of what he then called his "Mass on Things." During his first expedition to China he renamed his offering "The Mass on the World."

Teilhard's earliest drafts of his idea of a cosmic offering are found in his war diaries. They were given their first literary expression in July 1918 in "The Priest." That essay had been shaped by three moments of the Mass—consecration, adoration, and communion. There Teilhard had written that, since he had neither bread nor wine nor altar, he was taking the whole universe as the matter of his sacrifice. "The Mass on the World" opens with almost identical words:

> Since once again, Lord—though this time not in the forest of the Aisne but in the steppes of Asia—I have neither bread, nor wine, nor altar, I will raise myself beyond these symbols up to the pure majesty of the real itself; I, your priest, will make the whole earth my altar and on it will offer you all the labors and sufferings of the world.[126]

This lyrical essay of great mystical power is simply signed "Ordos, 1923." A letter of 1929 mentions that, after writing "The Priest" and "The Mass on the World," he was contemplating another, third version of his offering, but it never happened. "Ordos" refers to a group of people belonging to the Mongolian nation—a people with its own territory and dialect. Strictly speaking, the designation of " Ordos" territory applies only to the region inside the Yellow River bend, on the eastern side of that great Chinese river. During their 1923 expedition Licent and Teilhard traveled on both sides of the river, and they also journeyed on the river by boat.

Sometimes it was possible to say Mass; at other times conditions were so impossible that the idea had to be abandoned. Digging at Sharaousso-gol meant a noisy camp life. There were more than twenty Mongol and Chinese helpers of whom some were parishioners of a Belgian missionary who had first attracted Licent's attention to this fossil site.

Teilhard on a very old bridge of the imperial road near Xianxian, 1924. (Fondation Teilhard de Chardin)

Licent's diary describes their early risings from the tent and their desert walks before sunrise. It is this early vision of the world at dawn that "The Offering" of "The Mass on the World" depicts when Teilhard writes:

Over there, on the horizon, the sun has just touched with light the outermost fringe of the eastern sky. Once again, beneath this moving sheet of fire, the living surface of the earth wakes and trembles, and once again begins its fearful travail. I will place on my paten, O God, the harvest to be won by this renewal of labor. Into my chalice I shall pour all the sap which is to be pressed out this day from the earth's fruits.

My paten and my chalice are the depths of a soul laid widely open to all the forces which in a moment will rise

"Mysticism remains the great science and the great art, the only power capable of synthesizing the riches accumulated by other forms of human activity."
—September 9, 1923

up from every corner of the earth and converge upon the Spirit.[127]

God as energy, fire, and power. God as blazing Spirit that molds every living thing. God as heart of the world, as innermost depth of everything there is. God as milieu in which we live and breathe, and in which all is made one. These are some of the great themes of this Mass that celebrates the world as living crucible, the place of divine incarnation and transformation. This great prose poem has rightly been called "a cosmic liturgy."

It also expresses with much power and beauty Teilhard's "one basic vision" of the union between God and the universe. It is a vision that culminates in the figure of Christ, seen so directly and concretely:

Glorious Lord Christ: . . . power as implacable as the world and as warm as life; you whose forehead is of the whiteness of snow, whose eyes are of fire, and whose feet are brighter than molten gold; you whose hands imprison the stars; you who are the first and the last, the living and the dead and the risen again; you who gather into your exuberant unity every beauty, every affinity, every energy, every mode of existence; it is you to whom my being cried out with a desire as vast as the universe, "In truth you are my Lord and my God."[128]

It is an extraordinarily powerful vision of great beauty. It was to stay with him for the rest of his life. The world, the whole world, is God's body in its fullest extension. This is the "cosmic Christ" that Teilhard proclaims as God's "incarnate Being in the world of matter." This is what he prays to, communicates with, and celebrates as the purpose of his being, the center and all-consuming love of his life. While others may proclaim God's splendors as pure Spirit, he has no desire, no ability, to preach anything but "the mystery of your flesh, you the Soul shining forth through all that surrounds us."[129]

Teilhard on the journey to Dalaï-Noor on the Mongolian border, 1924. (Fondation Teilhard de Chardin)

The words of "The Mass on the World" were probably written down in mid-July 1923 when Teilhard and Licent were spending some quiet time under their tent. Teilhard had been meditating on his inner experience when slowly traveling by boat or on the back of a mule. The leisurely pace of their journey with its lack of distraction favored solitary reflection and enabled him to express his inner vision from the depths of his soul.

He kept meditating on the words of his Mass, present in him as a living experience. He told his friends, "I keep developing, and slightly improving, with the help of prayer, my 'Mass upon things.'"[130] Writing from his tent to Léontine Zanta, he mentioned: "As I travel on mule-back for whole days on end, I repeat, as in the past—for lack of any other Mass—the 'Mass on the World' which you already know."[131]

The British evolutionary scientist and philosopher, Sir Julian Huxley (1887-1975), a friend of Teilhard in later years, once described the "Mass on the World" as a "truly

"The people who first created these desert retreats were doubt-less really great men, prophets who discovered something of great beauty in the world, and beyond the world. Today one scrutinizes the dull faces of their successors in vain to find the most fleeting trace of that long-faded vision."

—July 1923

"My Mongolian journey has confirmed me in my faith in the future. The world holds no interest for me unless I look forward, but when my eyes are on the future it is full of excitement."

—October 23, 1923

Teilhard with a young Chinese friend. (Georgetown University Library)

poetical essay . . . at one and the same time mystical and realistic, religious and philosophical." Father Thomas M. King, S.J. (1929-2009), a great devotee and interpreter of Teilhard, provided his own spiritual reflections on the "Mass on the World" in a book of essays that also include an informative study on "The Scientific Work of Teilhard while Writing 'The Mass on the World'."[132]

The praise and thanksgiving so characteristic of the Catholic Mass are expressed in the "Mass on the World" as an immense cosmic offering, bursting forth like the melodies of a great symphony. The sacred, sacramental nature of the cosmos, symbolized by this offering of the Mass was for Teilhard an ever-living fountain of renewal for all his life and work.

Writing in late August 1923 to Abbé Breuil from one of the mission stations on their journey, Teilhard stated, "I am a little too absorbed by science to be able to philosophize much; but the more I look into myself the more I find myself possessed by the conviction that it is only the science of Christ running through all things, that is to say true mystical science, that really matters."[133]

The "Mass on the World" encapsulates Teilhard's mystical experience and vision. His faith in the presence of Christ in all things inspired all his efforts, including his scientific research. It truly sustained him throughout the vicissitudes of a long life. This deep certainty of his Christian faith enabled him to remain always faithful to his calling, however difficult this was at times.

Crisis and Exile

*I've been keeping up appearances but, inside me, there's
something like real agony, a real storm. . . . It's essential that
I should show by my example that even if my ideas appear an
innovation, they still make me as faithful as anyone else
to the traditional old attitude.*

By October 1924 Teilhard was back in Paris, teaching at
the Institut Catholique as before, giving many talks to
students at other colleges, visiting old friends, and meeting
new ones. Foremost among these was a young woman geologist, Ida Treat, whom he met that winter at the museum.
She had come to work with Marcellin Boule, but he asked
Teilhard to supervise her research.

He and the newcomer, with almost opposite worldviews,
soon got involved in deep discussions. Ida Treat, of American background, was a professed atheist married to Paul
Vaillant-Couturier, a leading member of the French Communist Party and later director of the Communist newspaper *L'Humanité.* What a powerful and passionate exponent
of Marxist ideas she was! The force of their differences made
them almost collide and oppose each other. Ida was of lively
temperament, full of energy and completely committed to
the spread of communism. Her arguments challenged Teilhard to find out more about communism worldwide, to
think in more consciously political terms and learn to look
at the world from the perspective of an atheist. How could
he convey his convictions to her? In what sense could one
explain Christianity to a committed atheist?

The heat of their debate, at a time when he himself was
having difficulties with his own order, soon led to strong
mutual attraction. Ida was an attentive listener besides enjoying a powerful argument. Teilhard learned to trust her so

Institut Catholique in Paris.

completely that he shared his thoughts with her and gave her some of his essays to read. He later confided to his friend Père Valensin that the turbulent nature of their encounter was so strong that it was really difficult to explain, and his definite departure to China was in some ways a providential blessing since it helped him to get over this new emotional entanglement.

Nonetheless, they always remained good friends. When Teilhard left Paris, Ida Treat became one of his favorite correspondents with whom he exchanged letters through all the years between 1926 and 1952.[134] In 1933, when working on a political report, she even went to visit him in Beijing.

He always encouraged her to have faith in life, but made it quite clear that his own life was completely turned toward God, in and through science itself. Yet he also needed an outlet to communicate his ideas to others. How best to do this? He was well aware of his possibilities and limitations when he wrote to Ida Treat in October 1926:

> As I have, unfortunately, no aptitude for either music or poetry, nor even (which I regret most of all) the talent or art of the novelist, I have up to now tried to express myself in all kinds of philosophico-literary essays of which I have had occasion to show you only an infinitesimal part. Unfortunately, these essays are almost all destined to perish in my desk drawers. . . . It seems to me that I have arrived at the point in my life when the best outlet would be speech. To awaken a spirit, a flow of passions in a group of people, this is what I would like to do. Not, I think, for the simplest enjoyment of acting and influencing, but because I seem to have, deep inside myself, something that needs to emerge and be disseminated: a certain enthusiastic vision of the immensity and promise of the World, a certain relish, a certain intoxication with real concrete "being" as it is revealed to us in the Universe.[135]

"The fundamental evil that besets us . . . is our incapacity to see the whole . . . I sometimes get vague and undefined longings to gather a small group of friends around me and . . . give the example of a life in which nothing would count but the preoccupation with and love for, all the earth."

—Letter to Léontine Zanta, October 15, 1926

Shortly before he wrote this passage, he had expounded his scientific and religious view of the world in the essay "My Universe," an important summary that Ida Treat may perhaps have seen. There he describes his experience as that of someone standing "at a privileged cross-roads in the world; . . . in my twofold character of priest and scientist, I have felt passing through me, in particularly exhilarating and varied conditions, the double stream of human and divine forces," a "favored position" which outstanding friends helped to develop and long periods of leisure allowed to mature and stabilize.[136]

Yet he was acutely aware that the essays buried in the drawers of his desk, apparently so hidden, could take on a life of their own and that their explosive power had unforeseen and dangerous consequences. With his consciousness of living on the frontier of two different worlds Teilhard tried to reconcile the latest discoveries about human origins with the traditional Catholic doctrine of original sin, a problem his listeners asked about when he gave talks about his travels in the East and the history of human evolution. In 1922 one of his colleagues, a professor of dogmatic theology, had asked him after some discussion to write a brief explanatory paper on original sin for the benefit of qualified theologians. Thus Teilhard had reluctantly agreed to draft his "Note on Some Possible Historical Representations of Original Sin" the only paper he wrote during 1922. In this brief draft he points to the difficulties with the traditional teaching on original sin and discusses several possible, new ways of understanding this doctrine.[137]

To date, no-one has been able to discover how this note somehow reached Rome, where the Holy Office and the Jesuit headquarters already held a file on Teilhard. The Roman censors were severe, and so were the authorities of his own

Pope Pius XI.

"There is a twofold and serious difficulty in retaining the former representation of original sin. It may be expressed as follows: 'The more we bring the past to life again by means of science, the less we can accommodate either Adam or the earthly paradise.'"
—"Note on Some Possible Historical Representations of Original Sin," 1922

Father Teilhard in the 1920s. (Courtesy Teilhard Study Center, Georgetown University)

order. They reproached him over his daring speculations regarding a possible rapprochement between science and religion. Shortly after his return to France, in November 1924, Teilhard had received an urgent letter from his Jesuit provincial, Père Costa de Beauregard, summoning him to Lyons to provide some explanation and sign a pledge to keep silent on these matters in future.

A crisis was at hand. Deeply concerned, Teilhard wrote to his close Jesuit friend Auguste Valensin asking for counsel. Fully aware of the delicacy of the situation, he had to speak to him personally in order to weigh up this serious matter before seeing his provincial. He experienced great anguish of conscience: "They want me to promise in writing that I will never say or write anything against the traditional position of the Church on original sin." He felt this was both too vague and too absolute. "I feel I should, in conscience, reserve for myself (1) the right to carry on research with professional men . . . ; (2) the right to bring help to the disturbed and troubled." He hoped to present an alternative version of the formula to reassure the Roman authorities and protect his freedom of scientific inquiry, something like "I bind myself not to spread (not to carry on proselytism for) the particular explanations contained in my note."[138]

Nothing was settled at the meeting in Lyons. Substitute formulas were exchanged over the coming months between Paris, Lyons, and Rome; new censors were appointed and the affair dragged on and cast its shadow over the whole of 1925. Teilhard carried on with his scientific work and teaching, writing yet more new papers, including the key essay "Hominization," which he finished in May of that year.

Copies of his essays were quietly distributed and discussed. His celebrity grew, especially among the young Jesuit students in Hastings whom he visited during a field trip at Easter. They asked eager questions and kept him talking for hours, referring to him and other advanced Jesuit thinkers of their time simply as *La Pensée*. This did not help his cause. A group of French conservative bishops were so disturbed by his growing influence that they complained to the Holy Office, which in turn put more pressure on the Jesuits. Despite the efforts of the rector of the Institut Catholique and also of his immediate superiors, Rome's severe stance showed no relaxation. Eventually Teilhard was asked to sign six propositions, of which only one caused real difficulty. On the advice of his counselors he signed it in the end. Nonetheless, his license to teach at the Institut Catholique was permanently revoked, and he never taught there again.

It was a blow, and he took it badly. He felt disappointed and in a really deep dilemma, pouring out his anguish in letters to his friend Auguste Valensin:

> If I separated myself, or kicked over the traces in any way whatsoever (humanly speaking, it would be so simple and so "easy"), I would be disloyal to my faith in Our Lord's animation of everything that happens. . . . Moreover I would be compromising . . . the religious value of my ideas. People would see it as turning my back on the Church, as pride, who knows what? . . . Which is the most sacred of my two vocations?——the one that I followed as a youngster of eighteen years?——or the one that revealed itself as the true spouse in the fullness of my manhood? [139]

These words clearly express his acute pain and inner tension. Was being a Jesuit or a scientist his true vocation? In the end he found the strength to remain faithful to both his great loves. He submitted to his superiors, but not without feeling tempted to quit the Society of Jesus: "I weighed up the enormous scandal and damage that an act of indiscipline on my part would have caused."[140]

He felt that this was perhaps "the moment of the great choice of my life." Could he be sure that he would not "des-

"It is no exaggeration to say that, in the form in which it is still commonly presented today, original sin is at the moment one of the chief obstacles that stand in the way of the intensive and extensive progress of Christian thought."
—"Reflections on Original Sin," 1947

Teilhard on a Chinese side street.
(Georgetown University Library)

ert" or leave prematurely?[141] He asked Valensin to pray for him "that, come what may, I never let myself wish for anything but 'the Fire.'"[142] In spite of his disappointment he was without rancor, for he felt supported and encouraged by the sympathetic attitude of his immediate superiors and friends. They all agreed with him on what he knew deep in his own heart: that it was only through the church and his order that he could live and grow in that particular spiritual life that he had chosen as his special vocation.

But what to do next? It had been agreed that from now on he would confine himself to purely scientific publications, and that he would leave Paris. There was nowhere to go but to return to China and work with Licent. Tianjin was the place the Roman authorities suggested to him. It proved a convenient and not unattractive exile at this critical turning point in his life. Yet it was a great trial of faith, to be intensified by further incidents and obstacles to his work over the next ten years and more. His close friend and Jesuit commentator, Henri de Lubac, later judged that henceforward Teilhard's life "was dogged by external difficulties and disappointments which formed an almost endless web around him"[143] from which he was never able to extricate himself.

One of his later superiors in Paris and a great supporter of Teilhard, Father René d'Ouince, described the eventful year of 1926 in retrospect by saying that this time Teilhard's departure for China had something of the aspect of a disgrace. He had been removed from Paris by the prudence of his superiors, to whom he had been denounced for propagating dubious ideas, and who feared a censure that would be equally prejudicial to the career of the young scientist and the good name of the Order. Thus he was leaving France under a cloud for an indefinite time, and he saw the momentum of his influence broken just as it was beginning to prove fruitful. The penalty imposed on him seemed unjustified. It was hard for him to "bend." He obeyed in a spirit of faith, but without understanding.[144]

In April 1926 Teilhard sailed on the *Ankor* from Marseilles via Sri Lanka and Singapore to Shanghai; from there he went back to Tianjin and soon planned a new expedition to Western China. Between June and August he traveled with Licent across the provinces of Shansi and Kansu, within range of Chinese Tibet, and after their return, between November 1926 and December 1927, he wrote his book *The Divine Milieu*. It was a most creative way of working through his own inner crisis since this book bears such vivid testimony to his active spirituality of transformation and adoration.

"I am not able to hide from myself that there is, developing within me, an inborn and profound opposition to what is usually regarded as the form, the hopes and the interests that are Christian. What can you expect: in the 'Christian world' as it is presented in our ecclesiastical documents and the catholic gestures or conceptions, 'I suffocate' absolutely, physically . . . . We are no longer in fact 'catholic'; we are defending a system, a sect."
—Letter to Auguste Valensin,
June 27, 1926

The Divine Milieu

The perception of the divine omnipresence is essentially a
seeing, a taste. . . . It is a gift, like life itself, of which it is
undoubtedly the supreme experiential perfection.

"All the communions of a life-
time are one communion. All
the communions of all men now
living are one communion. All
the communions of all men,
present, past and future, are one
communion."
                    —*The Divine Milieu*

The idea of a milieu as both a *center* and an *environment* of transformation had always fascinated Teilhard. He chose the expression "the divine milieu" to describe the diffuse presence and influence of God at all levels of created reality, in all areas of human experience. In essence this is really a spiritual and mystical idea, conveying an all-pervasive sense of the divine. One can think of it as a field of divine energy that has one central focus—God—from which everything flows, is animated, and is directed.

In a biological and social context a "milieu" can refer to an environment of growth, of influence, a web of relationships, something that can be at once organic, personal, and collective. For Teilhard the idea of the "divine milieu" was particularly important in capturing the universal influence of Christ through God's incarnation in the world, in its matter, life, and energy—an extended, cosmic understanding of the incarnation that far transcended the historical limitations of time and place associated with the person of Jesus.

The powerful, vibrant attraction of this large vision of a milieu of God's universal presence and action had already found expression in his war essay "The Mystical Milieu" (1917). It had been celebrated in "The Mass on the World" (1923) and was explained yet once again in the personal vision of his faith, "My Universe" (1924), the second essay of this title, which he had set down on paper in Tianjin shortly before his return to France. Up till then he had always spoken of a "mystical milieu," but he went on meditating and reflecting on it as "this rich and living ambience" with seemingly the most contradictory attributes "of attachment and detachment, of action and contemplation, of the one and the multiple, of spirit and matter"[145] that are reconciled within it.

Once again back in China, during his second period in Tientsin, it was only natural to continue working on this idea, articulating his deepest thoughts by writing them down, giving them expression, structure, and form. As soon as he and Licent had returned from their latest expedition, Teilhard could settle down to a quiet period of study and reflection, which also heightened his spiritual awareness. He catalogued and studied the fossils they had collected, revised his scientific theories, and wrote down his philosophical thoughts. He informed his cousin:

> I have finally decided to write my book on the spiritual life. I mean to put down as simply as possible the sort of ascetical or mystical teaching that I have been living and preaching so long. I call it *Le Milieu divin*, but I am being careful to include nothing esoteric and the minimum of explicit philosophy. . . .
>
> I have settled down to my little book. I want to write it slowly, quietly—living it and meditating on it like a prayer.[146]

This prayerful action was cathartic, almost a form of therapy. His reflective activity sustained his spirit and helped to heal his inner pain. It could see him through many moments of doubt and give him energy for his day-to-day activities. His trial of faith became transformed into a story of spiritual strength, which in turn could inspire and strengthen others in their most trying moments of need. It is miraculous how Teilhard worked through these critical months of his life; we can really see the divine milieu in action here: it gave him his deepest energy resources and the necessary powers of resistance to fight against the corrosive forces of doubt, despair, and hopelessness. As he wrote to Ida Treat, he needed a posi-

"What I cry out for, like every being, with my whole life and all my earthly passion, is something very different from an equal to cherish: it is a God to adore."

—*The Divine Milieu*

Statue at Ming tombs outside Beijing. (Photograph by Ursula King)

113

"To adore . . . That means to lose oneself in the unfathomable, to plunge into the inexhaustible, to find peace in the incorruptible, to be absorbed in defined immensity, to offer oneself to the fire . . . and to give of one's deepest to that whose depth has not end. Whom, then, can we adore?"

—*The Divine Milieu*

tive "outlet" that could animate his inner efforts rather than consume his powers in negative resentment.

Going back to China, traveling across its vast spaces, freed his spirit and also made him dream of writing "the book of the Earth" which would resonate with "the note of the All," a book for people like Ida Treat who were far removed from the Christian faith, but could perhaps be made to see the vibrant life and energy that animated what he then simply called "the divine milieu." He wrote to her in October 1926,

> The only book I want to and need to write would not be the book of China, but "the book of the Earth." In short, I would like to speak as I think, without concern for what is accepted, with the sole idea of translating as faithfully as possible what I hear murmuring in me like a voice or song which are not of me, but of the World in me. I would like to express the thoughts of a man who, having finally penetrated the partitions and ceilings of little countries, little coteries, little sects, rises above all these categories and finds himself a child and citizen of the Earth.[147]

In the following years he was to think more about the earth and its citizens, the global dimension of human reality within the vast context of life and its natural environment, but for the present he concentrated on writing *The Divine Milieu*. It bears the subtitle "An Essay on the Interior Life" and the dedication "For those who love the world." Written at his darkest hour, it is Teilhard's spiritual masterpiece, celebrating the diaphany of the Divine at the heart of the universe, in and through the world, through matter, life, and every experience we are likely to encounter. The mystical vision of communion and union with God can give every human being access to a new "milieu" in which everything becomes potentially divinized, transformed into fullness and plenitude that find their culmination in Jesus Christ. For Teilhard "the great mystery of Christianity is not exactly the appearance, but the transparence, of God in the universe. Yes, Lord, not only the ray that strikes the surface, but the ray that penetrates, not your Epiphany, Jesus, but your *diaphany*,"[148] the shining through and disclosure of something divine in all things and moments of experience.

Like so many of Teilhard's writings, *The Divine Milieu* is born out of a practical, pastoral concern. He poses the problem of how Christians can best sanctify action and what value all human endeavor has in relation to God. Pointing out the unsatisfactory nature of traditional solutions for seeking holiness and perfection, he comes up with a twofold answer that provides him with the structure for his book: "the divinization of activities" and "the divinization of passivities" represent a continuous process of transformation whereby we can find communion with God in the world. Some wonderful passages speak of our passivities of growth as well as those of diminishment, about attachment and detachment, the transfiguration of our failures, the meaning of the cross, and the spiritual power of matter:

> Immersion and emergence; participation in things and sublimation; possession and renunciation; crossing through and being borne onward—that is the twofold yet single movement which answers the challenge of matter in order to save it.[149]

After this description of the rhythm of Christian life, its renunciation and development, his book culminates in the discussion of the attributes, nature, and growth of the divine milieu. This part is preceded by a quotation from St. Paul, whose passages about Christ Teilhard was particularly fond of quoting. Here it becomes fully apparent how the presence of God reaches all the elements of the world exclusively through and in the body of Christ. Elsewhere he had written:

"This is the point we must bear in mind: in no case could be cosmos be conceived, and realized, without a supreme center of spiritual consistence."
—"My Universe"

Teilhard in 1931. (Courtesy Teilhard Study Center, Georgetown Study Center, Georgetown University)

"The presence of the Incarnate Word penetrates everything, as a universal element. It shines at the common heart of things, as a center that is infinitely intimate to them and at the same time . . . infinitely distant."
—"My Universe"

Whatever we do, it is to Christ we do it. Whatever is done to us, it is Christ who does it. Christian piety has always drawn strength from these words of universal and constant union; but has it, I wonder, always been able, or been bold enough, to give to that union the forceful realism that, since St. Paul . . . we have been entitled to expect?[150]

The divine milieu grows and is intensified through love, in the individual and in the human group, for ultimately there is a collective progress in this milieu; it grows into the communion of saints and the body of Christ:

Across the immensity of time and the disconcerting multiplicity of individuals, one single operation is taking place: the annexation to Christ of His chosen; one single thing is being made: the Mystical Body of Christ, starting from all the sketchy spiritual powers scattered throughout the world. . . . Our salvation is not pursued or achieved except in solidarity with the justification of the whole "body of the elect." In a real sense, only one man will be saved: Christ, the head and living summary of humanity. Each one of the elect is called to see God face to face. . . . In heaven we ourselves shall contemplate God, but, as it were, through the eyes of Christ.

If this is so, then our individual mystical effort awaits an essential completion in its union with the mystical effort of all other men. The divine milieu which will ultimately be one in the Pleroma, must begin to become one during the earthly phase of our existence. . . .

To what power is it reserved to burst asunder the envelope in which our individual microcosms tend jealously to isolate themselves and vegetate? To what force is it given to merge and exalt our partial rays into the principal radiance of Christ?

To charity, the beginning and the end of all spiritual relationships. . . . It is impossible to love Christ without loving others. . . . And it is impossible to love others (in a spirit of broad human communion) without moving nearer to Christ.[151]

The pages of *The Divine Milieu* speak eloquently of Teilhard's passionate sense of the world being full and vibrant with God. The developments of the world and humankind do not take place in competition with God, but culminate in God as their spiritual and divine center. Teilhard was not a man of little faith who dared not venture into the unknown for fear of warnings and prohibitions. On the contrary, "We must try everything for Christ; we must hope everything for Christ. . . . To divinize does not mean to destroy, but to sur-create. We shall never know all that the Incarnation still expects of the world's potentialities." Teilhard can see the ferment all around him "in laboratories, in studios, in deserts, in factories, in the vast social crucible, . . . the waters, the flood and the sap of humanity" welcomed by and into Christ's arms and heart. He has no more fear but, casting his mind back over his own difficulties, concludes his essay:

Teilhard inspecting an artifact in China. (Georgetown University Library)

> The temptations of too large a world, the seductions of too beautiful a world—where are these now?
>
> They do not exist.
>
> Now the earth can certainly clasp me in her giant arms. She can swell me with her life, or take me back in her dust. She can deck herself out for me with every charm, with every horror, with every mystery. She can intoxicate me with her perfume of tangibility and unity. She can cast me to my knees in expectation of what is maturing in her breast. . . .

> But her enchantments can no longer do me harm, since she has become for me, over and above herself, the body of Him who is and of Him who is coming.
>
> The divine milieu.[152]

Could this cherished text be published? Teilhard sent the manuscript to his provincial in Lyons who, after its positive assessment by two colleagues, gave his approval. Teilhard's friend, Father Pierre Charles, was to include *The Divine Milieu* in his series Museum Lessianum, published by the Jesuits in Louvain, Belgium. To be on the safe side, he gave it to two colleagues to read. One suggested a few changes, which were adopted; the other was enthusiastic about the successful way in which traditional, well-established ideas about Christian spirituality were here combined with a really new and original approach. But a church official who was to issue the ecclesiastical imprimatur on behalf of the local bishop had his reservations, knowing that a file about Teilhard existed in Rome. He therefore decided to send the manuscript to the Roman authorities, who then forbade publication in spite of the acknowledged orthodoxy of the text. Its unusual new perspective was deemed to demand too much of the faithful!

The book incurred many revisions over the following years. Teilhard, who so much hoped to see his work in print, corresponded about the text again and again with supporters and church officials without making any headway whatsoever. His friends were rightly incensed, but made sure that more and more copies of *The Divine Milieu* were quietly reproduced and distributed, traveling freely from hand to hand among those interested in its thought. But the book was never publicly recognized either inside or outside the church until it was finally published in 1957, two years after Teilhard's death. He could not have known that in March 1927 when he signed the last page of his manuscript in Tianjin.

New Horizons

To discover the new spirit that is struggling to emerge from the ruins of the old crenelated towns and the old pagodas; to recognize and reveal that specific and essential element which the East must bring to the West so that the Earth will be complete.

Soon after *The Divine Milieu* was finished, Teilhard and Licent planned another expedition. They set off from Tientsin in May 1927 to revisit eastern Mongolia, first explored in 1924. They were satisfied with the fossils they found near the south-eastern limit of the Gobi desert, not far from Dalai Nor. Returning in August, they judged their expedition a success. Teilhard had gathered detailed information on the geological structure of a hitherto little-known region, never before visited by a geologist. At least three-quarters of his observations were new, he remarked in a letter. The weather had been magnificent, the countryside bewitching—an immense basaltic plateau of 1,700-1,900 meters in height surrounded by stark rocks and abrupt wall-like ridges, with wide-open pastures and vestiges of forest. Once again he had thought himself in the Auvergne,

Teilhard with members of an expedition team. (Courtesy Teilhard Study Center, Georgetown University)

> but a bigger, more lonely Auvergne. . . . At that season the prairies were in full flower: a carpet of red and amber lilies, scarlet primulas, white peonies, bright-leaved rhubarb. This was Europe, or at least Siberia, rather than China. Toward Ting-pang, of course, the landscape changes; white sands appear, filling the valleys and clinging like snow to the mountains—this being, already, the Gobi.[153]

Both scientists were fully aware of the unrest and strife in China. They experienced the insecure state of the country where many areas were under the military regime of local warlords. Many regions were devastated by war or infested

"Go on reminding geologists that, in all prudence, after so much analysis, the moment has perhaps come for synthesizing. We were so busy counting the waves that we were beginning to forget the tide."
—"The Face of the Earth"

by bandits who obstructed their travel. On their return they could cross the mountain ranges only with the help of a military convoy they were lucky enough to meet. Teilhard's many letters to his friends describe some of the political chaos, the extreme poverty, and the growing support for the communist movement. The Nationalist Party, or Kuomintang, and the Communist Party were fighting each other, yet remained united in their struggle against the foreign presence and imperial powers in the country. By 1928 the nationalists had set up their own government in Nanjing, a former Chinese capital on the Yangtze river in eastern China, whereas the communists established their rural bases in central China. During their expeditions Teilhard and Licent saw much of the "Chinese China"—the traditional, rural population of the countryside, so markedly different from the educated elite in the modernized urban centers of Beijing and Tianjin.

Teilhard's attitude to China was now quite different from his critical appraisal during the first visit in 1923. By 1927, when the Kuomintang expelled the communists and there was much unrest in the country, he was convinced that "there is going on here, at this very moment, a human development of almost geological dimensions; to participate in it would be a rare chance indeed." This made him regret even less that he was not returning permanently to Paris, for he had a feeling that life was opening up for him in the Far East and that, if the ongoing Chinese revolution was not to destroy their projects, the possibilities of working more closely with the Chinese Geological Survey were to be very promising, "both in the realm of science and in the realm of contact with and action upon the mass of humanity here."[154]

While he deplored the scourge of militarism and the great suffering imposed on people by the Chinese warlords, he welcomed some of the good developments associated with the communist awakening, though he criticized the movement for its "internationalization *through hatred*"[155] rather than through sympathy and love. But he was well aware

Teilhard in the field. (Courtesy Teilhard Study Center, Georgetown University)

that a tremendous social upheaval was taking place, giving birth to a new China, a new Asia, where soon nothing much might be left of Western establishments and missions. However, he thought that it was not so much the countryside but the great urban centers with their young intellectuals that were the crucible for change. Confiding his thoughts to Léontine Zanta he wrote, "One feels that the country's intellectual élite is casting its skin. In a century the change will have happened. What will it give? A China capable of helping the West in its research, or merely an imitative China? Who can say?" Or on another occasion:

> I find it more and more difficult to form any exact idea as to what sort of greatness or renewal we should expect from the New China. Sometimes I feel pessimistic. What seems clear to me is that we must look with favor on the "birth" of a new human group that nothing can prevent. Later we shall see what can be done with the baby. Apart from some disagreeable symptoms (such as a narrow hatred of foreigners), I have been fortunate enough to come across all sorts of reassuring indications in the past three months as to the possibility of frank spiritual collaboration between East and West. Look: we just can't breathe in our different compartments, our closed categories. Without destroying our more limited organisms, we must fuse them together, synthesize them: the human being, nothing but the human being as the context of our ambitions and organizations.[156]

In early 1927 Teilhard had sent "a moderately pro-China and humanitarian article"[157] to a new Catholic journal, *The Week*, published in Calcutta. Perhaps the editor had invited him to contribute a piece based on his experience of working in China. He certainly felt he could say more in this Indian article than in a French publication when describing the contemporary crisis and intellectual tendencies of modern China.

He characterized the gigantic upheaval and fermentation

"It is impossible habitually to keep one's eyes on the great horizons discovered by science without an obscure desire arising to see a growing knowledge and sympathy so linking men that, as a result of some divine attraction, there shall be only one heart and one soul on the face of the earth."
—"The Face of the Earth"

"By the expression 'The Phenomenon of Man' we mean here the
empirical fact of the appearance
in our universe of the power
of reflection and thought. . . .
Man knows that he knows. He
emerges from his actions. He
dominates them in however
feeble a way. . . . He reflects. He
thinks. This event can serve as
a point of departure for many
philosophical, moral or religious
trains of thought. We would
only view it here . . . as a simple
point in history and science."
—"The Human Phenomenon,"
1930

Teilhard in the Gulf of Tadjoura
between Obock and Djibouti,
January 1929. (Fondation Teilhard
de Chardin)

occurring all around him as the modernization of a people.
Quite different from either conquest or colonization, he understood this modernization as the organization, the coming
together of humanity as a whole. This sudden and complete
transition was still lacking a strong internal focus and the
right kind of guidance, but however chaotic it might initially
be, one must not forget that Western Europe took ten centuries to find itself! It now was not for Westerners to interfere
in Chinese affairs except to help them while respecting the
individuality and originality of the Chinese soul. Here was a
new, vibrant energy at work. It was not only the success of
China that was presently at stake but the interest of humanity as a whole. In other words, for Teilhard in the late 1920s
contemporary events affecting China internally or externally
were of extraordinary importance for the future progress of
the world. Humanity so much needed the whole earth, East
and West, to draw on its most living energies and organize
itself. He saw these energies at their best among the scientific
community, in the relatively recent research associations the
Chinese had founded, and the pioneering work they were
doing in the very international milieu in Beijing.

It was not long before Teilhard was a full member of this
milieu, working in China and traveling regularly between
East and West. By October 1927 he was returning for another
year's stay in France where he renewed his scientific and personal contacts and continued to write. He revisited the places
of his childhood, continued to exchange ideas with Édouard
Le Roy, frequented the French Geological Society, visited
Marguerite and Léontine Zanta, conducted retreats for students based on *The Divine Milieu*, and gave an address at a
wedding. It was in Paris, in September 1928, that he drafted
his first essay on *le phénomène humain*, a most important subject that was to occupy his thoughts more and more. What is
the real significance of the human phenomenon, the emergence and specific nature of the human dimension within the
vast process of evolution? The widely used English translation

of this expression as "the phenomenon of man" does not truly capture the rich inclusiveness and many-layered differences of his thought at this time; its subsequent rendering as "the human phenomenon" is much more appropriate.

Teilhard argues against the disciplinary compartmentalization of the sciences that prevents an integral study of the human being, and the full recognition of the human being's place in nature:

> They treat man as a small separate cosmos, isolated from the rest of the universe. Any number of sciences concern themselves with man, but man, in that which makes him essentially human, still lies outside science.
>
> Nevertheless, we have only to think for a moment of the tremendous event represented by the explosion of thought on the surface of the earth to be quite certain that this great episode is something more than a part of the general system of nature: we have to accord to it a position of prime importance, from the point of view both of using and of understanding the motive forces of the universe.[158]

For Teilhard the development of humankind is not an anomalous element of the universe, but it is

> a fundamental phenomenon—the supreme phenomenon of nature: that in which, in a unique complexity of material and moral factors, one of the principal acts of universal evolution is not only experienced but lived by us.[159]

In November 1928 he embarked once again from Marseilles, but not immediately for the Far East. The explorer Henry de Monfreid, whom he had met on a previous boat journey, had invited him to French Somaliland. Teilhard was pleased to take up his invitation:

> It was just by chance that I tried this visit to Somalia and Abyssinia, guided by the general principle of my life that one should lose no opportunity of trying out or finding

Teilhard in Africa, December 1928. (Fondation Teilhard de Chardin)

"There is a science of the universe without man. There is also a science of man as marginal to the universe; but there is not yet a science of the universe that embraces man as such. Present-day physics . . . does not yet give a place to thought; which means that it still exists in complete independence of the most remarkable phenomenon exposed by nature to our observation."
—"The Human Phenomenon," 1930

123

> *"The importance of the human milieu escapes us because we are immersed in it. Born in it and breathing nothing else, we have difficulty in getting a just impression of its dimensions, of sensing its extraordinary qualities."*
>
> —"The Human Phenomenon," 1930

Dead City in the Gobi Desert. (Photograph by Ursula King)

out things: and it proved to be longer and more fruitful than I anticipated.[160]

He stayed until early February 1929, using his time for exploring a new world. Teilhard and de Monfreid traveled in a small, primitive boat on the Red Sea, enjoyed the scenery and rock paintings on the coastal mountains, took a slow train through different parts of Somalia and Ethiopia, and spent time prospecting in important geological areas. Teilhard collected enough fossils to send a whole case of specimens to Boule at the Paris museum. This was his second contact with the continent of Africa but in a different region than before. Here he was confronted with

> natural scenes wholly different from those I have seen before. Once the strip of coastal desert is crossed, the traveler immediately encounters typical African bush, with its sparse mimosaceous growths, its giant candelabra-shaped, cactus-like spurges, its antelopes, its many-colored birds, and its ant-heaps.[161]

Much of the landscape was wild, barren, full of rocks and stones, and in order not to scare some of the "still extremely barbaric tribes," Teilhard wore a turban during part of the expedition.[162] He admitted to a friend how delighted he was with his visit: "I am by no means bored with life in Africa, so different from Mongolia (which I haven't forgotten either!)."[163]

He sailed from Djibouti to China at the beginning of February 1929 and arrived back in Tianjin on March 15. On the long journey to the Far East he worked on another essay, "Le sens humain" or "sense of the human," translated into English simply as "The Sense of Man." Here the train of thought begun in the essay on "The Human Phenomenon" is continued, pointing to the awakening of "the human sense" as a specific event of the twentieth century in which "terrestrial thought is becoming conscious that it constitutes an organic whole, endowed with the power of growth, and both capable of and responsible for some future."[164]

After describing the modern awakening of "the human sense" and its characteristics, Teilhard calls it a faith and a summons, a faith that is disturbing and challenging to the established religions. He writes at length about the growing indifference of people to Christianity, the "sickness of Christianity," and the misunderstanding of contemporary developments by the official church that does not do enough to feed and sustain the zest for life, so essential to being human. For Teilhard faith in the world must, however, culminate in a principle of spiritual coherence and energy with a face and a heart that he can find only in Christ. It is Christ alone who stands ahead of human progress and can give a sense of direction to the modern world. Christ

> would not be divine if his spirit could not be recognized as underlying the processes which are even now re-creating the soul of the earth. It is only an extraordinary lack of faith that can have belittled, feared, or even condemned "the spirit of today." The awakening of the sense of man cannot be anything but the dawn of a new epiphany. . . . Today the Church, drifting in a backwater of abstract theology, of a sacramentalism whose standard is quantity rather than quality, of over-refined piety, has lost contact with the real. The guidance provided by the clergy, and the interests of the faithful, are gradually being confined to a little artificial world of ritualism, of religious practices, of pious extravagancies, which is completely cut off from the true current of reality. . . .
>
> Christianity will never cease to stagnate, will never begin once more to spread with the vigor of its early days, unless it makes up its mind to gear itself to the natural aspirations of the earth. Faith in Christ, a faith given vitality by man's faith (now born, and never to be lost) in some universal progress—faith in the world, a faith vindicated by the solid, exactly defined reality of Christ—the mutually supporting passion for Christ and

"The light of Christ, far from being eclipsed by the growing brilliance of the ideas of the future, of scientific research and of progress, is coming into prominence as the very central core destined to sustain their ardor."

—"The Sense of Man"

125

passion for the world—these are now emerging as the twin poles of the religion of the future.[165]

Here his critique of the church is strongly pronounced. It is a theme to which he returned more than once in order to emphasize how the Christian gospel must be understood and lived in the modern world.

Far away from the centers of Western intellectual life, he nonetheless remained in touch with current ways of thinking, sharing a deep passion for his scientific work with his collaborators and friends in Beijing. On his return to China he was appointed Scientific Adviser to the Chinese Geological Survey and soon got involved with their excavations. In May 1929 he was off on one last expedition with Licent, this time for a month in Manchuria. From June to September 1929 he was working under harsh conditions with a young Chinese geologist, C. C. Young, in the province of Shansi, exercising for the first time his official function as adviser. Another, more comfortable expedition followed in March 1930, this time with George Barbour, a Scottish geologist based in the United States, to undertake a geological survey of the southern part of Shansi.

Soon afterward, during the months of April and May, he accompanied five Chinese geologists on a tour around Manchuria, and in June 1930 he took part in the Central Asiatic Expedition organized by the Americans to the eastern part of the Gobi desert, which he joined as prehistorian. It was exhilarating. The new environment with its new opportunities for scientific research challenged every fiber of his being. This time they traveled by car, and he wrote to his cousin Marguerite:

> This is a very different experience from last year's, when I was the master of my ten mules. I am in excellent shape physically. Rain, storms and dust and icy winds have only whipped up my blood and brought me rest. Andrews has presented me with a thick fur coat and a sheepskin sleep-

"It was not physical fatigue that I felt at the beginning of my June expedition, but a sort of spiritual weariness, as though everything were growing old. . . . There are times, you see, when you have to be blind and deaf to what is going on within you and will soon be lost in action, in a passionate and blind abandonment to life's currents."

—Letter to Marguerite, October 30, 1929

ing bag which enable me to face the cold, until the time comes when we're roasting again. . . .

We are now a hundred miles farther to the northwest, well into the Gobi. Our blue tents are pitched at the edge of a fossil-bearing cliff, looking out over the immense flat surfaces of Mongolia. . . . There is nothing in sight but a few yurts beside the streams, and we work in absolute solitude, our only companions the wolves, eagles and gazelles, which always provide the bulk of our diet. The same gaiety and family spirit prevails in the camp. . . . Personally I am managing to link together satisfactorily the geologies of China and Mongolia . . . and I am vastly extending the horizons I include in my vision.

Although cut off from correspondence, and with his Paris and Louvain hopes concerning the publication of *The Divine Milieu* dormant, he felt in that faraway region that nonetheless

all that world is living and growing unseen, in the depths of my being. When I turn my eyes in that direction it seems to me that I have never attained such simplicity, clearness of vision or controlled tension in my interior effort. I look more and more to God to find the best point at which to apply it all most fruitfully, when the time comes. And meanwhile I can see quite clearly that I am still gathering my strength for action. If the action has to be brief—well, no matter.[166]

Shortly after their return, by September 1930, he was on his way to Paris again, traveling by Trans-Siberian railway this time. It gave him some satisfaction to see that a different version of his essay "The Human Phenomenon" had appeared in the November issue of the French journal *Revue des Questions Scientifiques*. During 1930 he published some eighteen scientific papers on his expeditions in Africa and China, a permanent record and visible proof of his great activity and constant hard work. During his brief stay in Paris he was busy too, planning yet another major expedition for the following year.

In the valley of the Téla, near Obock. Teilhard is at the left wearing a turban (December 1928). (Fondation Teilhard de Chardin)

Peking Man

Teilhard in 1931. (Fondation Teilhard de Chardin)

"Africa, and we shall soon, perhaps, have to add . . . central and eastern Asia are the great laboratories in which humanity must have been made. Europe, the center of modern civilization, was never, in the past, anything but a blind alley, in which the great movements of life, born in the broad continents, came to die."

—"Fossil Men"

However coldly and objectively we may study things, we must still conclude that humanity constitutes a front along which the cosmos advances.

The years between 1929 and 1931 were a very busy, complex period in Teilhard's life. His earlier collaboration with Licent now came to an end. He left Tianjin to take up permanent residence in Beijing where he could work much more closely with Chinese and foreign scientists in his field. Beijing reminded him of Paris, whereas he "was less charmed with Tianjin, that city of bankers and warehousemen, a sort of endless shopping center in which any intellectual or spiritual contact was inconceivable."[167] Beijing, by contrast, was a lively center with many possibilities for collaborative work and stimulating contacts. There were many international research organizations based in the city: the Geological Survey with Chinese, American, and Swedish personnel; the Peking Union Medical College, founded in 1906 by British and American missionaries, and funded by the Rockefeller Foundation, with North American and Chinese staff; the Free Chinese University, an American foundation; the Geological Society; the Natural History Society; the Institute for Prehistoric Studies; and also a number of visiting missions from Sweden and America that stayed around for brief periods.

Teilhard thought highly of the Chinese Geological Survey, founded in 1916 by three or four Chinese scientists after their return from studying in Europe. He commented that they all shared "the same inclinations, the same superior education, the same national pride; in addition, they had influential contacts and a great capacity for administration."[168] Their work was reinforced by that of the Geological Society, which counted more than two hundred members in the mid-1920s, with a spacious building, a splendid museum, laboratories, and a fine library at their disposal. The West was no longer the only center of scientific research; Beijing, with some assistance from the West, grew increasingly important and Teilhard now became more and more a Chinese geologist. In 1929, when he was made official adviser to the Geological Survey, he was given an office in Beijing and invited to become a corresponding member of the Academia Sinica and the National Research Institute in Nanjing.

This recognition was the result of his open attitude toward the Chinese and his enlightened thinking about collaboration between people from East and West. In 1923, when Teilhard had first arrived in China, he had come as a student of Marcellin Boule with the support of the Paris National Museum. Boule expected this link to be permanent and hoped that Teilhard would eventually become his successor. Because of this, he was opposed to Teilhard's fuller integration into Chinese organizations, whereas Teilhard was averse to a separatist attitude. Already in 1926 he had urged Sven Hedin "to trust the Chinese and work with them." The Swedish scientist was grateful for this advice because, as a result, he gained "the full confidence of even the most anti-foreign Chinese." Teilhard felt confirmed in his own line: "I have decided . . . I too (like the Church, for that matter) am going over to the Chinese."[169] He met with Boule's displeasure but retorted:

> Let me tell you that my preoccupation with swelling the fossil collections of France, though I keep in mind my obligations in justice in this matter (for after all I am being partly paid for that very purpose), has had to take a second place to my concern with and interest in co-operating with the Pan-Pacific's enormous project in geology. . . . I now find myself (with several others, of course) heading the geological advance in China.

"Let us never give the impression that we are afraid of something which may renew and enlarge our ideas of man and the universe.
The world will never be vast enough, nor will humanity ever be strong enough to be worthy of Him who created them and incarnated Himself in them."
—"The Vision of the Past"

Teilhard on the rail line used to transport supplies between Beijing and Zhoukoudian. (Courtesy, Teilhard Study Center, Georgetown University)

The same letter mentions:

Boule has lately written to me . . . that he is cutting off my funds for this year. . . . I have learned from a reliable source . . . that Boule is dissatisfied: (1) because I left France against his advice (as if it were any of my doing!) and (2) I can now see that everything I have been telling him about my finds here (they are more valuable to Beijing and geology in general than to his show-cases) has only served to annoy him. I feel a really filial affection for him as I always shall—so when I answered I did what I could to pacify him.[170]

Of special interest and excitement were the ongoing excavations at Zhoukoudian, then called Chou-Kou-Tien, some thirty miles southwest of Beijing at the edge of the Western Hills. It was an area full of limestone quarries and coal mines that had been worked for thousands of years. Bones were particularly abundant in humps of limestone, which the locals called Chicken Bone Hill and Dragon Bone Hill, and were gathered by people for medicinal purposes, a practice that attracted the attention of paleontologists.

Zhoukoudian was only a day's mule trip from Beijing and thus far more accessible than remote Central Asian sites. Soon there was even a railway connection, which made it easy to introduce excavation machinery. With some financial assistance from the Rockefeller Foundation, John Gunnar Andersson, a Swede, prospected in Zhoukoudian in 1918. He was then looking for coal, but he found instead rich deposits of fossil mammals in a perfect state of preservation. Efforts were made to investigate the site more thoroughly, and systematic excavations of the Zhoukoudian caves took place from 1922 onward. In the late 1920s Teilhard became increasingly associated with the geological and paleontological aspects of this work. In May 1929 he proudly wrote to his cousin:

> Things have so turned out as to make me take a further step in the direction I was telling you about—a new co-operation with the Chinese. A letter . . . urgently begged me to get down to Zhoukoudian . . . to study with two Chinese the geology of the site and supervise the organization of the year's new excavations. To take charge of Zhoukoudian is too important a job for me to think of refusing. . . . A little Ford took me and my two companions over impossibly bad roads to a village near the dig. Well, one way and another, I'm pretty satisfied. In the first place, from the technical point of view, I think I have been able to throw a little more light on the history of what will in future be a very celebrated site.[171]

The systematic excavation work at Zhoukoudian over several years eventually bore fruit. The year 1926 proved to be a turning point when two teeth were found. Davidson Black, a lively Canadian with whom Teilhard had struck up a close friendship, considered them to be human remains to which he soon gave the name *Sinanthropus*, or Peking Man. Teilhard, more prudent in his interpretation, was rather skeptical about the human quality of these teeth. But the find of these fossils intensified the systematic excavation of the Zhoukoudian site. The scientists were thrilled when on December 2, 1929, a real treasure was discovered. The Chinese scientist Pei Wenzhong came upon the first complete skullcap, embedded in porous rock from which it had to be carefully freed. Full of excitement, he sent a message to Black in Beijing: "Found skullcap—perfect—looks like a man's." Teilhard was assigned the task of determining the age of the formations in which the skull had been located. His role was an important and, at times, a decisive one, but the actual discovery was the result of teamwork and collaboration between

"The famous Sinanthropus skull is proving more and more to be a find of the first order—a solid fact that's going to be highly embarrassing to many out-of-date minds."
—Letter to Léontine Zanta, April 3, 1930

Excavation at Zhoukoudian, Dragon Bone Hill.

The skull of "Peking Man," discovered at Zhoukoudian.

"*The problem whether Sinanthropus was a thinking being seems immediately and positively resolved by the very conditions of his 'environment.' Fire and tools on the one hand; and on the other the manifestly intentional selection of skulls that we find. Are there not abundant proofs of intelligence on the Zhoukoudian site?*"

—"The Discovery of Sinanthropus"

Teilhard treating the foot of a Chinese soldier in 1931. (Courtesy, Teilhard Study Center, Georgetown University)

Chinese and Western scientists. Black and Teilhard sent a triumphant telegram to Boule in Paris: "New Year Greetings. Recovered Zhoukoudian uncrushed adult Sinanthropus skull entire except face. Letter follows."[172]

It was a significant breakthrough that stimulated much scientific discussion about human origins. Asia was then seen as the most promising area in which to find the earliest home of humankind. More work was devoted to excavating the fossils, and later finds included fourteen skullcaps, facial bones, limb bones, and teeth of about forty individuals as well as shaped stone, bone, and antler tools. Was Peking Man perhaps the earliest human being, or did other cultures exist before? The dating of the remains has ranged from 700,000 to 200,000 years ago, with 450,000 to 500,000 often given as the most likely.

Ash, cinders, charred animal bones, and the remains of hearths found in association with human bones seemed to indicate the domestic use of fire, but there was still room for doubt. By the winter of 1930 Teilhard brought a cinder with him to Europe and compared it with finds from prehistoric sites on the European continent. Thus the scientists eventually arrived at the conclusion that Peking Man had without doubt used fire. It was a landmark in human cultural history. For indeed there exists no earlier evidence for the use of fire anywhere else in the world. Teilhard must have been thrilled, for the image of fire meant so much to him, the spark and blaze of a roaring fire! A real step forward in the history of human evolution—to light a fire, to keep it alive and burning, to control it and put its powers to beneficial use, for heating, cooking, clearing the ground, starting agriculture, developing pottery, and melting metals. What a breakthrough it was, and here was Peking Man, the first human ancestor to make and use fire! When the great prehistorian Abbé Breuil came to examine the fossils, he asserted that this use of fire as well as that of bone and the presence of antler artifacts were evidence of a Peking Man culture, including hunting and communal domestic activities. In March 2014, the Archaeological Institute of America announced that new analyses have shown that Homo erectus pekinensis, or Peking Man, could control and use fire some 770,000 years ago.

The extensive finds, celebrated as an important Chinese discovery in prehistory, were of great significance for scientific research, and the work is being carried on today by the Chinese, who have built a museum at Zhoukoudian and are still working there with the staff from the Institute of Vertebrate Palaeontology and Palaeoanthropology of the Chinese Academy of Sciences. One of its distinguished members, Jia Lanpo (1908-2001), who became the field director of the Zhoukoudian excavations from 1935 onwards, worked as a young scientist as Teilhard's assistant on the site. Writing in 1990 about their association, begun in 1931, he commented:

Excavation in Zhoukoudian, where Peking Man was discovered in 1931. Photographed by Teilhard. (Fondation Teilhard de Chardin)

> My age (twenty-three) and my position prevented me from feeling comfortable. . . . Naturally I did not have much to talk to Teilhard about in the beginning. But this scientist of towering stature quickly put me at ease with his amicable manner and his patience and tirelessness in educating the young learner. . . . The scholar was to teach me much more on scientific matters, while in return I became his assistant, helping with the measurement of specimens that he was studying.

When Lanpo had written a twenty-page paper in English—"an awesome job"—on some of the fossils, as requested, and handed it to Teilhard, "he went over every sentence, making comments in his fine handwriting between almost all the lines—certainly a more painstaking job than if he had written the paper himself. But Teilhard spared no effort in educating the young." Lanpo also bears witness to Teilhard's personal qualities, mentioning how much he was at home

"No paleontological considerations can ever rival the dazzling greatness of the existence of present-day men. Human paleontology is only striving, after all, to rediscover the embryogenesis of the human species."
—"Sinanthropus Pekinensis"

on the back of a mule, and how many hardships he could bear, but especially that

> Teilhard felt deeply for the sufferings of the Chinese people during the war. When he was informed of the tragic death of three Zhoukoudian workers at the hands of the Japanese aggressors in 1937, . . . he immediately stopped typing: his face turned pale, his lips trembled and his eyes stared at me. He sat motionless for a while, then slowly stood up, and with his head bending low, began to pray. I had known him for a few years by then, but this was the first time I had ever seen him in prayer. That over, he solemnly stalked out of the room, uttering not a word. The spontaneous grief he manifested for his fellow men at that grim moment moved me so much that I can see it in my mind's eye to this day.[173]

"The scientific solution of the human problem will never be attained by the study of fossils, but by a more careful consideration of the properties and possibilities that permit us to foresee in the human being of today the human being of tomorrow."
—"Sinanthropus Pekinensis"

Teilhard wrote several articles about the important discovery of Peking Man and the numerous geological strata in which the fossils were embedded. In these remains one could observe the geological history of life, the ceaseless movement of evolution, and what the scientists now call the "deep time" of millions of years of the universe. What a vast canvas it was, and how it stretched human imagination and knowledge. It was an immense extension of vision into the faraway past and early human beginnings. He pointed out that all discoveries,

> especially in paleontology, owe something to chance. In the case of *Sinanthropus*, it should be noted, this chance has been reduced to a minimum. What started with a stroke of luck, method has patiently completed. The discovery of *Sinanthropus* is not, as some people have believed, the result of a happy stroke of the pick. It represents three years of systematic and devoted work.[174]

The extraordinary story of the discovery and subsequent disappearance of the skull and all other Peking Man fossils has been retold in great detail in Amir D. Aczel's book *The*

Jesuit and the Skull: Teilhard de Chardin, Evolution, and the Search for Peking Man (2007), a real detective story whose mystery has not yet been solved.

Around the early 1930s Teilhard was thrilled to be associated with this important work. How changed his situation was now from a few years before! He wrote with confidence to one of his correspondents, the Abbé Gaudefroy:

> Since I came back to China a year ago, things, as you have perhaps suspected, have moved a great deal and changed for me. . . . There is continually more work, more possibilities, more results, more offers. And there comes this Sinanthropus skull, which I did not, of course, discover myself, but which I was in the nick of time to deal with from the geological and paleontological angle. Such coincidences "madly" increase my faith in the presence of God in our lives. If I was offered whatever chair in Paris tomorrow, I wonder whether I'd dare accept it as long as I haven't felt the end of the seam which is still growing richer here for me every day.[175]

He obviously felt at ease, perhaps even somewhat at home, even though he continued to travel back and forth between China, France, and the United States. But it was not for nothing that the Chinese had their own name for him, using three Chinese characters standing for "morality, sun, progress" that were translated as "Father Daybreak Virtue." Unconventional though this name was, in the opinion of one of his Western colleagues, "to the Chinese it stood for the man, and was more prophetic than his unknown donor guessed."[176] Other Chinese simply referred to Teilhard as "the smiling scientist," an indication of the kind and happy presence in their midst. They must have seen a great deal of him, not only at Zhoukoudian, but also when working from one of his three other offices in Beijing. All this might have been enough to keep him busy, but soon other research demands were to be made on him as well.

Teilhard in China. (Georgetown University Library)

Yellow Expedition

I have virtually doubled my knowledge of Asia.
Ten months of my life, even at the age of fifty,
are not too much to pay for that!

Teilhard in 1931, about to depart
on the Yellow Expedition.
(Fondation Teilhard de Chardin)

*"The Chinese now definitely
have the self-awareness, if not
the capabilities, of a modern
nation."*

—Letter to
Joseph Teilhard de Chardin
April 19, 1931

Teilhard was now at the height of his scientific career. Actively involved in expeditions and excavations, he devoted most of his energies to scientific work, writing reports, presenting papers, and publishing specialized articles. There was thus far less time for religious and philosophical essays than during other periods of his life. He had become more independent of French institutions; Paris and Marcellin Boule seemed far away, though not forgotten. Besides the Chinese he also had the support of the Americans. His research was mostly financed by American and Chinese money and, scientifically, he now was more at home in China than in France. But Paris remained his religious and personal home where he had friends and followers, people who really understood him, whereas in China he felt alone.

Toward the end of 1929 he received an invitation from the Citroen car firm in France to take part in an experimental expedition across Central Asia and to be the official geologist for their Croisière Jaune, or Yellow Expedition. Its main purpose was to try out the capacity of Citroen caterpillar vehicles under extreme geographical conditions in Asia, following an earlier experiment of a Croisière Noire across Africa. But it also provided many opportunities for new scientific investigations, so that, besides engineers and motor mechanics, a certain number of scientists were asked to join the team. Teilhard, now almost fifty, was at first somewhat reluctant to go but he eventually accepted what turned out to be one of his most important and unusual expeditions, lasting much longer than planned.

In preparation for this journey he spent a few months in Paris at the end of 1930, followed by a brief stay in the United States in January 1931, where he lectured at the American Museum of Natural History in New York and Columbia University, visited the Field Museum in Chicago, being shown around by the founder's grandson, and crossed the States by Pullman to reach San Francisco. He was delighted to travel through the Colorado desert during this trip, but regretted not having the time to see the Grand Canyon.

He confided to Abbé Breuil:

Citroen caterpillar for the Yellow Expedition.

> I liked America: doubtless, of course, because I was made a fuss of. . . . But still more because everyone engaged in research gave me the impression of freshness and keenness without an eye on a chair or some other academic advantage.[177]

He liked New York, whose skyscrapers he thought very beautiful, and Michigan Avenue and its neighborhood by the lake in Chicago also seemed magnificent. In San Francisco he boarded the liner, *President Garfield*, to cross the Pacific, but stopped in Hawaii and Japan, where he visited the ancient Buddhist temples in Kyoto before returning to China.

During the voyage across the Pacific he wrote "The Spirit of the Earth," an interpretative essay on the world much admired by his friends. It inquires into the future of the spirit on earth, the further spiritual evolution of humankind in the long history of life, and the role of religion in this process:

> There is . . . a spirit of the earth. But in order to take form and shape, this spirit needs a powerful concentrating agent to bring human beings together and increase their powers. . . . We can already see before our eyes the first coming together of the human layer taking place in the form of an interpenetration of thoughts and interests.

Teilhard argues here that the "birth and progress of the

"The age of nations has passed. Now unless we wish to perish we must shake off our old prejudices and build the earth."
—"The Spirit of the Earth"

Teilhard in beret with members of the Yellow Expedition team. (Fondation Teilhard de Chardin)

idea of God on earth are intimately bound up with the phenomenon of hominization." Though religion can become an opium and be simply used to soothe human woes, its true function is "*to sustain and spur on the progress of life,*" which grows "continuously with human beings themselves."[178]

By May 1931 the expedition was ready to start. The plan was that two groups would set out from different directions: the "China group" was to leave from Kalgan, northwest of Beijing, go westward across the Gobi desert through Xinjiang, or former Chinese Turkestan, and reach Kashgar, where it was to meet up with the "Pamir group" that had traveled from the West via Syria, Persia, Afghanistan, and India over the Hindu Kush and Pamir Mountains. The logistics were complicated, the political situation unstable, the obstacles immense. Little did they know how colorful, varied, and dangerous their adventures would be. Much of it has been recorded in the official history of the expedition and the documentary films made during this journey, a valuable visual record of a vast and remote Chinese area before it was opened up to modern rail and road travel.

Teilhard was part of the China group, which set off from Beijing on May 8, 1931. Almost forty expedition members, mostly French, traveled together across the breadth of northern China. But besides the French there had to be an official Chinese delegation of eight, consisting of several scientists and political agents, one, a member of the central committee of the Kuomintang, the other, a minister of General Chiang Kai-Shek's nationalist government. Not surprisingly, this led to considerable difficulties during their travels through the different regions, and during the disputes among the Chinese, Teilhard often had to act as mediator because he was respected by all sides.

The Citroen convoy consisted of ten heavy vehicles, which reached the Gobi desert in mid-June. Ten days later they were brought to a halt when caught in a fight around the oasis of Hami where a major battle was taking place that was part of the Muslim uprising of the 1930s. Hami (or Kumul) is an ancient oasis city on the famous Silk Road that has always functioned as an important gate of China to the West. Today it belongs to the Eastern Uyghur Autonomous Region of Xinjiang and represents one of the largest industrial and agricultural centers of the entire region. Between 1927 and 1930, when it was much less developed, the Muslim conflicts were part of the Chinese civil war of that time, and the members of the French Yellow Expedition ran into considerable trouble. Their road was blocked by human and animal corpses, and they met with distraught children and women weeping for the dead. Teilhard came into his own as volunteer nurse, tending about thirty of the maimed and wounded, but could do little for the most seriously injured. Eventually the convoy was able to continue, and shortly afterward they arrived at the beautiful ancient oasis of Turfan, also a Muslim settlement, not far from the famous Thousand Buddha Caves at Bezeklik, which Teilhard visited on their return journey.

Here they could take some rest, and Teilhard was able to send one of his rare letters during this trip. He told Marguerite that he was writing in great heat, facing a most impressive view:

> In the foreground rows of tapering poplars; behind them a wall of red and grey cliffs encircling a depression below sea-level, . . . beyond them a long snow-capped barrier,

How will spiritual evolution of our planet end? . . . Perhaps . . . in a psychic rather than material turning about—possibly like a death—which will in fact be a liberation from the material plan of history and elevation in God."

—"The Spirit of the Earth"

Teilhard taking geological samples on the Yellow Expedition.
(Fondation Teilhard de Chardin)

the Bogdo-Ula, a continuation of the Tien-Shan. So here at last we are, at Turfan in the heart of Chinese Turkestan. It has been a long, long road from Suchow, across deserts more deserted than any I knew. The whole countryside becomes more majestic in outline. . . . It is a shock to find yourself among people who remind you more of the Near East than the Far East: a negligible minority of Chinese, and a predominance of Arab, Turkish and Persian types. They are practically all Muslims; you see mosques and minarets and hear the muezzin.[179]

When they reached Xinjiang, the governor refused the French permission to enter his territory until the members of the Chinese delegation had been sent home. The expedition finally reached Ürümqi, the capital of Xinjiang, that great northwest region that represents one-sixth of China, making it the size of Alaska or three times that of France. The city lies at the foot of the mighty, snow-capped Tien-Shan, or Heavenly Mountains, with some of the highest peaks in China, rising to nearly seven thousand meters. But despite the agreement negotiated earlier, the governor decided not to let the French proceed, but to hold them prisoners for three months, between July and October 1931. Their caravan was halted, and they camped in their tents outside Ürümqi which means "beautiful pasture" in Mongolian. It was then still a relatively small town surrounded by medieval walls and gates that have long disappeared, whereas it is now the largest city of China's western interior, a major cultural, industrial and commercial center with a population of more than 3 million.

The experience of this oasis town in the early 1930s will have been very different for the French Yellow Expedition, and camping outside its walls was a most frustrating experience. They were reduced to a passive period of waiting and eventually had to use subterfuge to contact by radio their parallel Pamir group, which had arrived in Kashgar. But in spite of repeated pleading with the governor, they were

Teilhard during the Yellow Expedition, 1931. (Fondation Teilhard de Chardin)

not permitted to continue their journey to meet up with the other group as expected. Instead, a small liaison group with four vehicles, while not allowed to travel to Kashgar as planned, was to meet the other group in the nearer locality of Aksu. Only technical personnel could go except for Teilhard who, thanks to his official position in China, was the only scientist of the party. A similar trust was shown when he was given permission to join another small group led by Joseph Hackin, then director of the oriental art collections at the Musée Guimet in Paris, to study some of the dead cities, rock caves, and Buddhist cave paintings in the Gobi desert. For the purpose of a comparative study of Bud-

"The more scientifically I regard the world, the less can I see any possible biological future for it except the active consciousness of its unity. Life cannot henceforth advance on our planet . . . except by breaking down the partitions which still divide human activity and entrusting itself unhesitatingly to faith in the future."
—"The Spirit of the Earth"

On the Yellow Expedition in the Gobi Desert. (Fondation Teilhard de Chardin)

dhist iconography they were allowed to take photographs of the mural paintings, but it was explicitly forbidden to take pictures of the indigenous population. However, for most of their expedition they had the services of the painter Jacovleff, who produced beautiful color studies of the various ethnic types met during their "extraordinary journey across the most inaccessible parts of China, at a time when the most terrible chaos prevailed and there was no law but the law of the strongest."[180]

Yet on other stretches of their expedition they had met with quite different conditions and had visited Mongol

Spirit of Fire

"Contemporary man has passed through a period of great illusion in imagining that, having attained a better knowledge of himself and the world, he has no more need of religion. . . . In reality . . . the great conflict from which we have just emerged has merely strengthened the world's need for belief."

—"The Spirit of the Earth"

camps, Chinese temples and inns, and many Buddhist lamaseries. At some of them they had the opportunity to observe elaborate religious ceremonies, especially the celebration of the Chinese New Year, which occurred in the presence of local dignitaries and the Panchen Lama, the second highest Tibetan spiritual authority after the Dalai Lama. Teilhard and his colleagues encountered many Chinese Buddhists and Muslims and talked to Taoist priests, Buddhist lamas, and quite a few Muslim dignitaries. Besides collecting scientific data there was ample room for gaining new insights into the rich diversity of people, cultures, and religions.

On their return journey Teilhard wrote:

A scene from the Yellow Expedition. (Fondation Teilhard de Chardin)

At last we have got out of Xinjiang, though not without difficulty. . . . But new delays, political or mechanical in origin, keep cropping up, and I have little hope of being back before the end of January. It's very difficult to do any work during this journey. . . . We are on our way back. The fascinating crests of the Tien-Shan are behind us and we are slowly making our way east in bitterly cold but clear weather. . . . These last nine months will remain among the hardest and most rewarding of my career.[181]

The expedition had lasted ten months. The return journey across the Gobi had to take place in the depths of winter, and more delays meant that they eventually got back to Beijing on February 12, 1932. Teilhard felt not dissatisfied, but he suffered from the after-effects of the sheer physical strain of this journey and regretted many a missed opportunity for research, due to the general political upheaval in China. They had endured extremes of heat and cold, a harsh winter in the desert with temperatures -20 to -30 degrees Celsius, and been subject to imprisonment, attacks, and robbery. The physical and climatic conditions endured during this expedition had a permanently adverse effect on Teilhard's heart, though he had greatly increased his knowledge of the Asian continent. He had been tirelessly active along the whole journey, never without his geologist's hammer, his magnifying glass, and his notebook. The scientific data collected were of considerable value for geology, for he could now combine the geology of China with that of Central Asia. He wrote to his brother:

> Climbing onto the caterpillars as though I were mounting a camel, I asked only one thing of the expedition: to take me across Asia. . . . So far as that goes, I have had what I asked for. I often strained at the bit when I was unable to follow up the marvellous opportunities that presented themselves. But, as someone truly said, the drawbacks of a thing are part of the thing itself.[182]

He also had to cope with personal loss, for soon after his return to Beijing he learned that his father had died on February 11, 1932. Deeply sad that one more precious link with his family was now broken, he thought of his early years at home when his father had guided his studies before he went away to a Jesuit boarding school. He owed his father such "an enormous number of things: certain clearly envisaged ambitions, no doubt, but still more a certain fundamental balance on which everything else was built."[183] Had he not given him the first taste for natural history, the true germ of his vocation to science, and the foundation of his life's work? This was his father's true inheritance, the father whose life had been made up of so many sorrows and disappointments, but who

"Without mysticism, there can be no successful religion: and there can be no well-founded mysticism apart from faith in some unification of the universe."
—"The Road of the West: To a New Mysticism"

in his old age could rejoice over the scientific achievements and successes of at least one of his sons.

There could be little doubt about Teilhard's standing and success, although he always remained modest about this himself. The orientalist art historian Joseph Hackin invited him to participate in a study tour of Japan during the following year, and the expedition leader Georges-Marie Haardt wanted him to accompany the French group on their return journey via Indo-China, but Teilhard was unwilling to go. These plans changed in any case, for soon he learned of Haardt's unexpected, tragic death in Hong Kong, which moved him greatly. Speaking as a friend and pastor he wrote:

> There was something fine in being struck down by death in the full vigor of activity. The desert would have been a nobler tomb for him. . . . To me, personally, the sudden loss of a man whose generosity and warmth of heart had captivated me is a real grief, deepened by my regret at not having been able to be with him in his last moments. From what I knew of him, he would have turned to me for support and I am sure that I could have eased his passing. It is a real sorrow to me.[184]

On the Yellow Expedition, beside the Yellow River between Tchoung Ouei and Ning Hia. (Fondation Teilhard de Chardin)

By July he was on another expedition to Shansi, and by September he returned to France for four months. That gave him an opportunity to revisit his family and friends, recharge his energies, and reflect more deeply on his work. For months on end, though with so many people on the Yellow Expedition, he had been on his own, the only practicing Catholic in an entirely secular, agnostic milieu. Although they were united in their scientific endeavor, some expedition members had held it against him that he was a priest and a Jesuit. Yet not a single one of them had stayed away when Teilhard had celebrated a New Year's Mass at one of the Christian mission stations on their return route in January 1932.

Life in constant company could be quite a spiritual trial, as he indicated in one of his letters:

> One of the disadvantages of this trip is the virtual impossibility of being recollected, in view of the numbers and the complexity of the group. They are a very agreeable lot (though the mechanics keep together in a different sort of gang of their own) but the trouble is you're never alone, either physically or morally. My life is identical with my work. Well, thought and reflection will come after it is all over, I suppose. . . . I have a vague conviction that it will help to free me from many fetters, or from narrow and intemperate views.[185]

He had used the enforced stay in Ürümqi to make notes on the nature of what he called a "personalistic universe" and to reflect on the state of the various religions in the world. Increasingly he came to see that Christians must, above all, rethink their own religion. After such close contact with people of different backgrounds and beliefs he felt

> struck by the difficulty of making certain universalist lines of thought intelligible to men who have never been Christians or who have escaped any deep-reaching Christian influence: for Christianity emerges as the only spiritual current capable of developing in souls the sense of the Absolute and the Universal, conceived above all as personal, in other words the true "mystical sense."[186]

He planned to make some minor adjustments to *The Divine Milieu* with a view to eventual publication, but above all he hoped "to write something new on the fundamental metaphysical and religious question: 'What is the Multiple, and how can it be reduced to Unity?' " to which he saw an "Eastern solution" and a "Western solution." There was

"The Divine Milieu seems thoroughly dead and buried. It should have been printed a year ago! But I'm philosophical now, not exactly stoical, but deeply convinced of the 'inexistence' of human obstacles as against the march of truth."
—Letter to Léontine Zanta, August 22, 1930

Inspecting rocks on the Yellow Expedition near the Toksun Gorges, 1931. (Fondation Teilhard de Chardin)

enough solitude and time for reflection traveling westward on his boat journey from China to France for developing these ideas into his essay "The Road of the West: To a New Mysticism."[187] Signed Penang, September 8, 1932, it is the first major piece written after the Yellow Expedition, and also the first explicitly concerned with a comparison between East and West. Its main question is what kind of unity is sought in different types of mysticism. Though apparently remote, this question is closely linked to assessing the present situation of the world with its overwhelming diversity. How to find a greater unity in the current state of disorder, how to embody the spirit of one earth with people from East and West coming closer together? Underlying is the problem of action: Where to find the energy for the right kind of action? How far can it be provided by religion and spirituality? For Teilhard the zest for life and action was best developed in the West, best sustained and nourished by a rightly understood Christianity pointing to a unity of richness and complexity, not one of impoverishment and simplicity.

These ideas had their starting point in the experiences described in his early war essays "Cosmic Life" and "Mystical Milieu," but they were now far more condensed and abstractly expressed. The comparison between West and East was from now on to stay with him. He approached it again and again from different angles, and in doing so, he gained ever further clarifications and nuances to his understanding of the place of religion and mysticism in the modern world.

Lucile Swan

You and I, we are two wild birds on the Mother Earth.
May be, for years, our paths are going to run close to each
other. May be, also the wind is going to separate our external
ways. . . . Be patient . . . peaceful, and happy—I know that
what is born between us is to live forever.

Teilhard loved visiting France, but he also greatly enjoyed living in the East. As he once said in China, "The West fascinates me: but once west of Turkistan, I . . . dream of the East."[188] He enjoyed the stimulating contacts of the international milieu of Beijing where scientists, artists, diplomats, travelers, and many an expatriate befriended him. There was never any shortage of lively social occasions and congenial company, meals with friends, excursions and picnics in the Western Hills, birthday parties or celebrations on special days of the year.

In the autumn of 1929, Dr. Amadeus Grabau, an American geologist of German origin, "father of all the institutions of natural history in China, and frequent host to gatherings of scientists,"[189] gave a dinner party at his house at which Teilhard found himself seated next to Lucile Swan, a recently arrived American sculptress and portrait artist from Iowa. Traveling the world with a friend, Lucile was at that time seeking a new meaning for her life after her marriage to another artist had broken down and been dissolved some years before. Teilhard and Lucile were soon deep in conversation. He was then forty-eight, intelligent, attractive, easy, and most interesting to talk to; she was thirty-nine, full of warmth and vivacity, a reassuring presence and lively personality with a mind of great openness and many questions. The meeting changed Lucile's life and was to have great significance for Teilhard in the years to come.

"By the love of man and woman a thread is wound that stretches to the heart of the world."
—"Sketch of a Peronalistic Universe"

Teilhard at a party in the home of Professor Grabau in Beijing, 1936. (Fondation Teilhard de Chardin)

"Love is the most universal, the most tremendous and the most mysterious of the cosmic forces. . . . Is it truly possible for humanity to continue to live and grow without asking itself how much truth and energy it is losing by neglecting its incredible power of love?"

—"The Spirit of the Earth"

Lucile settled in Beijing in an abandoned temple in the west of the city where she gave lessons in sculpture to members of the Western community and got on with her own artistic work. She and Teilhard met again at several social gatherings, and their friendship grew. Teilhard first wrote to her when, on return from the Yellow Expedition, he was on his way to France. It was a real joy to him to find her reply in Paris: "That means so much to me to feel your frank and strong friendship in my life; and I like so much to hear from you what you do, and what you think in the quiet recess of your small temple!"[190] He also mentioned his work on the essay "The Road of the West."

Their friendship grew much stronger during the following year when Teilhard was back in Beijing and Lucile sculpted a first bust of him. The regular sittings deepened their conversation, closeness, and intimacy. What first had been only a spark now grew into a passionate fire, a great and mature spiritual love, the like of which is very rare indeed. From 1932 to 1941, during the "Chinese phase" of their relationship, they were in daily contact when Teilhard was in Beijing; when away, they wrote each other frequently with great openness and warmth. Lucile's little house became a real home where Teilhard went every afternoon at 5:00 p.m. for tea and talk after a day's work at his laboratory or office. When weather permitted, they went for walks along the city wall or in the beautiful park of the Imperial City. There were many walks and talks whose beauty stood out in Lucile's mind in later years. Teilhard taught Lucile to share his vision of life, of love, of God, and in retrospect, she felt that they gave each other the very best they had.

Some of Lucile's searching questions found new answers. Having left her Episcopalian background, she never returned, but Teilhard helped her to find a new understanding of God, so that eventually she gained inner peace and harmony. In one sense he gave her spiritual advice and direction as he did for so many others whom he brought back to faith or simply helped with advice. Many people experienced what characterized Teilhard as a spiritual director:

> broad forbearance, an extraordinary capacity for sympathy. His first step was to put himself almost unreservedly in the place of the person who came to him, to attune himself to that person's feelings, and to share the weight on that person's mind . . . Teilhard had the gift of starting from scratch . . . out of love of truth and through a need to reconstruct the truth, piece by piece, under the eye of God. He never dodged a difficulty, but faced it squarely; he was open, he never disguised what he really thought, and he shared his correspondent's quest.[191]

These valuable qualities are very evident in the correspondence of more than twenty years between him and Lucile, a correspondence conducted almost entirely in English. Teilhard's lines to Lucile include the true spiritual direction of a searching soul, of a conscience, not unlike the spiritual advice given in the letters to Marguerite during the First World War and in those to Léontine Zanta. Yet at another level these most personal, most intimate letters speak of a depth and intensity of love as never before in Teilhard's life. Lucile and Teilhard were dear and precious to each other; in fact, Lucile read Teilhard's initials—P.T. for Pierre Teilhard, but also Père Teilhard—to mean "precious Teilhard," for she

"Love is the free and imaginative outpouring of the spirit over all unexplored paths. It links those who love in bonds that unite but do not confound, causing them to discover in their mutual contact an exaltation capable, incomparably more than any arrogance of solitude, of arousing in the heart of their being all that they possess of uniqueness and creative power."
—"The Grand Option"

Teilhard in the 1930s. (Georgetown University Library)

149

"The importance of virginity or material integrity of the body has become as unintelligible to us as respect for a taboo . . . we are finding a successful venture into experience more attractive than preservation of innocence; we now estimate the moral value of actions by the spiritual impulse they provide."
—*"The Evolution of Chastity"*

felt that no other word described him quite so well. There was something special about him, about his presence, his warmth, his constant belief in life that gave him a precious quality that his essays cannot convey in the same way.

Lucile loved him deeply and wanted his presence forever. She longed for a fuller giving, a complete union, not only spiritual love and friendship. But Teilhard's heart was given to an all-embracing, universal vision, a deeply burning love of God and Christ in all things, which Lucile did not at first understand. As he wrote to her in November 1933:

> The fundamental bearing of my life, you know it, is to prove to the others and to myself, that the love of God does not destroy, but exalt and purify any earthly power of understanding and loving. I dream of going to God under the pressure of the strongest and the wildest spirits of the world.
>
> That will explain you, perhaps, why, when I met you, I accepted you as a marvellous gift. I thought (as I still more think now) that I had found a wonderful thing, which would help me to live more intensely,—so that I could give myself more efficiently to the divine work of enlarging the World around me. Thus I can be yours, really yours, in getting more spirit from you, and in growing into the same spirit with you.
>
> But because your friend, Lucile, belongs to Something Else, he cannot be yours . . . just and merely for being momentarily happy with you.
>
> Do you remember a thought expressed in the short page I gave you . . . "to conquer the things, not for merely enjoying them, but for converging with them into something or somebody ever higher."[192]

He was aware that this might appear as selfish and make her suffer, but he was trying to discover a new path along which the world might move. Soon afterward, in March 1934, when replying to a "glorious letter" from Lucile, which provided him with one of the most precious minutes in his life, he declared his deep love:

> You have entered more deep than ever, as an active seed, the innermost of myself. You bring me what I need for carrying on the work which is before me: a tide of life.
>
> But, just because you are forever such a dear treasure for me, I ask you to do your best for not building too much your material, or external, life, on me. . . .
>
> Sometimes, I think I would like to vanish before you *into* some thing which would be bigger than myself,—your real yourself, Lucile,—your real life, *your* God. And then I should be yours, completely.

He assured her, then and again and again, that "what is born between us is to live for ever."[193]

Lucile was fully aware of Teilhard's great difficulties with his church and order, with the ongoing tensions and obstacles over publishing his work. He was greatly distressed when in July 1931 four books of his friend Édouard Le Roy were put on the Index, while he himself made no headway with getting his *Divine Milieu* published. At the same time he was forbidden to let his name go forward for a position at the Collège de France in Paris. Conservative circles reported him once more to church authorities in Rome, and he even received a letter laying down his line of conduct. The profound lack of understanding and the unjustified suspicions weighed deeply on him and provoked many a doubt and critical statement. Perhaps the harshest judgment he ever made was:

> The only thing that I can be: a voice that repeats, *opportune et importune*, that the Church will waste away so long as she does not escape from the factitious world of verbal theology, of quantitative sacramentalism, and overrefined devotions in which she is enveloped, so as to reincarnate herself in the real aspirations of mankind. . . . Of

"Christian chastity is ultimately a transposition into religion of the lover's fidelity."
—"The Evolution of Chastity"

151

course I can see well enough what is paradoxical in this attitude: if I need Christ and the Church I should accept Christ as he is presented by the Church, with its burden of rites, administration and theology. . . . But now I can't get away from the evidence that the moment has come when the Christian impulse should "save Christ" from the hands of the clerics so that the world may be saved.

He was scornful of speakers and writers whose "dead prose" is never brought to life by any "religious sap," and in whom only "truths already digested a hundred times and with no living essence" are to be found.[194]

Teilhard with Lucile Swan in her home in Beijing. (Fondation Teilhard de Chardin)

Lucile, who knew him better and closer than anyone else at this time, gave him continuing support, but also questioned his unswerving loyalty. She reacted with a spontaneity and freshness that must have made her all the more attractive. He had to probe deeper when she challenged him. She would get impatient because the church would not allow him to print his essays. This seemed to her most arbitrary and unfair; in her view he gave his life to a dead thing. But he strongly denied this. She noted in her journal that there might be a definite break with his order; in fact, she had subconsciously counted on it, but it did not come.

Teilhard loved her deeply and reciprocated her words of love over and over again. Thus it seemed only natural that, given their deep love for each other and the trying difficulties he continued to experience, she should wish him to leave his religious duties for a more permanent union between them. But Teilhard remained unswerving in his fidelity to his church and order.

Lucile expressed her own difficulties in a note to herself saying,

> You've become more important in my life every day. Yes. The live, physical, real you, all of you. I want you so terribly and I am trying so hard to understand and incorporate into my being your philosophy, your views on life. . . . I can't have you. Not really, so I must learn your way of having each other.[195]

He frankly admitted,

> The problem, I told you, exists for me just as for you,—although, for some complex reasons, I believe to have to stick somewhat to an old solution. My line of answer, let me observe, does not exclude the "physical" element,—since it is not some abstract spirit,—but the "woman,"—which I discover in you.[196]

Lucile sometimes felt that Teilhard's friendship was better than his ideas, that he was more interested in the human phenomenon and love in general than in individual people and personal love. Their letters often speak of the fire of love, but for Teilhard this implied first and foremost a fundamental faithfulness to his vocation and vision, the power, strength, and sincerity of the mystic priest and pioneer he had been in the trenches when he had so deeply experienced the call to follow "the road of fire." As he wrote to Lucile:

> In our particular case . . . we can find some kind of happiness in thinking that what we have to suffer or to miss expresses (and pays for) the work of discovering something which is grand and new,—the "new discovery of the Fire."[197]

Their spiritual intimacy was so great that Teilhard even

"Chastity, then, is a virtue of participation and conquest, and not a schooling in restriction and avoidance."
—"The Evolution of Chastity"

lent Lucile his personal notebook. Reading it helped her to understand him and his ideas better. She noted in her journal:

> I would like to love God in the way P. T. does—perhaps that will come in time—For certainly he has an inner strength and integrity that is unique—it is because of his feeling for God or just because he is that—probably both—His "credo"—or whatever it is still seems to me the best expression of a faith that I have yet found.

Shortly afterward, in July 1934, she expressed in another note to herself her deep desire and longing:

> Perhaps it is because I have been trying to contemplate and write about the spirit of the world, God, and also because I have read your notebook and realize how much of you is unworldly. And I wrote you just before you left in which I spoke of the "physical." Please don't think I mean just sex, although that is very strong. It would make a bond between us that would add a strength that I believe *nothing* else can give. However, that is only a part. I want to be with you and when you are well and when you are ill. Go see beautiful things with you and walk through the country. In other words, I want to stand beside you always, to laugh and play and pray with you. Don't you realize what a big part of life that is, and how that is what is right and normal and God-given. But I cannot.[198]

For him it was a question of giving fire its share, of animating her life, but "without interfering in anything with its normal external course."[199] The fire of his love and the fire of his vocation had to burn together, merged in their flames, for he saw it as his special calling to synthesize the love of the world, the love of God, and also the love of his church and order. He had once written to his friend Père Valensin that he had offered himself to the Lord "as a sort of testing-ground" to bring about the fusion between the two great loves, of God and the world, without which no Kingdom of God is possible. He modestly saw himself as a channel that could be made use of. The religious possibilities of the world were immense, and he asked God to give him the strength "to baptize that soul of the world which has become my own true soul."[200]

When their relationship was in its early, most intense and passionate stage, Teilhard was working on his essay "The Evolution of Chastity," dated February 1934. Here, in the light of a new understanding of matter and its spiritual power, he speaks of the nature and value of chastity and virginity, of the creative transformation of human love. If the feminine is "matter in its most virulent form,"[201] then Lucile represented perhaps the most virulent form of the feminine for him. He admits in the essay that he had been "through some difficult passages. But I have never felt any impoverishment of being, nor that I had lost my way."[202]

It is a splendid essay, though not without controversial aspects in its exploration of the moral significance of chastity in relation to Christian holiness and living. Left to his own judgment, Teilhard was not at all clear "about what is not allowable." Yet in his search for a higher road of spiritualization, he suggested:

> Spiritual fecundity accompanying material fecundity ever more closely—and ultimately becoming the *sole* justification of union. Union for the sake of the child—but why not union for the sake of work, for the sake of the idea? . . . Is not this spiritual use of the flesh precisely what many men of genius, men who have been true creators, have instinctively found and adopted, without asking the moralists for their approval?

At the same time he felt it was indispensable "to disclose some perfection that resides in virginity by *nature*" and that Christianity has staked its authority on the belief "that physical chastity brings with it a sort of absolute superiority." Perhaps now the time has come when "man and woman—on whom life has laid the charge of advancing to the

Bronze bust of Teilhard by Lucile Swan, 1936.

155

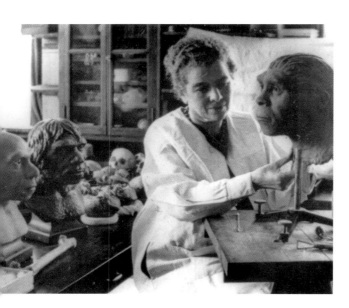

Lucile Swan modeling a head of Peking Man, 1937. (Fondation Teilhard de Chardin)

highest possible degree the spiritualization of the earth—will have to abandon that way of possessing one another which has hitherto been the only rule for living beings" in order to rise together so that their complete giving would coincide with their meeting with the divine.

Though aware of the difficulties, Teilhard thought that the transformation of love has to be ventured, for love is going through a "change of state" in the noosphere. If we are not paralyzed by a "lack of faith and lack of audacity," then the day will come "when, after harnessing the ether, the winds, the tides, gravitation, we shall harness for God the energies of love. And, on that day, for the second time in the history of the world, human beings will have discovered fire."[203]

During 1932-1941 Lucile was closely involved with the production of Teilhard's essays at a time when he wrote such important texts as "Christology and Evolution," "How I Believe," "Sketch of a Personalistic Universe," "The Phenomenon of Spirituality," "Human Energy," "The Mysticism of Science," and many others. Most important was his magnum opus written during 1938-1940, his great book *The Human Phenomenon*. He always liked to discuss his ideas with Lucile and referred to each nez essay as "another egg" he had produced, but acknowledged that it was her work too, with each essay being "a new result of our 'spiritual union,'"[204] as if their work consisted "in a single and common activity."[205] This is why their correspondence is so uniquely important: it provides many new clues as to Teilhard's way of thinking and working; it also shows how all his ideas were deeply embedded in personal experience and nourished by interpersonal relationships.

Lucile was able to question him and challenge his ideas like nobody before. She gave Teilhard more than many a partner provides. She discussed, read, and translated his essays, got them typed, printed, and sent out to numerous friends, shared his walks and talks, and provided a place of intimacy and warmth in her home. She also helped with the work at the laboratory where she, in collaboration with Teilhard's colleague Weidenreich, modeled the head of *Sinanthropus*: "The reconstructed individual (a complete head including the mandible) is a female: we call her Nelly," Teilhard wrote to one of his friends.[206]

Lucile gave much light, energy, and warmth to Teilhard, who called her his "star," his "sounding board," his "spark," a "tide of life" and "rejuvenation," the "very expression of his life." He wanted her womanliness, as he once said, but he did not want to be the center of her entire life. But she wanted more than anything else his presence, for ever. Although she had her own creative work, her social life and travels, these were somehow subordinate to her love and tenderness for Teilhard. She wanted all of him, but in the end she had to fit in with his ideas: he wanted the world, and wanted it for God. But he also was a helpful critic of her own work and always encouraged her to achieve the best; he gave her life direction, leading her to a fuller understanding and love of God. Their relationship expressed to the full what Teilhard always taught, that "union differentiates."

Their great love for each other was a trial by fire in which Teilhard remained faithful to his vows until the end. After 1941 they went their different ways, but Lucile always remained very dear to him, and he continued writing to her until his death. The later history of their relationship, in its second, "American phase," was more complicated and troubled than their "Chinese phase," but their letters are a lasting testimony to the inspiring and transforming powers of love—love as the greatest source of human energy, love as power of union, communion, and spiritual transformation, especially when human love is so closely intertwined with love of the divine.

(Georgetown University Library)

Travels between East and West

It is better, no matter what the cost, to be more conscious than less conscious. . . . The only reality in the world is the passion for growth.

Teilhard with Abbé Breuil near Ming tombs outside Beijing, 1935. (Fondation Teilhard de Chardin)

During his second decade in China much time was taken up with traveling, attending international conferences, and writing scientific papers, After the Yellow Expedition he had enjoyed a refreshing break in France, though there was disappointment over the fate of his writings. Two censorship reports on *The Divine Milieu* had both been favorable except for "a request for precision on the 'Sense of the Cross,' which I can easily satisfy, I think. Pity that the whole thing must be held up."[207] By March 1933 he was back in Beijing, accompanied by his friend Abbé Breuil, who came to study the excavations at Zhoukoudian.

This was the fifth return to his chosen exile, but the atmosphere in Beijing was more difficult now. Many inhabitants were leaving the city in a panic because the Japanese were threatening China. As a measure of security, the scientific material of the Geological Survey was moved from the Chinese laboratories to the Rockefeller Foundation, where work could be carried on as usual. Fortunately an agreement with the Japanese was signed, and life soon returned to normal. Teilhard took advantage of the calm for another expedition to the province of Shansi, and by June he was traveling with his colleague Davidson Black to attend the International Geological Conference in Washington. They were joint authors of a monograph, "Fossil Man in China," dealing with the Zhoukoudian cave deposits, which they could now get published. Teilhard was also able to write several essays with a religious theme, dealing with modern unbelief and Christianity in the world, but also a short pa-

Teilhard with faculty from the University of Tianjin, 1935. (Fondation Teilhard de Chardin)

per, "The Significance and Positive Value of Suffering," written at the request of his favorite sister, Marguerite-Marie, or Guigite, permanently ill since the age of twenty. Teilhard loved her greatly and learned much from her about physical pain and suffering.

Guigite was for many years the leading light of the Catholic Union of the Sick, and it was for their bulletin that Teilhard produced his essay. It contains the encouraging message that even pain and suffering can be transformed into spiritual energy and help to build up the world: "Illness naturally tends to give sufferers the feeling that they are useless or even a burden on the earth. Almost inevitably they feel as if cast up by the great stream of life, lying by sheer ill-luck incapable of work or activity," as was the experience of his sister.

> What a vast ocean of human suffering spreads over the entire earth at every moment! Of what is this mass formed? Of blackness, gaps and rejections? No, let me repeat, of potential energy. . . . The whole question is how to liberate it and give it a consciousness of its significance and potentialities.[208]

"But what an absurd thing life is, looked at superficially: so absurd that you feel yourself forced back on a stubborn, desperate, faith in the reality and survival of the spirit. Otherwise—were there no such thing as the spirit, I mean—we should have to be idiots not to call off the whole human effort."
        —Letter to Abbé Breuil,
           March 18, 1934

"In my distress following Black's death, and in the stifling atmosphere of 'agnostic' condolences that surround it, I swore to myself, on the body of my dead friend, to fight more vigorously than ever to give hope to man's work and inquiry."
—Letter to the Begoüens,
April 10, 1934

In November he returned from Washington via San Francisco to Beijing, where there was more work waiting for him. Newly found fossils from Zhoukoudian required further study and interpretation. By Christmas he had completed an essay, "Christology and Evolution," "strictly limited in intention for some intimate friends in my own profession."[209] It discusses how to understand the Christian teaching on incarnation and redemption in the contemporary world. While he believed Christianity to be immortal, he recognized that it is at present "reaching the end of one of the natural cycles of its existence."[210] Lucile later translated and typed the controversial text to which Père Maréchal, whose advice Teilhard had sought, provided a long and detailed critique. But despite their disagreement Teilhard felt encouraged because Maréchal had said in one of his letters: "There is no-one today who has such a grasp as you have of all the material bearing on the problem of evolution—theological, philosophical and scientific." Teilhard only wondered, "Surely it should be to the Church's interest to make use of my acknowledged reputation, even if it's not justified?" He could see only one answer: "to keep pressing on, in ever-increasing faith. May the Lord only preserve in me a passionate taste for the world, and a great gentleness; and may He help me persevere to the end in the fullness of humanity."[211]

That fullness was marked by loss and diminishment when suddenly, in March 1934, Davidson Black, his close friend and collaborator, was found dead in his laboratory due to sudden heart failure. It was a great shock. Teilhard was so fond of him, his good sense of humor, his intuitive mind, his congenial company, his great professional expertise. He had been like a brother to him, one of those he loved most apart from his own family. They did not share a religious faith but had experienced in their work a deep "communion in science." Though untimely, it was a noble death, in the full force of activity. Yet Teilhard felt a leaden sadness and revolted in spirit. He wrote to Lucile:

Either there is an escape, somewhere, for the thought and the personality,—or the world is a tremendous mistake. And we must stop.—But, because nobody will admit that we must stop,—then, we must *believe*. To awake this belief must be, more than ever, my duty. I have sworn it to myself, on the remains of Davy,—more than a brother, for me.[212]

Black had been world famous for his research on Peking Man, and his death left a terrible gap. Peking Union Medical College had lost an outstanding colleague whose brilliant achievements in science had done great credit to the college. The Chinese greatly respected Black for his contribution to research on the early history of humankind and so much admired him as a person that the Chinese scientist Jia Lanpo later described Davidson Black as "the Man Who Forgot his Nationality."[213]

While waiting for Black's successor to be appointed, Teilhard went on two expeditions with George Barbour, one along the river Yangtze with its famous gorges, the other to central China. But in spite of the great geological interest of their work he still felt a deep grief: "I miss Black very much. Missing him is like a shadow, or an emptiness that I carry with me wherever I go."[214] The death had left him with a sharp and concrete realization of the utter vanity of human effort, except if there exists an outlet whereby the universe is moving toward some immortal consciousness. Death's large shadow was further lengthened when his brother Victor died in October of that year from the after-effects of gas poisoning suffered during the First World War.

It is under these circumstances that Teilhard completed on October 28, 1934, his important essay "How I Believe." He called it the history of his faith. Written at the special request of Msgr. Bruno de Solages, it is almost as if Teilhard here found the height of his creative powers to express what he had sworn on the mortal remains of his friend to be his

"I believe that the universe is an evolution. I believe that evolution proceeds toward spirit. I believe that spirit is fully realized in a form of personality. I believe that the supremely personal is the universal Christ."
—"How I Believe"

Georges Barbour in New York, February 1934. (Fondation Teilhard de Chardin)

161

"All the sufferers of the earth joining their sufferings so that the world's pain might become a great and unique act of consciousness, elevation and union. Would not this be one of the highest forms that the mysterious work of creation could take in our sight?"

—"The Significance and Positive Value of Suffering"

task, to awaken belief in others by describing the development of his personal experience: "Today I believe probably more profoundly than ever in God, and certainly more than ever in the world. . . . I am going to broadcast the seed, and let the wind carry it where it will." Here we find the key stages and central elements of his faith expressed in great detail. His vision of the universal Christ and his belief in Christianity are celebrated with great power, but "Christianity takes on its full value only when extended . . . to cosmic

Teilhard with Abbé Breuil.
(Fondation Teilhard de Chardin)

dimensions." The clarity and security of his faith are fully visible, but its glory is not without penumbra:

> Certain though I am—and ever more certain—that I must press on in life as though Christ awaited me at the term of the universe, at the same time I feel no special assurance of the existence of Christ. Believing is not seeing. As much as anyone, I imagine, I walk in the shadows of faith.[215]

At the beginning of 1935 he wrote to Lucile that his thoughts were progressing, especially "concerning the value (and emptiness) of the past. I think that I have crossed a critical point in my internal evolution, those past months,—with you."[216] Lucile helped him through some of his most difficult and darkest hours, but she was also there to discuss the ongoing work on his essays.

The new year also brought new opportunities for travel. After an expedition to southern China, Teilhard traveled once again, this time with Abbé Breuil, on the Trans-Siberian railway to Paris where he stayed for a few months. In August he was able to have a holiday with his two brothers in the Auvergne, meet his family again, and enjoy the "old houses, full of familiar scents and noises,— surrounded by quiet fields and large oaks."[217] But soon he was again traveling the world. From September to December he represented the Peking Institute on the Yale North India Expedition, led by Helmut de Terra. Teilhard took a boat from Marseilles to Bombay, went by rail to Rawalpindi, and from there by car to Srinagar in Kashmir, accompanied by the English scientist T. T. Patterson. They joined de Terra on a houseboat he had rented with his wife and young daughter. After some field work on the glacial series of the Himalayas, they went down to western Panjab, visited part of Sind and Baluchistan, and later worked in central India before traveling to Calcutta. They saw some of the prehistoric drawings in the Indus Valley and visited the famous

Excavations at Mohenjo-Daro in the Indus Valley

excavations at Mohenjo-Daro, which left a deep impression on Teilhard. Their research led to the discovery of a number of early pebble industries, and he felt they had a hand in laying the foundations of prehistoric studies in India.

As he traveled by camel or car in the Salt Range of what is now Pakistan, the semi-desert conditions reminded Teilhard of his earlier stays in Egypt and Abyssinia, of the Nile valley and Cairo. He loved the wonderful luminosity of the landscape but commented more harshly on the country's population, only met from afar. Helmut de Terra, who later wrote about their journey, was of the opinion that if there was any foreigner "who could have roused ancient India to new life, it was Teilhard," for "in this superstition-ridden Indian world, he seemed like a new species of human being."[218]

From India Teilhard went to Burma, now called Myanmar. After spending Christmas in Rangoon, now known as Yangon, he sailed to Java to study the sites where Pithecanthropus, or Java Man, had been found in the late nineteenth century, and where Ralph von Koenigswald was now undertaking more excavations. The trip gave Teilhard the unique opportunity of examining the close relationship between these newly unearthed fossil bones and those found near Beijing. He loved being in Java and was convinced he was made for life in the tropics. On his return to China in January 1936 he wrote:

> I have just spent four really *exciting* months in India and Java: masses of new stuff, good solid stuff in the loveliest settings in the world. . . . Now I am hurrying back to Beijing to see what effect the Japanese penetration is likely to have on conditions at the Geological Survey.[219]

The trip had also given him something else. The meeting with Rhoda de Terra, Helmut de Terra's wife, who lovingly looked after the well-being of the scientists, led over the next few years to a new friendship. Their exchange of ideas is reflected in a considerable correspondence of letters written

"In itself, to be frank, the problem of personal survival does not worry me greatly. . . . I can say in all sincerity that my personal happiness means nothing to me. It is enough for me in that respect that what is best in me should pass, there to remain forever, into one who is greater and finer than I."
—"How I Believe"

between 1938 and 1950,[220] after which Rhoda lived close to Teilhard in New York where she saw him regularly.

He was barely back from his exciting travels when the news reached him that his mother had died on February 7, 1936. Yet another link with his past and his beloved family was broken, another bereavement difficult to bear. On this as on other occasions he was never able to go home, although he had known the end was near. That was perhaps the greatest strain, the highest cost he had to pay for his exile in the Far East. He described her as "My dear and saintly mother, to whom I owe all that is best in my soul."[221] He saw in her something of Mary, a *Mater Dolorosa* who had experienced so much loss and suffering in her life, but this pain was transformed and redeemed for both of them in the sufferings of Christ and his mother.

Lucile was a constant, loving presence, providing compassionate support during his greatest hours of need. After several months of daily contact in Beijing he wrote to her from an expedition to eastern Shantung, where he renewed "a loathsome acquaintanceship with Chinese inns and Chinese carts."[222] He commented that

> we have been so much together during the past months that we need perhaps those days for assimilating the treasures accumulated by the physical presence. So far as the spiritual presence is concerned (and this is something essentially physical, too!), you know that I never get out of it,— because you have become a part of my deepest own life.[223]

Shortly afterward, on August 17, 1936, his beloved sister Marguerite-Marie died, liberated at long last from her many

"Illuminated by the invisible light, Marguerite lived so as to be led and to lead others towards that center of creative power which shines upon us through the shadows of death."

—Teilhard about his sister

Teilhard's sister Marguerite toward the end of her life, 1936. (Fondation Teilhard de Chardin)

(Georgetown University Library)

years' illness. It was another blow, though he knew it was coming.

> But I feel that a great void has opened up in my life—or rather in the world around me—a great void of which I shall become increasingly aware. . . . The only way of making life bearable again is to love and adore that which, beneath everything, animates and directs it.[224]

To another correspondent he wrote:

> Toward the middle of August I lost my younger sister (the last surviving). I was only too well prepared to learn of it. She and I understood each other particularly well, and her death leaves me with a great emptiness (as Black's did, though in another way). There are now only we three brothers out of the ten in 1900.[225]

Marguerite was an example to him of how suffering and sickness must not only be mastered, but can also be transfigured through becoming an expression of love and union, as he movingly expressed it in a brotherly testimonial written for her. Unfortunately Marguerite destroyed all Teilhard's letters to her, but years later he wrote:

> O Marguerite my sister, while I, given soul and body to the positive forces of the universe, was wandering over continents and oceans, my whole being passionately taken up in watching the rise of all the earth's tints and shades, you lay motionless, stretched out on your bed of sickness: silently, deep within yourself, you were transforming into light the world's most grievous shadows.[226]

To some extent their two different lives, each in its own way, embodied what he had called in *The Divine Milieu* the "divinization of activities" and the "divinization of passivities"—truly beautiful, inspiring examples of the spiritual empowerment and transformation of a life lived from the depths of Christian faith.

Spiritual Energy

The definitive discovery of the phenomenon of spirit is bound up with the analysis (which science will one day finally undertake) of the "mystical phenomenon" that is of the love of God.

After a year of family losses, toward the end of 1936, Teilhard wrote to his youngest brother, Joseph:

> From the narrowly personal point of view, 1937 looks like being a laborious and complicated year, and my own life in general an unending pilgrimage. But I can see quite clearly that it would be a betrayal on my part not to take up my staff again and accept the routine of perpetual separations.[227]

He worked for most of 1936 in the Beijing laboratories, writing scientific reports and several essays, mostly not published until after his death. During September he was busy with "Some Reflections on the Conversion of the World," which, in substance and brief form, restated some ideas of his earlier "Christology and Evolution" for the benefit of some high officials in Rome.[228]

In February 1937 he sailed again for America, visiting Seattle and Chicago from where he went to attend a symposium on Early Man sponsored by the Carnegie Foundation in Philadelphia. He was "a welcome guest at the suburban house" of Helmut and Rhoda de Terra.[229] His visit was an occasion to strengthen the friendship between them. Teilhard wrote, "De Terra and I understand each other like a couple of brothers," whereas de Terra later declared, "Teilhard was my friend, the most cherished and revered human being I ever met."[230]

While in Philadelphia, Teilhard expounded his views

Teilhard, inspecting a skull, at a symposium on Early Man in Philadelphia, 1937. (Fondation Teilhard de Chardin)

"Christianity must at last accept unreservedly the new dimensions (spatial, temporal and psychological) of the world around us."
—"Some Reflections on the Conversion of the World"

"The world is being converted spontaneously to a sort of natural religion of the universe, which is wrongly turning it away from the God of the gospel; it is in this that its 'unbelief' consists."

—"Modern Unbelief"

On March 27, 1937 at Villanova in Philadelphia, Teilhard receives the Mendel Medal in recognition of his work. (Fondation Teilhard de Chardin)

on *Sinanthropus*, arguing that this was a true human being since Peking Man was capable of shaping tools and making and preserving fire. He was awarded the prestigious Mendel Medal in recognition of his work by the Catholic University of Villanova, but his views attracted considerable notoriety in American and Canadian newspapers when he was described as "the Jesuit who believes man descended from the apes." This had such an impact that the Jesuits at Boston College, who had also planned to honor him, withdrew their invitation.

Without seeming too upset, Teilhard made a few more visits and then departed for France to spend the summer there. By September he was back in China, where the Japanese were bombing Shanghai. This was the beginning of the Japanese invasion of China, and hostilities continued until 1945. At first Beijing was not so much in danger, and work at the laboratories continued as before, with Lucile Swan completing the reconstruction of Nelly, the female head of *Sinanthropus*. It is quite extraordinary how, amid the indescribable misery and suffering of the Chinese, with extremes of poverty and hunger, and with mounting hostilities and warlike conditions, Teilhard nonetheless continued to maintain such an attitude of hope and a deep belief in the future of humanity.

Between 1933 and 1936, his numerous experiences and encounters in China also included close contacts with Edgar and Helen Snow from whom he learned about Snow's visit to Mao Zedong, saw photographs, and received much information about the Chinese communist movement. He judged this new political phenomenon as an important manifestation of human energy and discussed with the Snows Mao's influence on Chinese villagers never before touched by Western influences, but now subject to a new, Western-derived political creed. Apparently, in 1937, Mrs. Snow described to Mao personally Teilhard's vision about further human cultural and social evolution. It seems that Teilhard also helped her to arrange the first exhibition of works by contemporary Chinese left-wing artists in Paris, just as he helped several students to go to France for their studies.

As was his wont, Teilhard used the leisure of his sea voyages to write some more essays. While sailing on the Pacific to the United States in early 1937, he completed "The Phenomenon of Spirituality," which he soon sent to Lucile for translation. Here, as elsewhere in his work, Teilhard presents his own kind of "phenomenology," which approaches all phenomena in a larger, more comprehensive framework, through seeing them ultimately on a cosmic scale within the vast process of evolutionary becoming. While different sciences analyze small, specialized areas of the real, he always argues for an all-embracing vision of synthesis that looks at the human phenomenon, the social phenomenon, the religious, mystical, and spiritual phenomenon as a whole, within the larger context of nature and the universe.

The essay proposes a theory of the phenomenon of spirit within evolution, a theory that appears as true to Teilhard "as any large scale physical hypothesis can be."[231] The spirit is not a passing, secondary phenomenon in the process of evolution, but the central phenomenon of the whole process. Therefore he investigates the possibilities of further spiritualization, the future of the spirit on earth. At present humankind has a great need for technicians and engineers "of the spiritual energies of the world" who can develop "by awakening and convergence, the individual riches of the earth." In a cosmos in spiritual transformation a new kind of spirituality is needed, one linked to a "morality of movement" that defines the value of human actions in three ways:

Japanese troops entering Shanghai.

"The true name for spirit is 'spiritualization.'. . . The phenomenon of the spirit is not . . . a sort of brief flash in the night; it reveals a gradual and systematic passage from the unconscious to the conscious, and from the conscious to the self-conscious. It is a cosmic change of state."
—"The Phenomenon of Spirituality"

"Spiritualized energy . . . is the flow of cosmic energy. It is consequently the most interesting part of human energy for organization."

— "Human Energy"

i.   *only* finally good is what makes for the growth of the spirit on earth.

ii.   good . . . is *everything* that brings a spiritual growth to the world.

iii.   finally best is what assures their highest development to the spiritual powers of the earth.[232]

The whole motivation of this essay is best summed up in his statement, "What we are all more or less lacking at this moment is a new definition of holiness."[233]

On his return journey to China in August 1937, sailing for a month between Marseilles and Shanghai, he wrote another long essay, "Human Energy." It sets out ideas that had preoccupied him for some time, namely, the need for a science of "human energetics." At a global level, humanity not only faces a problem of balance in terms of land, food, employment, and material resources, but it increasingly comes up against another problem, that of spiritual energies, of resources to feed the zest for life and build up the human community with greater strength. At present so much energy is used in the "most primitive and savage form of war," used for attack and victory. Teilhard argues not for the suppression of this energy, but for its transformation. He wishes that the moment may come, and he thinks it will,

Teilhard at leisure in Beijing.
(Georgetown University)

"when the masses realize that the true human victories are those over the mysteries of matter and life."[234]

He also argues that human energy "implies faith in some final completion of *everything* around us," that it is attracted to a higher pole, which he calls "the cosmic point Omega."[235] This is both a center and a summit:

Omega, in which all things converge, is reciprocally

that from which all things radiate. Impossible to place it as a point at the peak of the universe without at the same time diffusing its presence within each smallest advance of evolution. The meaning of this is nothing less than this: that *for him who has seen it* everything, however humble, *provided it places itself in the line of progress*, is warmed, illumined and animated, and consequently becomes an object to which he gives his *whole* adhesion.[236]

The highest form of human energy is the unifying and synthesizing power of love, which he sees at work at all levels of evolution. But above all it finds its expression in "the phenomenon of Christianity," which proclaims God as love, only to be finally reached in and through love.

During his visit to the United States de Terra had invited Teilhard to join him on another expedition to Myanmar. Teilhard initially had to postpone his departure because he fell ill with malaria. But eventually, in late December 1937, he was well enough to go to Myanmar, where he spent three months near the Irawaddy River, which runs between two massive mountain ranges. He felt soon restored to health and loved the place so much that, according to de Terra, it was hard in the end to take their leave,

> whether because of the idyllic river landscape, the wild expanses of tropical mountain forest, the Buddhist traditions of the country's graceful inhabitants, the colorful splendor of village festivals, or the harmonious and successful way in which we had carried out our researches.[237]

From Myanmar they went via Singapore to prehistoric sites in Java, where Teilhard had been two years before, and where recently a new *Pithecanthropus* skull had been found. He felt rather more exhausted by now and was anxious to rejoin his colleagues in Beijing, where he arrived at the beginning of May.

Life in Beijing was getting more and more difficult. The

"Our world entered the era of force at the same time as it awoke to consciousness of its evolution. It will collapse on itself if it does not discover as a way out some point of convergence above and ahead for its excess of power. It will no longer obey any morality but one of movement; and I cannot conceive of any such morality outside belief in the existence of a transformation which will bring the universe from the material to the spiritual state."
—"The Phenomenon of Spirituality"

Buddhist temple on the Irawaddy River in Myanmar.

Japanese military authorities had control over the city, and living conditions were changing for the worse. Although foreigners were relatively free from trouble, it was different for the Chinese. The Japanese cut all access to Zhoukoudian so that excavation work had to stop. The Chinese workers dispersed so as not to work for the Japanese. Teilhard felt concerned about the fate of the Geological Survey, where scientific research was now restricted to laboratory work only. He also changed his residence from living with the Lazarist fathers to Chabanel Hall, a teaching institution for newly arrived missionaries, where he was not too comfortably lodged in a room located in noisy outbuildings. However, there was a glimmer of hope on the horizon. He had received permission from Rome to direct a laboratory concerned with the study of continental geology in relation to human origins at the prestigious École des Hautes Études in Paris, which would give him a permanent platform in France to which he could regularly return. But somehow he felt only lukewarm about these developments and wrote to his brother in June 1938: "I look forward to returning to France this autumn, though without giving up China, where my true field of study still lies."[238]

Mao Zedong in 1937.

Meanwhile Lucile had gone to the United States to visit friends and relatives and to exhibit her recent work. Teilhard wrote to her about their "marvelous friendship" in which momentary separations "are a useful part in the process of what is growing between us." She now gave him even more than before because in the depth of their lives they were still closer, but also because, as Teilhard wrote,

> as I become "less young," I feel deeper the need of a full comprehension and support. . . . Keep this point very strong in your mind and your heart: You can and you must help me to go on straight ahead, by giving me light and warmth. Keep me alive on Earth, while I try to bring you closer to God. This seems to me to be the meaning

and the definition of our mutual union. Make me more myself, as I dream to make you reaching the best of yourself. . . . And thank you, so much, for forgetting as you do, for me, what you might, naturally, expect, but what, for higher reasons, I cannot give you. I love you so much the more for this "renoncement." And there is nothing I will not do for you, in order to repay you.[239]

Love was for Teilhard the greatest form of human energy, an intensely physical and spiritual energy. Without its warmth, its spark and fire, he could not have carried on his many tasks. When he went to France, in the autumn of 1938, he traveled via the United States, where he could visit friends at Harvard University and the American Museum of Natural History in New York, but also meet up with Lucile for three weeks. This was a specially valuable experience because they could share in a new environment their work and friends

> as if it were in a single and common activity. Art and science, your friends and my friends, are so closely mixed in my last experiences, that I can hardly separate them in my feelings and my memory. . . . More and more, I count upon you, for animating me, and directing me, ahead. Life must and will be for both of us a continual discovery—of ourselves, and of the true face of God who is the deepest bond between us.[240]

Teilhard spent the rest of 1938 and the first half of 1939 in the West where, apart from his scientific work, much of his time was taken up with writing his book *The Human Phenomenon*, which he had begun in China.

"Between man and woman a specific and mutual power of spiritual sensitization and fertilization is probably still slumbering. It demands to be released, so that it may flow irresistibly towards the true and beautiful. Its awakening is certain."

—"Human Energy"

Teilhard in Java, 1938. (Fondation Teilhard de Chardin)

The Human Phenomenon

Teilhard at the American Museum of Natural History.

"The true struggle we are witnessing is not between believers and non-believers, but between two sorts of believers. Two ideals, two conceptions of the Divine, are confronting one another . . . A religion of the earth is being mobilized against the religion of heaven."
—"Some Reflections on the Conversion of the World"

The best success I can dream for my life: to have spread a new vision of the world.

Throughout his life Teilhard was fascinated by the question of the significance of the human being within the vast cosmic process of evolution. What was the meaning of the human phenomenon within the overall history of life? How did human life begin; how could it grow and be sustained; what was its future on the planet, its ultimate purpose? What scientific and experimental knowledge could be gathered about human beings, and how could all the facts available to us be interpreted from a contemporary perspective of research?

Such questions had been formulated early, and two brief essays of 1928 and 1930 had been explicitly devoted to the *phénomène humain*, the human phenomenon. But this was not enough. He wanted to express his thoughts in a much larger work and bring together some of the fundamental themes that had preoccupied him for such a long time. His great book, the sum of his lifetime's work and experience, underwent a long period of gestation. By September 1937 he had consciously decided on the project, by October he began to jot down some ideas, by May 1938 he had preliminary sketches, and from June onward he was steadily working on it. In letters to his friends he regularly refers to his ongoing work on his "essay" or "book" on "Man," his great work that was to take up two years of his writing, from June 1938 to June 1940. On August 5, 1938, he wrote to his brother Joseph:

I am working steadily on the first chapter of *Man*, a page or two a day. For the last ten months I have been thinking about it a great deal, and it seemed to me that plan and inspiration had reached maturity. So far I have come up against no "fault" as the structure develops.[241]

He took the project with him when he left for America and France in September 1938. When he found any leisure between his travels and lectures, he continued working on it. He told his friend Père Valensin that beyond geology the true passion of his life was now the human phenomenon and that he hoped that this time "his quite long work" on "Man" would be published.[242] His main professional activities in late 1938 and early 1939 were centered on the Paris Museum, but also included giving lectures to French audiences and visiting British scientists in London and Cambridge. The recognition of his scientific work in Britain was evident from his membership of the Zoological Society in London, his honorary life membership of the Society of Vertebrate Palaeontology, and his election as an Honorary Fellow of the Royal Anthropological Institute.

Also very important for him was the meeting with Mademoiselle Jeanne Mortier, who had attended one of his lectures and already knew his unpublished book *The Divine Milieu* that was circulating in cyclostyled form. Deeply impressed by his vision, she wanted to meet this priest and wrote to him for an appointment. They met in Paris in January 1939, and she then offered to act as his secretary. Teilhard accepted her generous offer, and from then on she collected, typed, filed, and circulated his writings as Simone Begouën and Lucile Swan had done earlier. She became one of his regular correspondents, too, who could count on him to provide her with spiritual guidance.[243]

By early summer 1939 he was traveling by boat to the United States, accompanied by his cousin Marguerite, who was going to do some research for one of her novels. The boat stopped in Southampton, where they were joined by his old friend Pierre Charles, also bound for New York. They had not seen each other for years and were delighted to be

"Science was born . . . of the exuberance of an internal activity that had out stripped the material needs of life; it was born of the curiosity of dreamers and idlers."
—*The Human Phenomenon*

Jean Mortier (1964).
(Fondation Teilhard de Chardin)

"By making plain the splendors of the universal Christ, Christianity, without ceasing to be for the earth the water that purifies and the oil that soothes, acquires a new value. By the very fact that it provides the earth's aspirations with a goal that is at once immense, concrete and assured, it rescues the earth from the disorder, the uncertainties, and the nausea that are the most terrible of tomorrow's dangers. It provides the fire that inspires man's effort."
—"Some Reflections on the Conversion of the World"

Bronze cast of a bust of Teilhard by Malvina Hoffman.

together. Once in New York, Teilhard met the renowned sculptor, Malvina Hoffman, a student of Rodin's, who later made fine portrait busts of him, one of which is now in the Musée d'Art Moderne in Paris, the other in Georgetown University library. He worked for three weeks at the American Museum of Natural History in New York, visited the anthropologist Henry Field in Chicago, and attended a geological convention at Berkeley.

Much aware of the gravity of the international political situation, the imminence of hostilities threatening Europe, the Japanese occupation of Beijing, and war raging in China, Teilhard felt a certain disquiet but considered it his duty to return to the Chinese Geological Survey and his laboratory work there. He embarked from Vancouver, where Lucile, who had also been visiting the United States, joined him for the return journey across the Pacific.

By September they were back in Beijing, just as Europe was becoming engulfed by the Second World War. No more field work was possible, and the scientific laboratories in Beijing were in a pitiable state. Much of scientific life, along with Free China and the Kuomintang, had been transferred to Yunnan, in southern China, where some of the scientists had regrouped themselves, inviting Teilhard to join them. But he preferred to stay where he was and cope with the safe-keeping of the valuable specimens stored in the laboratories, now dependent on the Americans. Social life in the city first went on as usual, but from now until the end of the war Teilhard was virtually a prisoner in the city.

By mid-November he wrote to his cousin:

The civil invasion of Beijing continues without interruption under our eyes, and makes much more impact than the "western front." In fact what strikes one in this new war is a certain vagueness and even a certain ambiguity, in the aims of both sides. . . .

Lost in this sort of mental uncertainty I still find plenty to do while waiting for something better. I am going ahead patiently with my essay on *Man* which may come at the right moment when people again have time and inclination to listen.[244]

Life in Beijing, was "pretty monotonous," but he kept working every day, following the regular routine of looking after two laboratories, visiting Lucile in the afternoon, and writing a page or two of his book. By February 1940 he called it *The Human Phenomenon* and reported that he was

> beyond the half-way mark in the draft. What its value will be I don't know. But I long so much to finish it properly. I feel that I have seldom worked so entirely for God alone. I am sure that He will give me the light and the strength to complete as it should be completed what I wish to say *only for Him*.[245]

The writing was not without effort. He admitted that he had "to fight against a slight depression, mostly nervous," and that he was surrounded by an alarming "monetary and food crisis." But his book was making unhurried progress, and by Easter he was not far from three-quarters of the way through:

> The whole interest and point of the book is concentrated toward the end, which must be particularly lucid and carefully done. I hope that the Lord will help me, since it is entirely as an attempt to make His countenance seen and loved that I am taking such pains, which sometimes I could well be spared.[246]

It was his deep spiritual desire to draw closer to God that nourished his every effort in completing his great work. This period in his life was marked by inner and outer crosses and a certain dryness, though faith and hope continued to sustain him. As he wrote to one of his correspondents,

> the more the years pass, the more I begin to think that my

(Georgetown University Library)

"To those who only know it outwardly, Christianity seems desperately intricate. In reality . . . it contains an extremely simple and astonishingly bold solution of the world. In the center, so glaring as to be disconcerting, is the uncompromising affirmation of a personal God: God as providence, directing the universe with loving, watchful care; and God the revealer, communicating himself to man on the level of and through the ways of intelligence."
—*The Human Phenomenon*

177

Teilhard in Beijing with Mme. Raphael and Lucile Swan.
(Fondation Teilhard de Chardin)

"We can envisage a world whose constantly increasing 'leisure' and heightened interest would find their vital issue in fathoming everything, trying everything; . . . a world in which, as happens already, one gives one's life to be and to know, rather than to possess."
—*The Human Phenomenon*

function is probably simply that—on a much reduced scale—of John the Baptist, that is, of one who presages what is to come. Or perhaps what I am called on to do is simply to help in the birth of a new soul in that which already is. . . . And when it comes to taking an objective view of things, and of my particular capacities, I always come to this conclusion: what is required of me is, while following my individual line, to be at the same time ever more thoroughgoingly a Jesuit. If the great Christ is indeed what we think, and if he really wishes to use me to preach him, it is in the ranks of the thoroughgoingly faithful that he will seek to find me.[247]

While he was writing, he regularly visited Lucile in her little house for afternoon tea, and they discussed his work together. She then typed what he had revised, and by June 18, 1940, he brought her the whole manuscript. He was very happy that it was completed and Lucile read it, looking for its inspiration, on Teilhard's advice, in the Gospel of St. John. Teilhard hoped to get the book published in Europe, but he realized that

> I shall have the pure scientists against me as well as the experts in pure metaphysics. but as I . . . say in my conclusion, I do not see what else you could say if once you try to work out to its conclusion a coherent place for man in this universe of ours.[248]

How could he possibly get it published during the war? Lucile got three clean copies of the manuscript typed, ready for examination by Rome and the Jesuit general. But how to send the work there? An American visitor, passing through Beijing en route to Washington, took one copy with him while the other two remained for the time being on Teilhard's desk. It was only in April 1944 that *The Human Phenomenon* reached Rome; by August that year Teilhard learned the deeply disappointing news that ecclesiastical permission to publish had been withheld. The manuscript might be reconsidered if presented in a revised and more acceptable form. It was another major blow, another terrible diminishment—his work might never see the light of day! Had he not put all his heart and mind into this work in order to express something of his deepest, innermost experience? Had he not written to one of his friends?

> Pray that I can find the words I would like in order to express and make others see what I believe I see. In truth, I am conscious of not writing for myself, but with a desire (such as I have never felt before) to make Him appear greater—as He must be. But it is so difficult to translate a vision, however clear, of an ideal into sentences. . . . One would need the thought and style of Plato himself. Well, I'll do what I can.[249]

Although some expressions may be incomplete, the book conveys a glorious vision to its readers. As Teilhard wrote to Ida Treat in February 1940, the time had come for him to relate—his "best insights into the world of the heart and the spirit . . . I want so much to 'finish well' . . . to finish proving the value of the ideas I have defended!"[250] It is no coincidence that the book's prologue is called "Seeing." To see or to perish, to see the human phenomenon as the center of perspective and the center of construction of the universe. Vision as an increase in consciousness made possible through a whole series of senses: the sense of spatial immensity, in greatness and smallness; the sense of depth; the sense of number; the sense of proportion; the sense of quality, or novelty; the sense of movement; the sense of the organic—all these illuminate human vision. To see the human being in its relation to humankind, and humankind in relation to life, and life in relation to the universe—that is the basic plan of his book with its stages of "Pre-Life," "Life," and "Thought." These are immense processes in the past that point to a future stage, that of "*Survie.*" This does not simply refer to survival but to a higher form of life, a

"I am continuing to work towards a better presentation, clearer and more succinct, of my ideas on the place of man in the universe. Julian Huxley has just brought out a book . . . called The Uniqueness of Man, in a way so parallel to my own ideas (though without integrating God as the term of the series) that I feel greatly cheered."
—Letter to Abbé Breuil, July 12, 1941

Teilhard in the woods outside of Beijing. (Fondation Teilhard de Chardin)

"If the love of God were extinguished in the souls of the faithful, the enormous edifice of rites, of hierarchy and of doctrines that comprise the Church would instantly revert to the dust from which it rose."
—*The Human Phenomenon*

"super-life." In Teilhard's vision the human being is not a static center, but "the axis and the arrow of evolution—which is much more beautiful."[251]

Teilhard saw this book as the synthesis of his life's work, bringing together the insights of forty years of study, experience, and reflection. Mainly addressed to the contemporary scientific temper, it contains little explicit discussion of religion. It demonstrates how the rise of evolution is an immense movement through time from the development of the atom to the molecule and cell to different forms of life, and to human beings with their great diversity. This movement exemplifies how the development of ever greater structural complexity leads in turn to an ever greater "within" of things, an increase in consciousness and reflection. He speaks of this development as the "cosmic law of complexity-consciousness," now sometimes referred to as "Teilhardian law."

His countryman Pascal saw the human being as lost between two infinites, the infinitely great and the infinitely small, or what one might call macroscopic and microscopic reality. Following this line of thought, Teilhard posited a third infinite, the infinitely complex that affects the human mind and especially the new noosphere, which is the sphere of thinking and acting humanity encircling the globe. As this irreversible movement of complexification is still going on in the world, he speaks of a confluence of thought, the convergence of people at a higher collective level, the growth of a super-consciousness, and ultimately the appearance of some "ultra-human," which he calls the "Omega point." For him this point is God, an extrapolation going far beyond the scientific data with which he started. When his friend Père Leroy used to tease him about his newly coined word, "the Omega point," Teilhard used to reply, "God is a person, God is a person. We must think of him as we do of a person. A God not a person would not be God."[252]

No wonder it took Lucile a long time to read this new book, whose thought is not always easy to follow. Science is here tinged with mysticism, as he himself admitted while in the midst of writing *The Human Phenomenon*: "I should like to feel myself already free to forget nature's scientific aspects for a while, and to turn more directly to the consideration of its mystic overtones."[253] In his essay on "The Mysticism of Science" (1939) he argues that science and religion, reason and faith have been "two rival mysticisms" struggling "for the mastery of the human heart." He believed that a new mysticism is now developing where religion and science can animate and mutually transform each other. Religion is for Teilhard "the soul biologically necessary for the future of science. Humanity is no longer imaginable without science. But no more science is possible without religion to animate it."[254] His new vision of the world culminates in a vision of spiritual transformation brought about by the powers of love. The human phenomenon finds its living roots and center for him in the phenomenon of Christianity, to which he devotes the epilogue of his book. Not every reader can follow and accept this vision of faith. Although Teilhard's message is truly incomplete without it, the fascinating picture of the human story embedded in the long history of life on earth, described in *The Human Phenomenon*, can still set on fire, inspire, and enlarge many a mind and soul.

Teilhard in Beijing.
(Georgetown University Library)

War Years in Beijing

Since my last retreat, I have a kind of feeling of being closer to Our Lord. It seems to me so simple, and so simplifying, to look for Him by "communicating" with the becoming of things. . . . Thus I can get back a little more into the milieu divin . . . at a time when the course of events and probably increasing age are dimming for me life's radiance.

"*The very upheaval that is going on at this moment raises the question of the future of man on earth. And yet there is nothing being published to give a constructive, dynamically Christian interpretation of what's happening.*"
—Letter to Abbé Breuil, July 12, 1941

Between September 1939 and March 1946 Teilhard's activities were much curtailed, although he now had more time for writing and reflection than ever before. But he missed the living contact with field work, with his beloved rocks and the open air, the traveling, and the many international connections with the world at large, now severed by the events of the world war and the political turmoil in China. He commented that it was tedious "not having the stimulus and illumination of new material any more. We have just the old things to work on."[255]

The first few years were not too bad. There was plenty to do, especially with the transfer of Licent's museum to Beijing. Père Licent, who had built up a splendid museum in Tianjin, had to leave China for health reasons in 1938, and Père Leroy, Licent's assistant since 1931, took over. The size and range of collections were such that the museum was practically an institute of geobiology without being given this name. Due to the political situation, many young Chinese could no longer go for their studies to Shanghai or southern China but found themselves trapped in the North. This meant that the School of Advanced Commercial Studies, run by the Jesuits at Tianjin, enjoyed a record enrollment, and its museum premises were needed for additional student accommodation. Thus a new place had to be found for the valuable scientific collections which Père Licent had built up over the years and on which Teilhard had done much work.

Though in many ways temperamentally incompatible, the two Jesuit scientists had closely collaborated in their pioneering work. In the late 1950s, at a time when both were no longer alive, their joint contribution was praised by Teilhard's first biographer, Claude Cuénot:

> It was Licent who, before ever the Americans came, launched scientific research in China; and it was Teilhard who was responsible for its rapid development, gave it continental extension, created a vast network of scholarship, and so solidly educated Chinese scientists that geology and paleontology flourish today in Communist China.[256]

In 1939 there was considerable debate about what to do with Licent's Tianjin museum, but a solution presented itself when the French ambassador offered a house for the collections and an additional site for new developments near the French Embassy in the European legation quarter of Beijing. This meant that the contents of the Tianjin museum could be moved to Beijing. Thus Teilhard and Leroy

Teilhard and Lucile Swan in the Western Hills of Beijing, 1941. (Fondation Teilhard de Chardin)

The Institute of Geobiology in Beijing. (Fondation Teilhard de Chardin)

founded the Beijing Institute of Geobiology in 1940. The plan was to make it into a continental research center, "less cumbersome and more active" than Licent's museum.[257] Teilhard was responsible for much of the conversion. He spent several weeks packing the rock and fossil specimens in Tianjin for transportation to Beijing while working on memoirs and still completing *The Human Phenomenon*. The move also meant that he could leave his Beijing residence, the rather austere Chabanel Hall with its strict discipline, and live together with Père Leroy at the new institute. The new place meant a great deal to him for it was "a really pleasant, warm setting. A new feeling of having a home of one's own and of not being able to go out without running into friends on the pavement."[258]

The two Jesuits followed their own regular routine, with daily Mass at seven in the morning, followed by a cigarette and talk over breakfast, and work at the institute until lunchtime. Teilhard then left for his other laboratory at the Peking Union Medical College, where the Zhoukoudian fossils were stored and where some other scientists were still working. He spent hours emptying thousands of cases and carefully preparing an inventory of the fossils. At five o'clock Teilhard went out visiting, but only for three hours, for he had to be back by eight, when the doors of the Institute were locked. He often went with Père Leroy to have tea at Lucile Swan's.

In spring he enjoyed strolling through the imperial park where "all the cherry trees showed pink against the grey earth, under a dust-dimmed blue sky. A real Chinese spring, unconscious of the troubles of war."[259] In the autumn, when the weather was fine, Teilhard took to going once or twice a week to the Western Hills outside Beijing to do whatever little field work was possible. Although most of his American friends had left by now, not all the good old life was gone. There was still Dr. Grabau, and on Sunday afternoons quite a few people liked to gather at his house to spend an enjoyable few hours in lively company. There were other friends to discuss religions in East and West and talk about current ideas and events. There was also the continuing presence and support of Lucile who, unlike some of her friends, delayed departure in order to remain close to Teilhard.

By December 1940 he wrote to his cousin:

> The Beijing community has been greatly depleted by the recall of a large number of American women, chiefly wives of American diplomats or servicemen. In this exodus I have lost several good friends.

And again by the middle of May 1941:

> People are still leaving Beijing one by one. It's a sad business really. . . . Well, on the first of May I entered my sixties. It's incredible how quickly time goes: my whole spiritual life consists more and more in abandoning myself (actively) to the presence and action of God. To be in communion with Becoming has become the formula of my whole life. Incidentally, the people here marked the occasion most charmingly.[260]

(Georgetown University Library)

"The only true happiness is. . . the happiness of growth and movement. . . . The happiness of growing greater—of loving—of worshipping."
—"Reflections on Happiness"

Lucile had arranged a birthday picnic for a small group of friends amid the temples and flowering plum trees of the Western Hills and also a cocktail party for a larger number of people at her house. Perhaps this was one of the last really happy social occasions for Teilhard in Beijing, for Lucile was soon forced to make the necessary travel arrangements if she wanted to catch the last suitable freighter leaving for America.

When Lucile finally left the city on August 8, 1941, she and Teilhard had enjoyed almost two years in close proximity, two years without any travel since their return from the United States in 1939. Teilhard wrote a farewell letter

"Unless it receives a new blood transfusion from matter, Christian spirituality may well lose its vigor and become lost in the clouds."
—"Reflections on Happiness"

The Sacred Heart of Jesus.

in which he reminded her of these "two precious years of constant presence and uninterrupted mutual confidence," which sealed their friendship, so that it was now "strong enough to face everything." While she had come to accept his view of the world, transparent with divine glory in all moments of becoming and growth, and his deep love for the universal Christ, he in turn felt:

Thanks to you, I see more definitely what I believe, and what I have to fight for. I am convinced that your going to America is just a providential and necessary step in the constructive convergency of our lives. Go ahead in full peace, joy and hope.

He also gave her the only "pious" object left on his desk, a small picture of the Sacred Heart, hoping this was not too "Roman Catholic" for her, since it symbolically expressed "a vague representation of the universal 'foyer' of attraction which we are aiming for. In this atmosphere we can always love each other more and better."[261]

It is impossible to know what Lucile's feelings were, how this parting necessitated by the war affected her. Teilhard wrote regularly while mail still got through to the United States, but after 1942 this was impossible, and, apart from a few letters, there was then complete silence until 1945. He missed her deeply at first, writing a month after their farewell:

that makes such a difference for me not to have you, dearest, to tell and divide *everything*. So many things I have to keep for myself, now, and so many things probably, which do not get born in my mind because you are not there to give me (as Grabau would say) the "internal impetus."[262]

His closest contact was now with his collaborator and good friend Père Leroy, with whom he could discuss many of his ideas, though Leroy was little aware of the profound loss that Lucile's absence had created. But the younger Jesuit got to know many sides of Teilhard, which he later described with much love and affection, speaking of his liveliness, his simplicity and frankness, his sense of humor and wit, his appreciation of "good cooking and a good story." Living together softened the harshness of their isolation, and he admired Teilhard's great optimism, based on attributing to the universe a sense of direction in spite of the existence of evil and contrary appearances. But he also bore witness to Teilhard's agonizing distress and personal trials during these lonely years of war, with sometimes almost no heart to carry on, no courage to venture further. During this period Teilhard

> was at times prostrated by fits of weeping, and he appeared to be on the verge of despair. But, calling on all the resources of his will, he abandoned himself to the supremely Great, to his Christ, as the only purpose of his being; and so hid his suffering and took up his work again, if not with joy, at least in the hope that his own personal vocation might be fulfilled.[263]

It was a period of personal losses, too. On October 29, 1941, Teilhard's brother Gabriel died, but he only learned about his death a year later and was "at a loss to estimate the significance of this bereavement." Of all his brothers and sisters only the youngest, Joseph, now remained alive. He had been under the "false hope" that all was well with the family, but he could still affirm that at the moment "life demands of us that we shall live, that is to say, think and feel, on more than an individual scale . . . The very value and happiness of existence consists in passing on into something greater than self." He was certain, though, that life was much less hard in Beijing than it was for his brother in war-time Europe, but he hoped that "as soon as the road is open I may be able to go back to France and work at a reconstruction of the 'spirit.'"[264] On June 14, 1942, he also lost his good friend Léontine Zanta, whom he had last seen on his visit to Paris in 1938.

"The whole future of the Earth, as of religion, seems to me to depend on the awakening of our faith in the future."
—*The Future of Man*

Enjoying a picnic on the Western Hills above Beijing. 1941. (Georgetown University Library)

Father Leroy and Father Licent.
(Fondation Teilhard de Chardin)

"The different courses open to Man on the threshold of the socialization of his species. . . : to cease to act, by some form of suicide; to withdraw through a mystique of separation; to fulfil ourselves individually by egoistically segregating ourselves from the mass; or to plunge resolutely into the stream of the whole in order to become part of it."
—*"The Grand Option"*

He always found it of great benefit to discuss his ideas with her and, some years before, had confessed in a letter:

> I owe you *so much*, dear friend, and it is such sweetness, both for my mind and heart, to find you there again on each return to Europe—always wise, steadfast and loving. Oh if only women were all like you. . . . But then the conquest of Fire (a nice title for a novel, don't you think?) would be too easy.[265]

During these long years in Beijing Teilhard read an immense amount, as his notebooks show, and he continued producing one essay after another. The enforced period of leisure led to great intellectual activity, but at first he had hoped he might still be able to travel to the United States. But these plans were all brought to an end by the Japanese bombing of Pearl Harbor on December 7, 1941, an event that probably also led to the disappearance of the *Sinanthropus* fossils. These had been kept in strong boxes at the Peking Union Medical College but, given the war situation, it was decided to send them to America for safe-keeping. American soldiers took the boxes with them, but after Pearl Harbor all their goods were confiscated by the Japanese, and the chests with their important fossil specimens disappeared without trace.

During 1942 Teilhard could still do a little traveling in China, going to Manchuria during the summer and to Shanghai in the autumn. In 1938, he and Leroy had briefly met Claude Rivière, the correspondent of French Radio in Shanghai who in 1941 came to visit them at the Institute of Geobiology in Beijing. In mid-November 1942 Teilhard and Père Leroy set off on a long train journey to spend almost three weeks in Shanghai to give lectures at the Alliance Française. They stayed at the Jesuit university, L'Aurore, but for much of the time Claude Rivière acted as hostess, showing them around, introducing them to friends, and discussing Teilhard's ideas. She was one of his regular correspondents, too, exchanging letters with Teilhard in China during the years 1939-1946. He addressed her as a great friend, someone who responded to his reflections and animated his thought. During these quiet years of great isolation she perhaps took the place held before by Marguerite Teillard-Chambon, Léontine Zanta, and Ida Treat in Paris, by Lucile Swan and Rhoda de Terra in Beijing and America.

Claude Rivière later described their meetings and discussions in her book *En Chine avec Teilhard de Chardin,* in which she mentions that she interviewed some Buddhist monks in the Temple of the Great Jade Buddha in Shanghai, with Teilhard present. They got into a long discussion about the present state and the future of Buddhism, and apparently a Tibetan lama described Teilhard as a great "living Jesus" of the West who, one day, would become famous, and many people would be nourished by his message.[266]

A second invitation to lecture in Shanghai again the following spring was refused by Teilhard's Jesuit superiors, not only because he had been too enthusiastically received by his audience when lecturing before, but he had inadvertently left a copy of his 1933 essay "Christology and Evolution" in one of the drawers of his room at the Jesuit residence. The Jesuit fathers considered his ideas as too unorthodox and were unwilling to let him come again. Instead, in September 1943, Claude Rivière went to visit Teilhard and Leroy in Beijing. After the war, they saw each other again in Paris, and Teilhard helped her to find a teaching post at a university center in Nice.

In all his life Teilhard never published as many scientific papers as during these years of the war. Taking into account the unpublished philosophical and religious writings, he wrote twenty-seven articles between 1939 and 1946, apart from completing *The Human Phenomenon.* The titles of his essays range from "The Grand Option," "Some Reflections on Progress," "Christ the Evolver," and "Reflections on Happiness," to "Introduction to the Christian Life," "Centrol-

"These are just the years on which I was counting so much, and I see them slip by while I get practically nothing done. 'Everything that happens is adorable,' Termier was fond of saying. Properly understood, that idea sums up my whole religion."
—Letter to his brother Joseph, November 13, 1943

Teilhard in front of the Medical College, Beijing. (Fondation Teilhard de Chardin)

*"We must, it is true, sink
our roots deep into the rich,
tangible, material realities
which surround us; but in the
end it is by working to achieve
our own inner perfection—
intellectual, artistic, moral—
that we shall find happiness. . . .
Through and beyond matter,
spirit is hard at work, building."*
—"Reflections on Happiness"

Teilhard enjoys a glass of cognac.
(Fondation Teilhard de Chardin)

ogy," "Christianity and Evolution," and "The Planetization of Mankind." Much of his thought was now directed to the future, to global developments, to the problem of human action and the available choice of roads for shaping the human community at a collective level, but also the important contribution of Christianity in feeding the zest for life, in building one earth and a better life for all, in revealing a higher goal for all human effort and striving.

Though immersed in the epochal changes and troubles of China, Teilhard remained relatively distant from the great events of the Second World War, whether the battles in the Pacific, in North Africa, Russia, Germany, or Normandy, or the much closer atomic bombing of Hiroshima and Nagasaki, whose great historical significance he was quite unable to assess. With the German surrender to the Allies on May 7, 1945, and that of the Japanese on September 2, 1945, the end of the war had come. Hearing about the armistice in Europe, he was moved to write: "V-Day Relief, but not 'joy'; for, in itself, at least here and now, this brutal victory of Man over Man is not a victory on the part of Humanity."[267] But at least he could now consider returning to France. A curious anecdote relates that one evening when he felt more than usually depressed, he heard a clandestine BBC broadcast announcing on radio: "We have just learned today of the death of Father Teilhard, who was assassinated by brigands in Tibet."[268] It greatly amused him, but fortunately it was not true.

By Christmas 1945 he received official permission to return to Paris. He could go back to the Jesuit house at the *Études*, whose superior, Père d'Ouince, was one of his strongest supporters and, over the years, had faithfully collected all Teilhard's writings in spite of official censure. Père Leroy, who eventually intended to return to China, flew home on a British plane whereas Teilhard chose to go back by boat, accompanied by some of his luggage. Unfortunately he had to leave most of his books and papers, his diaries, and Lucile Swan's bust of him behind in Beijing. They eventually got lost, although another copy of the bust has been preserved elsewhere. Originally he planned to travel to France via America, as he had done several times before. Now that the political pressures on his life had lifted, he realized how much the last few years in the Beijing "fishbowl" had been like living in a "twilight." He wrote to Lucile that he wanted to travel via America to take stock with her:

> A bath of life, and a rejuvenation, before I reach the battlefield in Europe. I do not regret the last six months spent in Beijing, at the hot point of treble contact between Communism, Democracy, and the rising Yellow Mass. I saw, I thought, and I learned a lot. But now I must try to talk and act. You will give me the spark,—as you ever did.[269]

He flew from Beijing to Shanghai, where he took the first opportunity to board a boat bound for Europe, abandoning the American plan after all, for it would have delayed him too much. He sailed on the *Strathmore* on March 27, 1946, and on May 3, 1946, he was back in Paris. During the journey he wrote to his brother:

> The *Strathmore* is one of the finest P. & O. ships, converted (the lower decks, that is) into a troopship, so that we are living a gregarious existence, sleeping in hammocks. It's not a bad life, with plenty of simple food, but it's practically impossible to work. It will be the first time that I shall see the end of a sea-voyage without regret.

Looking back on the war years in Beijing, he told his cousin:

> These seven years have made me quite grey, but they have toughened me—not hardened me, I hope—interiorly. The first war started me on the ladder. This one has cut clean across my life, but I have a better grasp of certain distinct central points, and to these I wish to devote all that is left to me of life.[270]

"I do not give up the idea of starting some new periods of staying in China."
—Letter to Lucile Swan, August 31, 1945

Jesuit chapel in Beijing.
(Fondation Teilhard de Chardin)

191

Paris and Rome

You feel almost an exile in Paris.
The Eternal City has given me no shock, but I have been
impressed—and heartened—by Christianity's extraordinary,
really imperturbable confidence in the unshakable solidity of
its faith and truth. There is a remarkable phenomenon there,
unique, in fact, in this world.

Teilhard in 1947. (Fondation
Teilhard de Chardin)

"Since it has become human,
the world cannot continue to
advance towards greater
complexity and consciousness
except by making an ever more
explicit place for the forces of
expectation and hope,that is to
say for religion."
—"Man's Place in the Universe"

Teilhard was home at last, though older and less energetic, aware that he was now on the declining slope of
life with years diminishing fast. The hoped-for meeting with
Lucile had not taken place. Was the warm reunion with few
remaining family members and old friends enough to provide the necessary "impetus," the "spark" he needed to work
for the "reconstruction of the spirit" after the war, as he had
planned to do? Once back in Paris, he was much invited,
sought after, and celebrated. There was no shortage of activities, but his earlier idea of perhaps eventually returning to
work in China soon receded, not least because of changing
political circumstances.

The intellectual liveliness of Paris excited him. The French
capital provided every opportunity for meeting distinguished
scientists, artists, writers, and philosophers. He took part in
debates and symposia on all sorts of topics, whether science and consciousness, or cosmology and theology, or an
international meeting of the Society of Jesus. He also met
Julian Huxley and Joseph Needham, both then working at
UNESCO. Needham, with whom he became more and
more friendly, greatly sympathized with Teilhard's ideas and
later helped to make them better known in the Anglo-Saxon
world. Another encounter took part with General Jan Chris-
tiaan Smuts, the prominent South African statesman, military leader, and philosopher, whose pioneering ideas about

"holism" greatly attracted Teilhard, but whom he also wanted to meet because of his plans to visit prehistoric fossil sites in South Africa during the following year.

During this post-war period in Paris Teilhard was in some sense a kind of "freelance thinker," a great solitary figure, a well-acclaimed and brilliant lecturer, but also a much-consulted spiritual director and pastor. He continued his large correspondence and often explored his ideas in letters and talks before giving them a more final form in writing. But his order requested him to address only small, confined audiences. Thus he often spoke to small groups, meeting privately in someone's home. But the text of the talks was always preserved, and his reputation continued to grow.

There was still enough leisure to be creative in thought and writing. Many essays were produced, and his *carnets de lecture* in which he made notes about the books he read, show how much reading he got done, how wide-ranging his interests were, covering many disciplines, including scholarly works on Eastern religions and comparative mysticism. He was a regular reader in the library of the Musée Guimet, studying Eastern art and philosophy, and became a close friend of several French scholars on Eastern thought. These interests even motivated him to attend the international Orientalists Congress in Paris in 1948.

While living in the Far East, most of his interests and contacts had been in the field of science. His collaboration with Chinese scientists gave him little opportunity, and perhaps he also had little inclination, to learn in depth about traditional Chinese thought and culture. On the basis of his mystical experiences in earlier years he had a continuing interest

"What is carried along by the various currents of faith that are still active on earth . . . is no longer only the irreplaceable elements of a certain complete image of the universe. Very much more even than fragments of vision, it is experiences of contact with a supreme Ineffable which they preserve and pass on."
—"The Zest for Living"

Teilhard with friends in Paris.
(Georgetown University Library)

193

"What is really going on, under cover and in the form of human collectivization, is the super-organization of Matter upon itself, which as it continues to advance produces its habitual, specific effect, the further liberation of consciousness. . . . So what finally lies ahead of us is a planetary arrangement of human mass and energy, coinciding with a maximal radiation of thought."

—"The Planetization of Mankind"

in questions of comparative mysticism, where he always gave most attention to Indian monism and Vedanta. Now he had the time to do more reading in this area, and, with greater distance, he could reflect more critically on the spirituality of Eastern religions. The outcome was his essay "The Spiritual Contribution of the Far East," completed in February 1947. While fully aware that he could not lay any claim to "special competence in the history of Asiatic thought," he felt nonetheless able to offer "some personal reflections" concerning the three different types of Eastern spirituality found in India, China, and Japan. He pointed out that each of them had arrived at different solutions to the problems of "God and his transcendence; the world and its value; the individual and the importance of the person; mankind and social requirements," without having solved "the problem of the spirit" in its totality. He now envisaged a "confluence of East and West," a necessary coming together or convergence of the active currents of faith in the world around a powerful new mysticism that he, somewhat misleadingly, always called "the road of the West." What he really meant was a new and future synthesis of Eastern and Western spiritualities at present not yet existent, though beginning to emerge.[271]

His great interest in a dynamic, action-oriented spirituality with a genuine concern for pressing contemporary issues made him argue for a closer collaboration and a necessary dialogue between members of different faiths. During his Paris years he actively supported the Union des Croyants, the French branch of the World Congress of Faiths. His essay "Faith in Man" provided the inaugural address for the foundation of this interfaith association in March 1947. He later gave several other informal talks to this group and took an active part in committee meetings at which he encountered several Hindus, Muslims, and Bahais. According to him, such ecumenical working together was the "summit movement" of the future, indispensable for the future evolution of humankind and of religion.

One of his finest talks to members of the Union des Croyants is "The Zest for Living," which emphasizes the need for a will to live and love life, to sustain and advance it, warning that the greatest enemy is indifference and boredom, the loss of a taste for life, and the absence of inner resources. At the deepest level, the zest for life is linked to an act of faith:

> What is most vitally necessary to the thinking earth is a faith—and a great faith—and ever more faith.
>
> To know that we are not prisoners.
>
> To know that there is a way out, that there is air, and light, and love, somewhere, beyond the reach of death. . . .
>
> That, if we are not to perish smothered in the very stuff of our being, is what we must at all costs secure.
>
> And it is there that we find what I may well be so bold as to call the *evolutionary role* of religions.[272]

Pope Pius XII.

On his return to Paris Teilhard was understandably worried about the fate of his writings, especially the unclear position of *The Human Phenomenon*. In January 1947 he had spent several days with two old friends, the Jesuit Henri de Lubac and Msgr. Bruno de Solages, revising his book manuscript to make it acceptable to the Roman authorities. He admitted to Lucile:

> The most tedious work I have to face is to readjust the famous book on *Le Phénomène Humain*. My friends positively hope that I shall be allowed to print it. But now it is my turn not to be satisfied with the child. You know, my ideas have developed and improved (I hope) rather much since six years. People insist that I must publish nevertheless. But I do not like so much the idea. Practically, I will do my best to repolish the thing before Easter. And then I shall decide. In fact, I would prefer to write something entirely new. But where to find the time for it?

He also mentioned that Rhoda de Terra

made her appearance. . . . As you know I am sincerely fond of her. Unfortunately, I have very little time to spare. I do my best, but it is not easy, to see her. Luckily, if you think her possessive, she is not "demanding"; . . . she is quite able to find her own ways by herself.[273]

Unfortunately all the revision work on *The Human Phenomenon*, then and subsequently—the last page is dated August 4, 1949—was of no avail. Recognition continued to be withheld. In August 1947, the Jesuit general, Father Jean Baptiste Janssens, even threatened that his work might be put on the Index. But on the scientific side the situation was quite different. Here his achievements found greater acknowledgment. In June 1947, at the instance of the Foreign Affairs Ministry, he was made officer of the Légion d'Honneur with a citation praising him for

> outstanding service rendered in the propagation of French intellectual and scientific influence, through a body of writings, written and published for the most part in China, which have won the highest standing for him in international scientific circles, American and British in particular. He may be properly ranked today, in the field of paleontology and geology, as one of the glories of French science, the international prestige of which he has done so much, through his personal relations with scientists of other lands, to develop and maintain.[274]

But this honor reached him when he was recovering from a heart attack. He had felt under considerable strain for quite some time, and his health seemed to be worn out. On the evening of June 1, 1947, he had been at a friend's house where he had spoken "very movingly on the mystery of the Ascension, saying that it was the most beautiful feast of the year and that we did not celebrate it with enough solemnity, since it is the anticipated consummation of the Universe returning to the Father in the heart of the glorified Christ."[275] During the night he had a breathing attack and fell so ill that for fifteen days he was hovering between life and death. Suffering from high fever and brushed by the wings of death, he could hardly speak, but his zest for life and innate robustness soon prevailed. By July 5 he wrote to Lucile,

> I am just, or almost just, out of bed. . . . Yes, it is rather unusual to me to be sick. But here I am. On the whole, it seems that something went wrong with my circulation . . . a classical case, they say.[276]

He was ordered to take total rest until December. No coffee, tobacco, or plane flights were permitted. Plans for a visit to South Africa had to be abandoned. The only consolation during this period of recovery was the joy of being made a corresponding member of the French Académie des Sciences and an officer of the Légion d'Honneur.

He spent several months convalescing in a clinic outside Paris from where he wrote to Abbé Breuil: "Fundamentally, my real interest in life is moving irresistibly to a more and more intense concentration on this basic question of the relations between Christ and 'Hominization.' It has become for me a question of *'to be or not to be.'*"[277] By the end of the year he was well enough to contemplate traveling again to the United States. In late December he informed Lucile that his travel plans were still uncertain, but his letter also said:

> Do not forget that the discovery of God is something (like Art) which is never achieved, although trying to achieve it is probably the greatest joy man can feel; at least, that is what I am experiencing each year more. So you have to be steady, and patient, and chiefly *"confiante."* I suppose that the highest form of worship is active *"confiance"* in Life—*confiance* which brings peace.[278]

By late February 1948 he was at long last well enough to set off on his sixth visit to the United States, following his earlier ones in 1931, 1933, 1937, 1938, and 1939. He traveled by boat, and on arriving in New York his two women

"The birth and progress of the idea of God on earth are intimately bound up with the phenomenon of hominization."
—"The Spirit of the Earth"

Museum of Natural History in New York. (Fondation Teilhard de Chardin)

friends, Rhoda de Terra and Lucile Swan, were both waiting for him on the pier. It proved a somewhat awkward reunion, not without jealousy.

Teilhard's four months in the United States were not an altogether satisfactory experience. For much of the time he was in New York working at the Museum of Natural History and seeing scientific colleagues, but also personal friends. In Washington he stayed for a week in the Jesuit community at Georgetown University, with Lucile living in a house close by. They met many friends from China again and felt their getting together was like a family reunion. In New York he lectured "On the Trend and Significance of Human Socialization" to a group of anthropologists at a meeting of the Viking Fund. He thought he made a favorable impression but might do less well at Harvard. The lecture was the highlight of his stay and provided openings for future research. He felt more and more drawn to analyzing the biological value of the social phenomenon and the reality of what he called a "super-humanization," which he saw already taking place. He was also planning "a series of six lectures, next year, at Columbia or Harvard . . . provided the authorities don't put a spanner in the works."[279]

Unfortunately the plan came to nothing because the American Jesuit provincial referred this matter to Rome and no decision was made. He wrote to Pierre Leroy, his best friend since their years in Beijing, with whom he was in constant contact in Paris, that he now felt "a sort of nausea for the study of the past." What could he do in the United States? Very little apart from making contact with people. But perhaps Providence was awaiting him here to get engaged in one thing or another. He would have to wait and see.[280]

At a personal level it was not easy either. He and Lucile had not seen each other since August 1941. It had been such a long separation, and now he was older and in worse health. She had been longing to see him, but it was Rhoda who had helped to make the travel arrangements and organized the work at the museum. Lucile experienced disquiet and concern, but Teilhard assured her in an affectionate note, "You will see that we will 'rediscover' one another again—as it must be—according to the new times." But they had grown apart and were different people, as they discovered in their meetings and conversations. Lucile acknowledged this in a letter she did not send:

> I thank you for telling me the truth. I suppose I have really known it for a long time, but . . . I thought maybe I was wrong and one does not easily accept something that breaks the heart. You say you have not changed toward me: but of course that is not the truth, though you may believe. . . .
>
> Years ago when you wrote, not once but several times: "What is born between us is forever. . . . I know it." I feared you did not know (I think no one can know) but I so much wanted to believe and because of all the circumstances, and also even our ages, made it seem very possible, and so I built my life upon it.

IHS Monogram in the Church of the Gesu.

Recognizing the truth of their greatly changed situation must have been a shattering experience for Lucile, such a deep disappointment, but she was still convinced that the "years of working together will go on"; she still remained his "devoted and loving Lucile." Teilhard was again experiencing nervous depressions; he was not feeling very strong at all and was glad to return soon to France. But before his departure he assured Lucile that "we can build still higher," quoting a line from a letter of his cousin Marguerite, which he felt convinced, "is the expression of what is growing between you and me: 'Devant Dieu j'ai compris que je t'aimais *mieux* (that is in a better way) et ainsi que je t'aimais *plus*, ce que je n'aurais pas cru possible." This was written on the "feast of the 'Heart' of Christ," the feast of "Love-Energy," which he considered a good omen for the future of their relationship.[281] But it cannot have been an easy truth for Lucile to accept that there were other stars on Teilhard's firmament: there was Rhoda now, and there was still Marguerite, as close to him now in France as Lucile had been to him in Beijing.

Teilhard arrived grief-stricken and depressed in Paris, where he was glad to see his friend Pierre Leroy waiting for him. Was his depression a purely organic problem, "triggered by strong emotions," as his friend suggested? In Paris he was immediately back in a whirlwind, but perhaps he needed more rest and quiet. The summer of 1948 was spent in the Auvergne at his brother's property, Les Moulins, a wonderful place to be at complete peace, surrounded by the grandeur and beauty of a landscape he knew so well. When he had first gone back there after returning from the Far East, he told a friend:

> Perhaps, as you get older, you become more conscious of the need to get back to your own home. Those long years in China had made me feel as though I no longer belonged to Auvergne: now I see that was an illusion.[282]

The Auvergne was a place to restore his mind and heart. He could also make his annual retreat there, as was his wont, spending eight or ten days every year based on the Ignatian Spiritual Exercises. It gave him time for taking stock. He told Marguerite:

> For the moment my chief concern (increasingly so, for a long time now) is not to know what sort of beginning I have made but how to *end well*: and by that I mean the problem of ending my life in the spontaneous attitude or the gesture and providential circumstance which best bear witness to the sincerity and value of the vision for which I have lived. It is not a matter of saying that death sets the seal upon life; on that point we must have absolute trust in God, for the "good end" depends on Him alone. It is, in fact, on trust that I am going to focus my most earnest thoughts during the "retreat" I am taking the opportunity to make here.[283]

He used the summertime in the Auvergne for putting the final touches to his essay "My Fundamental Vision," which presents a clearly structured, concise summary of his views on the human phenomenon and on Christianity, philosophy, and mysticism. He prefaced it with this statement: "It seems to me that a whole life-time of continual hard work would be as nothing to me, if only I could, just for one moment, give a true picture of what I see."[284]

Another matter preoccupying him during that summer was the compilation of a list of his scientific publications, asked for by the Collège de France. He had been nominated for the chair in Prehistory, which had become vacant due to Abbé Breuil's retirement. It was one of the finest opportunities of his career, a crowning acknowledgment of the eminence of his scientific achievements and standing. Would he be allowed to accept it? He wrote to Rome to obtain the necessary authorization. But instead of answering yes or no, the Jesuit general asked him to come and see him personally to talk things over, indicating in his letter that Teilhard's book might be printed and permission given for lecturing in America and accepting the chair at the Collège de France. So, suddenly in October 1948, he had to go to Rome, for his answer concerning the chair was expected by mid-November.

Father Leroy with Teilhard on their visit to the Auvergne in 1948. (Fondation Teilhard de Chardin)

It was his one and only visit to Rome, where he spent about a month "living as the Romans live" and waiting an extraordinarily long time for the Jesuit general to see him. The reception was friendly, but no decision was made. He stayed on to see friends, followed up some scientific contacts, and had some meetings with Lucile. She was traveling in Europe at that time and came from Switzerland to see him for two weeks. On his return to Paris she also visited him a few times. Describing his impressions to Pierre Leroy, Teilhard wrote: "Rome has not given me nor will it give me . . . any shock, either aesthetic or spiritual. . . . So far as the past is concerned, I am immunized; and as for the

"*Let us imagine an observer standing on a star who has found the means of following by a sort of spectral analysis the gradual development around the earth of a sort of halo of thinking energy, which I have ventured to call the Noosphere. There is no doubt that for such an observer our planet . . . must at this moment be coming to an explosion . . . of ever increasing consciousness.*"
—"Man's Place in the Universe"

The Church of the Gesu in Rome.

picturesque, there is nothing to surprise me—after the great East."[285] And he told his brother Joseph:

> The city has made no great impact on me; I have been living too long in another world. But I immediately fell in love with the light and the climate and (old memories of Aix and Egypt perhaps?) I feel curiously at home among the umbrella-pines and cypresses in this Mediterranean setting. . . .
>
> Only two things have impressed me, St. Peter's and the Gesù (in spite of its orgy of marbles and moldings), because in them one feels from time to time . . . the security (that's a better word for it than fixity) of a faith that will not be side-tracked. At this moment in history there is no doubt that one of the poles passes through Rome, the prime pole of ascent of what in my jargon I call "hominization."[286]

He wrote to Père d'Ouince, his very supportive Jesuit superior in Paris who later documented in detail all the vicissitudes of Teilhard's life as those of "a prophet on trial":[287] "Pray that I may end well. . . . That is the grace of all graces—particularly when one has taken it on oneself, in however humble a way, to point out the road to others."[288]

Although he felt a strong awareness of "the extraordinary focus of spiritual radiation concentrated by two thousand years of history these places have witnessed,"[289] the visit to Rome gave him little reassurance. No decision was arrived at, and he returned empty-handed to Paris, soon settling back into his established routine. He simply had to go on waiting. Two further revisions of *The Human Phenomenon* were undertaken. Meanwhile he was invited to give a series of scientific lectures at the Sorbonne, delivered in February 1949. He used the opportunity to outline some of the central ideas of *The Human Phenomenon* in more summary form, and these lectures were later published as *Man's Place in Nature: The Human Zoological Group*.[290]

No sooner had he finished than he fell ill again and had to

return to a clinic. Between March and May he had to spend more time recovering his strength. During the summer, as usual, he had a long, restful spell with his brother in the Auvergne, where George Barbour came to visit, writing home:

> Teilhard has much improved, and hopes to go to Africa in 1951. Two unforgettable days, spent sauntering along the avenues, or sitting in the garden, while he spoke of his boyhood with his sister Marguerite, of the threat of hailstorms to the vineyards, . . . of his slow return to health, and of encouraging contact with mutual friends.[291]

Teilhard had to wait a long time for a reply from Rome. When it eventually came, it was all in the negative: he was not allowed to publish his book despite its further amendments; he was not permitted to accept the chair at the Collège de France. His friends organized clandestinely the production of two hundred copies of *The Human Phenomenon* for private circulation. Teilhard was particularly delighted when, the following May, he was elected non-resident member of the prestigious Institut de France, where he replaced a botanist at the Académie des Sciences. In a letter to Père Leroy he admitted: "Apparently, I was nominated less for my 'science' than for my ideas—which is infinitely more interesting."[292] He hoped that the honor of being an *académecien* would give him more freedom to pursue his projects.

Alas, this proved to be an illusion. His superiors in Rome now had even more reason for fearing Teilhard's ever growing influence and decided he could no longer reside permanently in Paris, but would only be allowed to visit the city from time to time. A second exile was in store. Considering Rome's attitude he reflected with regret that before 1940 "it was so convenient . . . to be able to return for some time to China in order to be forgotten."[293] But this was no longer an option. After the communist victory in China he could hardly return there again. He would have to find another solution, another "milieu" for his work.

St. Peter's Basilica in Rome.

"The old Marxist conflict between producers and exploiters becomes out-dated—at the best a misplaced approximation. What finally divides people of today into two camps is not class but an attitude of mind—the spirit of movement."
— "The Planetization of Mankind"

203

The Heart of Matter

Teilhard in 1947. (Fondation Teilhard de Chardin)

"Yesterday I drew the first sketch . . . of Le Coeur de la Matière . . . without knowing, of course, whether this outline will be final, or perhaps the nucleus of something bigger . . . I think that the Féminin will be presented and discussed as a kind of Conclusion . . . : not so much as an element by itself than as a kind of light illuminating the whole process of universal concentration: vraiment, as I wrote you: 'the spirit of Union.'"
—Letter to Rhoda de Terra, August 17, 1950

It is utterly impossible for me not to see (and to say) what I see. And I am so sure that God cannot be smaller than our biggest and wildest conceptions! Of course, I cannot print. But printing is not essential.

Permission to print *The Human Zoological Group,* which Teilhard had hoped to obtain more easily, was also withheld. The book meant much to him because he felt he had enriched his subject, focused it more, and expressed more concisely what he had tried to say at greater length in *The Human Phenomenon.* He gave more scientific lectures at the Sorbonne dealing with the geology of the Far East and, on another occasion, "the phylogenetic structure of the human group." While preparing scientific articles for publication, he continued to give talks and work on a wide range of philosophical and religious themes, resulting in numerous new essays, mostly unpublished, of course. It must have been an extraordinary cross to bear—yet the cross was for him always a sign of the effort of centering, a symbol of achievement and evolution as well as redemption. He was truly living under the "fire of the cross." His deeply spiritual nature and ardent faith enabled him to bear the pain of this cross and his gentle, warm disposition helped him to recover from many a shock. As he said: "It is absolutely necessary to keep smiling. The essential, and doubtless most fruitful, gesture is to smile, with something of love in the smile."[294]

He was much concerned with the future of human evolution during this time. The future of humankind as well as of religion seemed to him to depend on the awakening of faith in the future and in the collective responsibility of human action for shaping the noosphere. Several of his papers were written for UNESCO, such as "Some Reflections on the Rights of Man." A memorandum for Julian Huxley proposed an "institute for the study of human self-evolution" with theoretical and applied branches, dealing with such matters as "energetics" and "eugenics."

In his essay "The Spiritual Repercussions of the Atom Bomb," he pointed out that each new major breakthrough gives human beings a *"new* sense of power," implies "a change of epoch," and requires new moral choices, whether it is the "re-modeling of the human organism by means of hormones," "the control of heredity and sex by the manipulation of genes and chromosomes," "the readjustment and internal liberation . . . brought to light by psychoanalysis" or the splitting of the atom. What are the effects of these inventions on the inventor, transforming life as hitherto known?

The atomic bomb.

> By the liberation of atomic energy on a massive scale . . . man has not only changed the face of the earth; he has by this very act set in motion . . . a long chain of reactions which . . . has made him, virtually at least, a new being hitherto unknown to himself. . . . Exploding the atom . . . was also enough to ensure that the nightmare of bloody combat must vanish in the light of some form of growing unanimity. We are told that, drunk with its own power, mankind is rushing to destruction, that it will be consumed in the fire it has so rashly lit. On the contrary, I think that through the atom bomb war itself may be on the eve of being doubly and definitely destroyed.[295]

Most of Teilhard's post-war papers dealing with further human social evolution were eventually grouped together posthumously under the title *The Future of Man*, but quite a few got published at the time of writing and appeared in French journals such as *Revue des Questions Scientifiques* and the Jesuit review *Études*.

Other essays dealt with the role of religion in the contemporary world, the necessary renewal of Christianity, and the importance of an ecumenical working together for the development, greater integration, peace, and unity of the whole human community:

> Present-day Mankind, as it becomes increasingly aware of its unity—not only past unity in the blood, but future unity in progress—is experiencing a vital need to close in upon itself. A tendency toward unification is everywhere manifest, and especially in the different branches of religion. We are looking for something that will draw us together, below or above the level of that which divides. It may be said, in the aftermath of the war, that this need is spontaneously and unanimously arising on every hand. . . .
>
> A profound common aspiration arising out of the very shape of the modern world—is not this specifically what is most to be desired, what we most need to offset the growing forces of dissolution and dispersal at work among us?[296]

Teilhard always saw the need for greater unity and often perceived promising efforts toward greater human unification, despite increased difficulties and tensions. It was not uniformity and unity achieved through absorption and fusion he envisaged, but a unity of complexity with respect for pluralistic differences. True unity was not wrought through outside pressures and mere expediency; it had to be worked for and animated by the powers and energies of love.

Nowhere was the central, fiery role of love, its power of animation, transformation, and unification, more vividly expressed than in his autobiographical masterpiece, *The Heart of Matter*, tracing the journey of his inner development from childhood years to full maturity. He had thought about its central threads for years, alluded to his most formative experiences and insights in many essays and letters, and traced the outlines of his spiritual vision on several occasions. But it was only now, amid disappointment and depression, that he could sit down in the quiet country retreat of Les Mou-

"For some time now the principal interest of my life is no longer Fossil Man, but the Man of tomorrow; or, more exactly, 'the God of tomorrow,' since I am more and more convinced that the great event of our time is a kind of change in the face of God . . . I know that hundreds of people around me feel it (hence the success of the books I've circulated privately)."
—Letter to Ida Treat, August 30, 1950

lins and write from the depths of his heart with great lyricism and frankness in an utterly personal idiom and a partly prayerful mode, in a way he had not expressed himself since he had poured out his first torrent of thought during those extraordinary early years in the trenches.

He drafted most of the text in the Auvergne during August 1950, but completed the essay later in October in Paris. As he wrote to some of his friends:

> I have just spent a week of great calm at my brother's place, . . . an old family house of the seventeenth century, full of old tapestries and pretentious arms, but perfumed with age, full of old noises and surrounded everywhere by tall oaks with an admirable view. . . .
>
> . . . Facing the Puys mountains, far from every railway and in the midst of oak trees, . . . I am jotting down a first outline (definitive?) of an essay about which I have been thinking for a long time: "Le coeur de la matière" (not at all in the sense of Graham Greene!). It is an essay on the reconstruction of the psychological genesis which historically has brought me (since my childhood) to pass from a vague and general cosmic sense to what I now call "the Christic sense."[297]

Teilhard at a party to celebrate his election to a chair at the Academy of Sciences, 1950. (Fondation Teilhard de Chardin)

Many years earlier, on another Auvergne holiday spent in June 1937 at another family house, Murol, he had outlined some of the themes of his future essay in a letter to Lucile:

> Never before, perhaps, did I perceive so clearly the possible meaning of the deep evolution of my internal life: the dark

Teilhard at Les Moulins in the Auvergne. (Fondation Teilhard de Chardin)

purple of the universal Matter, first passing for me into the gold of Spirit,—then into the white incandescence of Personality,—then finally (and this is the present stage) into the immaterial (or rather super-material) ardor of Love.—And never before, too, did I realize in such a tangible way how much people, around me, are starving for the same light, which perhaps I can transmit to them.[298]

The same ideas, though somewhat differently expressed, are found in the introduction to *The Heart of Matter*:

Crimson gleams of Matter, gliding imperceptibly into the gold of Spirit, ultimately to become transformed into the incandescence of a Universe that is Person—and through all this there blows, animating it and spreading over it, a fragrant balm, a zephyr of Union—and of the Feminine.

The Diaphany of the Divine at the heart of a glowing Universe, as I have experienced it through contact with the Earth—the Divine radiating from the depths of blazing Matter: this it is that I shall try to disclose and communicate in what follows.[299]

It is a powerful, inspiring vision of fire, a vision of divine love and its fiery vigor that creates, connects, transfigures, and sets free. The essay begins with the burning bush, here transposed into a contemporary perspective of meeting the heart of God at the heart of matter. Teilhard describes the pattern of his spiritual journey, his discovery of the blazing fullness of God, through the successive integration of unfolding experiences of "the cosmic, or the evolutive," "the human, or the convergent," "the Christic, or the centric," concluding after a "Prayer to the Ever-Greater Christ" with "the Feminine, or the Unitive."

Fire and flame, fuel and spark, smoldering and burning, bursting into a blaze—these vivid images run through the entire essay, expressing an extraordinary intensity and vibrance, likening his vision to the brilliance of a great light, comparing the passion of his mystic love to the leaping of a flame welling up through the entire universe, through the heart of Christ, through every fiber of his being:

Christ. His Heart. A Fire: a fire with the power to penetrate all things. . . .

It is as if the fact of bringing together and connecting the two poles, tangible and intangible, external and internal, of the world which bears us onward had caused everything to burst into flames and set everything free. . . .

Lord of consistence and union, you whose distinguishing mark and essence is the power indefinitely to grow greater, without distortion or loss of continuity, to the measure of the mysterious Matter whose Heart you fill and all whose movements you ultimately control—Lord of my childhood and Lord of my last days—God complete in relation to yourself and yet, for us, continually being born— God, who, because you offer yourself

Château Les Moulins in Neuville, home of Teilhard's brother Joseph. (Fondation Teilhard de Chardin)

to our worship as "evolver" and "evolving," are henceforth the only being that can satisfy us—sweep away the last clouds that still hide you—the clouds of hostile prejudice and those, too, of false creeds.

Let your universal Presence spring forth in a blaze that is at once Diaphany and Fire.

O ever-greater Christ![300]

When the essay was ready, in the middle of December just after Lucile's birthday, which he marked every year by celebrating a special Mass for her on the feast day of St. Lucile, he sent her a copy of the text, describing it in his letter as "a sort of history of my spiritual adventure, 'the Quest of Spirit through Matter.' I wonder whether you will like it,—

but I think you *will.* Anyhow, these pages are an effort to express an internal evolution deeply impressed by you." Could there be a clearer statement about Lucile's significance in Teilhard's life? A more candid recognition of the mutuality of their love, the depth of their relationship, so important to both of them, however differently understood? He added that these pages were also

> a fairly good expression of my present state of mind.— Really, at this point (an approaching terminal point) of my life, I may say that nothing counts any more for me except a passionate interest for a better vision and discovery-of-God-through-evolving-Matter: this effort bringing me to a warm and rich feeling of some mysterious essence of human Research—and love.

Teilhard's letter gave Lucile a great deal of pleasure. Perhaps it reminded her of their earlier years of collaboration since she replied:

> How proud and happy I was when you said how much I helped to clarify your ideas, to talk them over with me and so it was OUR work—and you say so kindly in this last letter, the internal evolution so deeply impressed *by you.* Perhaps it was something like this that you meant when you wrote over and over again "what is born between us is *for ever.*"

She also wrote:

> Oh Pierre, I have recently been reading *Le Milieu Divin,* and I understand why it has been loved by so many people, and it is of special delight to me because it somehow so vividly recalls to mind the YOU as you were when I first knew you, the eager searcher, the mystic who was so full of the love of the world and to whom God was so close, so much a part of you so that everyone who came into contact with you was aware of His Presence. I like to

hold to this picture because it broadens my own feeling and vision.[301]

By early 1951 Teilhard felt restless. He was no armchair scientist but needed to be in the field, have his hands on the earth again, as he used to say. On his return from China, Abbé Breuil, who was a great authority on South Africa and had made three trips there during the war, had first told him about the important paleontological research carried out there in the preceding years. Teilhard was keen to go and see the fossils of *Australopithecus*, or the "southern ape," for himself and extend the network of research he had built up in the East. When sounded out about assessing the importance of the finds, "not to interfere, nor to tell them what to do, but to learn, and make available what I have been able to see and learn elsewhere,"[302] he was thrilled to go. But illness had prevented him on two previous occasions from going. By the summer of 1951 the idea of a trip to South Africa, which George Barbour encouraged him to pursue, seemed most attractive. It also provided a convenient "screen" to get away from the unsatisfactory situation in Paris.

Yet he hesitated. Was it wise to go, now that he was seventy and had experienced two serious illnesses in recent years? The strain of the journey might be too much for him. There was also the troubling concern about the fate of his writings. Would they ever be published? The Jesuits were unlikely to do so, and close friends urged him to take steps to ensure that his lifetime's writings would not be lost forever. Someone proposed setting up a foundation in his name to preserve his works; others suggested he ought to leave the Society of Jesus because he then would have more freedom as a secular priest. But he refused to do this, for it would mean "cutting myself off from my 'divine milieu'; I should be breaking the thread that binds me to the will of God, and I should no longer be able to entrust myself to its guidance."[303]

Several possibilities were debated. Father Jouve, the editor of the Jesuit journal *Études*, located at 15 rue Monsieur

"When all is said and done, I can see this: I managed to climb up to the point where the Universe became apparent to me as a great rising surge, in which all the work that goes into serious inquiry, all the will to create, all the acceptance of suffering, converge ahead into a single dazzling spear-head— now, at the end of my life, I can stand on the peak I have scaled and continue to look ever more closely into the future, and there, with ever more assurance, see the ascent of God."
—The Heart of Matter

211

where Teilhard was living, was only too aware that given Teilhard's recent history of heart problems, it was by no means certain that he would safely return from his South African trip, due to start on July 5, 1951. Realizing that it was unlikely that the Jesuit order would publish Teilhard's writings, Jouve hit on a solution by suggesting that Mademoiselle Mortier, who had been looking after Teilhard's essays for some years, should be made his literary executrix because otherwise his works would never see the light of day.

When Mademoiselle Mortier briefly called on July 2 to say good-bye before Teilhard's departure, this idea was put into practice there and then. Quite unexpectedly Teilhard asked for a piece of paper, but she was not prepared for this. He therefore went to get some notepaper himself, carrying the letterhead of *Études*. On this he wrote a short statement saying that in case of his death all rights over his non-scientific writings were made over to her, thus placing the preservation and future publication of all his essays into her hands.

Mademoiselle Mortier later interpreted this unexpected development as a "divine intervention responding to the limitless trust and obedience" of Teilhard as a religious who had such complete faith that he never did anything against what he understood to be the will of God and of his Society, his particular "divine milieu." As the initiative and wise counsel regarding his will had come from one of his Jesuit colleagues, backed by legal advice from the resident Jesuit canon lawyer, Teilhard was willing to respond, but in a spirit of complete detachment, "If my writings are from God, they will go on. If they are not from God, they can be forgotten."[304]

He could now depart with his mind at rest. It enthralled him to go to South Africa at long last, made possible through financial support from the Viking Fund in New York, later called the Wenner Gren Foundation of Anthropological Research. With the possibility of carrying out further research on behalf of this foundation, he was no longer so dependent

on Paris. Treated almost as an exile in France, he again envisaged his future work abroad, whether in South Africa or
America. But he needed more practical help now: "Fortunately Rhoda is there to direct me in an efficient way in the
preparations and formalities of this journey."[305]

Rhoda had been living in Paris for some time and was
able to give him help and support by accompanying him on
this and subsequent journeys. When Lucile had first heard
about this, she was not too pleased:

> So Mrs. de Terra is going to South Africa with you. I sup-
> pose I have known all along that she would, so I should not
> be so upset. . . . Probably this is what YOU want so I should
> be happy about it. I am so sorry my encounter with her last
> summer was so unsuccessful. It seems to me that now she
> has EVERYTHING that used to be mine, the daily visits,
> the sharing of all the intimate things and friends—well, all
> that makes life sweet and worthwhile, now that she has it
> all she could be a little more generous so that I could feel
> happier about your being with her so constantly. Perhaps
> this is also a part of the lesson that I have to learn. And you
> can see I have not yet conquered my EGO or I would not
> still feel so unhappy about it all.[306]

Lucile felt particularly hurt because Rhoda de Terra had
not been too friendly toward her. Nonetheless she still sup-
posed that they both shared the same interest in Teilhard's
well-being.

By the end of July Teilhard was in Johannesburg. As always, he had used the journey on the boat to write another
essay, "The Convergence of the Universe." Once he had
found his bearings, he explored the South African terrain
with much interest and enthusiasm. His headquarters were
in Johannesburg and Pretoria, where he had an opportunity
to visit all the important museums with paleontological collections. But he no longer enjoyed the vigor of his younger
days. He could not travel rough as he used to, but had to go

Capetown, South Africa.

everywhere by car, and at some of the barely accessible prehistoric sites he needed to be carried in a litter to visit them at all. But he managed to see most of what he considered essential and felt better than at any time during the three previous years.

In September he wrote about some of his impressions to Lucile:

Teilhard being carried by porters in Rhodesia, 1953. (Fondation Teilhard de Chardin)

In fact (and largely thanks to the helpful and calming presence of Rhoda) the journey is developing all right. Scientifically speaking, I am extremely interested by everything I see here in the line of both continental and human genesis. And, as a result of this new contact with field and field work, I feel a kind of mental rejuvenation (or excitation): the favorable atmosphere for a further (?) development of the ideas (or Weltanschauung) I have tried so hard to focus and to express for fifty years.

As always, his mind was still forging ahead, thinking of yet further possibilities and future growth.

The climate reminded him of "Beijing weather" and "Beijing colors." He had made several trips and felt really "caught" and "lured by this enormous and enormously worn out country, where the roads and the tracks can strike, right ahead through endless 'étendues' of a thorny jungle,—so perfectly similar to the Abyssinian bush. A curious mixture of contrasts and similarities with dear old Asia." But he felt cut off from the intellectual life of Europe and America and had "very few opportunities for interesting contacts" apart from the "technical discussions with geologist colleagues." It was "a big difference with Beijing indeed!—Probably due to their isolated location at the end of a continent, the people here seem to be curiously absorbed in their petty dissensions (white against natives,—Africaans against British,—bigoted Dutch Church against any form of spiritual liberty)."

He would not have liked to have been stuck there for a long time but a few weeks gave him a quiet time "hundreds of miles from Rome." This was a "rare and fine opportunity to collect and consolidate oneself internally,—far from any foreign pressure."[307] Thinking about his position, he decided to write a frank letter before his departure from South Africa to the Jesuit general, Father Janssens, dated Cape Town, October 12, 1951. Teilhard wanted to explain "what I am thinking and where I stand." He told the general that above all "you must resign yourself to taking me as I am." In the consciousness of the synthesis of all things in Christ,

> I have found an extraordinarily rich and inexhaustible source of clarity and interior strength, and an atmosphere outside which it is now physically impossible for me to breathe, to worship, to believe. What might have been taken in my attitude during the last thirty years for obstinacy or disrespect, is simply the result of my absolute inability to contain my own feeling of wonderment.

He assured the general that the immediate effect of his interior attitude

> is to rivet me ever more firmly to three convictions which are the very marrow of Christianity: The unique significance of Man as the spear-head of Life; the position of Catholicism as the central axis in the convergent bundle of human activities; and finally the essential function as consummator assumed by the risen Christ at the center and peak of Creation.

He recognized "that Rome may have its own reasons for judging that, in its present form, my concept of Christianity may be premature or incomplete and that at the present

"We must no longer seek to organize the world in favor of, and in terms of, the isolated individual."
  —"Some Reflections on the Rights of Man"

moment its wider diffusion may therefore be inopportune." But he could not abandon his own personal search—

> that would involve me in an interior catastrophe and disloyalty to my most cherished vocation; but (and this has been true for some months) I have ceased to propagate my ideas and am confining myself to achieving a deeper personal insight into them. This attitude has been made easier for me by my now being once more in a position to do first-hand scientific work.
>
> In fact I have every hope that my absence from Europe will allow the commotion about me that may have disturbed you recently, simply to die down.

Statue of Christ the Redeemer, Rio de Janeiro, Brazil.

He described his letter as simply "an exposition of conscience" not calling for an answer. He asked the general to look on it only "as a proof that you can count on me unreservedly to work for the Kingdom of God, which is the one thing I keep before my eyes and the one goal to which science leads me."[308]

After working in South Africa for eight weeks, he went to North America rather than back to France. But instead of traveling directly by boat from Durban to New York, he went via Buenos Aires, Rio de Janeiro, and Trinidad. This journey opened yet more new perspectives in anthropology and geology for him. He then settled for the winter in New York, staying with the Jesuits at 980 Park Avenue, a fifteen-minute walk from the Viking Foundation and conveniently situated for his work. Providence had lent a helping hand in providing a new research position at a particularly precarious time when his situation amounted in fact to a second exile. As he explained to Lucile, "Apparently, Paris has become too hot for me these days; and I must try to find a shelter here for the time being.—I may be here for months."[309]

American Exile

*I can tell you that I now live permanently in
the presence of God.*

He settled into St. Ignatius, the Jesuit house in New
York, wondering what his remaining years would
bring. Such an uncertain and unsettled existence! Like a
traveler between different worlds, or perhaps more like a
pilgrim, he was always journeying on, without a permanent
abode. It must have been a tremendous strain for a man of
seventy not having a home he could truly call his own, nor
having the warmth of his closest friends surrounding him
during the autumn years of life.

Maybe, at first, he still hoped that New York would
be only a temporary stage, that in the end he might return to France after all, but he soon learned that there
was little chance of that. He wrote to Jeanne Mortier in
November:

> I gather from the new provincial in Lyons (a firm friend,
> P. Ravier) that the situation at Rome, as far as I am con-
> cerned, is rather strained. . . . If I returned to France
> now, he could not leave me in Paris, but would have
> to send me somewhere into the provinces to be "in re-
> treat." . . . It so happens that . . . the director of research
> at the Wenner Gren Foundation which sent me to South
> Africa . . . is asking me (as a favor!) to join him as a "re-
> search associate." . . . I am not sure what will happen in
> the end. But everything is turning out so strangely for
> me, just as in 1923 when China was receiving me when
> I arrived from Paris. This time it's America, and I am 70.
> But perhaps this time again there is still something wait-
> ing ahead of me.[310]

St. Ignatius, the Jesuit church on
Park Ave., New York.

The Chapel of the Sacred Heart,
at St. Ignatius's, where Teilhard
liked to say Mass. (Fondation
Teilhard de Chardin)

"One might say that a hitherto unknown form of religion—one that no one could as yet have imagined or described, for a lack of a universe large enough and organic enough to contain it—is burgeoning in the heart of modern man, from a seed sown by the idea of evolution. . . . Far from being shaken in my faith by such a revolution, it is with irrepressible hope that I welcome the inevitable rise of this new mysticism and anticipate its equally inevitable triumph.

—"The Stuff of the Universe"

Courtyard at St. Ignatius. (Fondation Teilhard de Chardin)

Although less energetic than in earlier years, he remained strongly focused on his research, but also enjoyed numerous social contacts. Not only were there scientific conferences, meetings, and symposia, but he attended dinners and receptions, met artists and writers, distinguished scholars from many different fields, diplomats, and representatives from the new United Nations. Many people later gave witness to the wide-ranging conversations they had shared with him. For example, a Dutch parapsychologist who had undertaken research on Voodoo ritual in Haiti reported how Teilhard took him aside after dinner discussing for about two hours "scientific methods of studying 'paranormal' phenomena. I was surprised that Père Teilhard was familiar not only with all the literature on such phenomena . . . but also with the laboratory work and the statistical computations . . . .Again I was greatly impressed by his wide knowledge and appreciation of Jung's theories" and also how "he made a sharp distinction between the theories of Freud, Adler and Horney, and the ideas of Jung, with which his own thought had something in common."[311]

Teilhard always remained open to new ideas right to the end of his life. Always interested in the most recent developments in science, psychology, sociology, and religion, he was forever questioning established orthodoxies, whether scientific, religious, or political. Evidence of the versatility, range, and depth of his mind can be found in his carefully crafted essays, but nowhere is it more strikingly visible than in the densely covered pages of his diaries, written in a small, fine handwriting, full of condensed notes and abbreviations. Rarely do these pages relate personal or public events; instead, they are packed with ideas and critical reflections, up to three days before his death. He kept writing, writing, writing—unto the last. He wrote many letters to his friends; he wrote scientific papers and notes; he wrote more religious and philosophical essays in the years 1946-1955 than during any other period of his life—his bibliography lists over ninety titles for this time.

During the summer of 1952 he decided to take a vacation visit to the western United States, going via Chicago to California, especially Los Angeles and Berkeley, visiting his colleague George Gaylord Simpson near Albuquerque, New Mexico, traveling to Glacier Park in Montana, and then returning east, spending a few days in Maine at a holiday place that belonged to Rhoda de Terra's sister. Being in San Francisco made him feel nostalgic. The Golden Gate was now closed to him—there were no more embarkations to China. But he was thrilled to be given a close view of the great cyclotron at Berkeley and was so much impressed by it that he drew on this experience in one of his essays. He commented in a letter:

Glacier Park, Montana.

> You really have the feeling in such places of being out of your depth in this new human thing; in the complexity and power of one machine—mathematical speculation, laboratory research, the wide scope of industrial enterprises, military ambition, medical hopes of therapy—and even the secret hope of finding the ultimate explanation of things. . . . The first chance I get, I must make the acquaintance of the great computers at Harvard—the last word in systematization after the last word in energy.[312]

He could see that here, in the work of the nuclear energy research center, "the barriers between Laboratory and Factory, between the Atomic and Social, disappear; also, I might add, between the Local and the Planetary."[313]

He was still pursuing his scientific interests, but he nevertheless had a curious feeling of a profound change within and without, for "from now on geology has been unmistakably replaced for me by the human and ultra-human . . . the 'neo-anthropology' of which I dream has now first place in my thought and conversation."[314] He was largely preoccupied with the theme of "human energetics," but also with developing a christology that affirmed the absolute primacy of Christ in the mystery of creation. Christ was Alpha and

Portrait of Teilhard taken in 1952.
(Fondation Teilhard de Chardin)

With A. G. H. Goodwin in Jaldaerba, South Africa, 1953. (Fondation Teilhard de Chardin)

Omega, human, divine, and cosmic. Christ was the center of the universe, the center of humankind, the center of each person. This was the heart of Teilhard's faith, animated and sustained by a fervent cosmic Christ-mysticism.

Sometimes he thought of returning to Europe, but he was soon planning a second visit to South Africa for the summer of 1953. At his suggestion the Wenner Gren Foundation was financing excavations in Pretoria, and it seemed important that he should have first-hand contact with the new developments. Yet a crisis of anxiety paralyzed him in making decisions about the trip. He also still felt troubled emotionally, as he admitted in a letter to Lucile, now in Washington. Frequent meetings seemed to be too disturbing, and telephoning strained his nerves. Therefore he suggested meeting less often, "let us say once a month," and being in touch by letter. His doctor was quite optimistic, even though Teilhard was "still the easy prey of the most amazing variety of 'anxieties,'—an old disease of mine, which (if only I was a more spiritual man!) should force me into an evergrowing 'abandon' in the hands of God. Pray for me. I am praying for you."[315]

When he finally left for South Africa at the end of June, again accompanied by Rhoda de Terra, he faced a long and tiring sea crossing of seventeen days before he reached Cape Town. During the journey he wrote "The Stuff of the Universe," a brief essay in which he tried once again "to grasp and express rather more thoroughly the real heart—which always seems to elude me—of what I feel, of what I see, of what I live." It was completed "in sight of St. Helena, on passage from New York to the Cape."[316] He also began thinking about drafting a new book "on the singularity (singularities?) of the human species," wondering at the same time whether it might be preferable to work out "the principal axes of what has become 'finally and fundamentally' my form of adoration?"[317]

Being back in the field in South Africa greatly pleased him and provided him with important insights:

> All that I have seen and heard . . . confirms me in the idea that *I did well* to come. I have arrived just at the time when research into human origins is being reorganized and has received a new impetus—and that in a critical region of the earth. I believe that I can be of some use in this field, in organizing and inspiring. In any case, I am learning a great deal—and ideas are coming. All I now have to do is continually to put my trust more completely in the guiding influence of the "Milieu Divin."[318]

He visited several important centers of excavation and studied fossils and geological strata. From South Africa he flew to what was then still Northern Rhodesia where he visited important excavation sites. He also went to see the Victoria Falls in Southern Rhodesia, but unfortunately he never managed to get to Kenya. He realized that over the last two years "the problems concerning Early Man have certainly become clearer in S. Africa; and an eager team of young researchers is just there, ready to be used. Somewhat a duplication of the situation I found in China thirty years ago!"[319]

Once again he was happy. As he told Lucile, there was no better way for rejuvenation, and even "adoration," than to be "in close contact with old mother Earth." Although very busy with research, this did not prevent him—on the contrary—

> from maturing further on, as much as I can, the "philosophical" and religious side of my ideas. As you know, Early Man, for me, is only the gate leading to "Future" Man,—the existence of such a "Future Man" being, in my opinion, the strongest foundation on which to build

"How can we fail to be struck by the revealing growth around us of a strong mystical current, actually nourished by the conviction that the universe, viewed in its complete workings, is ultimately lovable and loving?"
— "The Singularities of the Human Species"

Victoria Falls.

"I am so much convinced . . . that nothing can be obtained any more in the line of making Man happier and better except by visualizing a 'new dimension' of God: the God of a moving and growing World—the true Spirit of Matter."
—Letter to Lucile Swan, January 22, 1951

the new faith in God which is so urgently needed by the Man of today.

Lucile was probably less pleased to learn that

Here, as you may suppose, Rhoda is of an immense help for me. In fact she helps me a lot, even in my work for the Foundation, on the most essential social and psychological planes,—a plane where, as you know, probably, I am not particularly gifted.[320]

How happy Lucile would have been if she could have changed places with Rhoda!

On his return he sailed again from Cape Town via Buenos Aires and Rio de Janeiro to New York. His original plan to visit Chile and the Andes unfortunately had to be abandoned. He got some more writing done during the journey, completing a short paper, "The God of Evolution," signed "At the Equator, 25 October (Christ the King) 1953." Back in New York City, of which he was decidedly very fond, he wrote to Jeanne Mortier:

I am back to my normal existence between the Wenner Gren Foundation and Park Avenue (in the same microscopic room which I like)—and, more important, always under the same roof with P. de Breuvery. . . . And now, with you in mind, I am going to tidy up two short essays written during the journey: one is called "The Stuff of the Universe" and the other "The God of Evolution."[321]

He also decided to pursue his earlier idea regarding a "book" on "the singularities of the human species."[322] It was completed in March 1954 and turned out to be a sizeable monograph, providing an excellent introduction to his mature ideas on the significance of human evolution, the birth of the noosphere, the power of co-reflection, and the nature of point Omega.

At the end of 1953 he learned that Piltdown man had been a hoax. The story took him back to the early stages of his career when he had first become so passionately devoted to the search for fossils. Had his life now come full circle? Learning the truth about this strange find affected him much less, though, than the loss of his dear friend and confidant, Père Auguste Valensin. His death in December 1953 was followed shortly afterward by that of another friend, Père Charles from Louvain. Teilhard wrote: "Another one: when will it be my turn?"[323] The three friends had known each other since their first year of studying theology and had been in touch ever since. Now only Teilhard was left. The year before, Père Licent, his collaborator during his early years in China, had died too. Life was fast diminishing all around him and he felt "a bit shaky, these days," he told Lucile.[324]

Their friendship continued, but it was fraught with tension. Perhaps Lucile did not understand him sufficiently well anymore; perhaps he was expecting too much of her, for she was unlikely to take up a "motherly" role toward him now, during his declining years. She sounded almost angry when she asked him to find time for

Teilhard in Hopefield, South Africa in 1953. (Fondation Teilhard de Chardin)

> a CALM talk about "us." We meet and act as if nothing had ever existed between us . . . until just as we are parting some chance remark brings on others and the time being so short and the feeling of pressure so great, things are said that are too strong or not explicit. . . . So we part with a feeling of frustration and ill ease.

He responded that she was absolutely right in her diagnosis, except that he would put it differently:

> In the "Chinese phase" of our life, not only you needed me—but we needed each other.—And now, apparently, we need each other (and we can help each other) in a different way.

Some months later he apologized for having been so "terribly silent," but his "nerves are stupidly somewhat tense these days. But I try to forget it, and to lean on God,—the

"During these last years I have tried . . . to pin down and define the exact reason why Christianity, in spite of a certain renewal of its grip on backward-looking (or undeveloped) circles in the world, is decidedly . . . losing its reputation with the most influential and most progressive portion of mankind and ceasing to appeal to it."

—"The God of Evolution"

closer for it." He was pleased, though, that his "booklet on Man" was finished and he was trying "to have it published in some technically scientific series,—without having to ask any special permission of my Order."[325] It was "The Singularities of the Human Species," which eventually appeared in 1955 in the *Annales de Paléontologie*.

His New York routine was interrupted when the Jesuits decided to modernize their house, and so living in Park Avenue was no longer possible. Having to move again was another strain. The only consolation was that his friend Father de Breuvery was moving with Teilhard to the accommodation they found in Hotel Sixteen, where the two shared a flat on the sixth floor. At least the company was congenial. Like Teilhard, Father de Breuvery had spent time in China and was now, since 1952, working at the United Nations so that the two fellow Jesuits shared some common experience and interests.

After his return from South Africa Teilhard had weighed for several months whether to make another visit to France. He decided to go, and by January 1954 he had arranged a definite booking for a crossing by sea, with the plan to spend the months of June to September in his home country. His friends were delighted to learn of his forthcoming return to Paris. Rhoda de Terra, who now lived close to Teilhard in New York and helped him in so many practical ways, accompanied him also on this last trip.

By early June Teilhard was back in his old room on the rue Monsieur at the house of the *Études*. One of the Jesuits had organized a public lecture for him and he spoke, somewhat reluctantly, to a large audience "On Africa and Human Origins." There was some criticism about his presence in France; he was tired and under strain, and although well organized, his lecture was not as interesting and well received as might have been expected. Père Leroy soon took Teilhard away from Paris to Lyons to visit the Jesuit theology students and faculty, not least his old friend Henri de

Lubac. He found his provincial, Père Ravier, very helpful and understanding and enjoyed discussing his ideas with the young Jesuit students.

Teilhard and Leroy were traveling by car. From Lyons they drove on to the Auvergne to pay a brief visit to Sarcenat, the place of Teilhard's birth. He wanted to see it once more, for the last time. He insisted on entering the old house alone. He walked through the park, visited the little church at Orcines where all the family was buried, and came back very tired, confiding to Leroy, "I shall never see Sarcenat again."[326]

But it was important to him to have made this visit. It was a return to the very beginnings, to his roots in the quiet ancient family chateau of Sarcenat, surrounded by its wooded hills and wonderful views. Here he had lived so long ago surrounded by a large family that was no more; it was here that the young child had first searched for treasures, for fragments of metals and stones, and the world had gradually caught fire for him. This was the place where he had first discovered the "glow of matter," the promising light of the spirit that shone at the heart of all things and disclosed the face of God. It was this initial childhood vision that had first set him on his life's long journey, exploring the far corners of the earth, the depths of time, the vast dimensions of life, the origin and destiny of humankind. A great and splendid adventure! Was not the motto on his family's coat of arms the ancient line from Virgil, "Fiery is their vigor, and of heaven their source"? His vision of heaven and earth was truly one of fire, and its source was the noble, ancient setting of a remote and unknown hamlet in the volcanic mountains of central France.

Perhaps he would have liked to linger on, but their journey continued to the region of the Dordogne where they visited the famous prehistoric caves of Lascaux. Teilhard had never seen these caves, discovered only in 1940; thus he was very pleased to get to know these remarkable examples of the first-known paintings in the world of some twenty-five thou-

Examining a rock in Rhodesia, 1953. (Fondation Teilhard de Chardin)

"Let us turn back to the Cross— and look at the crucifix. What we see nailed to the wood—suffering, dying, freeing—is that really still the God of original sin? Is it? Or is it not the God of evolution?

Or rather, is not the God of evolution—the God for whom our neo-humanism is looking for . . . the very God of expiation?"

—"What the World Is Looking for from the Church"

sand years ago. By traveling to this part of France, he was not only returning to his own personal roots but was at the same time able to visit a specific cradle of the human race where artistic creativity, so specifically human, had found one of its earliest expressions. As he later wrote to Leroy, these visits had been the highlight of his journey to France.

He had hoped to stay until September, but he was not welcome in Paris. Several signs indicated to him that it was preferable to leave. So he traveled in early August to England, paying a visit to Dr. Kenneth Oakley, who had discovered the Piltdown man fraud. He then returned to New York. There was trouble there, too, since the U.S. immigration authorities refused to give him a visa as permanent resident, but would only extend it for six months. He kept himself busy with writing, worked for the Wenner Gren Foundation, and in the autumn took part in a colloquium on "The Unity of Human Knowledge," where he met Niels Bohr, Julian Huxley, Étienne Gilson, and other well-known figures among the participants.

Had he made the right decision to return so suddenly to the United States? He would have liked to go to France once more, even though some of his recent experiences had been disappointing and harrowing. It was difficult to regain his inner balance and harmony as he felt tired and not too well. But he kept thinking about how best to follow his Christic vision. As he wrote to Jeanne Mortier on his return from France:

> I can retain nothing from this too hasty visit to Paris except a mass of more or less chaotic impressions from which nevertheless a few clear or clarified points stand out, namely: (1) That through all that is most alive in me, I feel that I am more and more dedicated to my vocation of devoting my life (what remains of my life) to the discovery and the service of the Universal Christ— and that in absolute fidelity to the Church. (2) That— for the immediate future at least—it is most certainly in

"Not only among the Gentiles or the rank and file of the faithful, but even in the religious orders themselves, Christianity still to some degree provides a shelter for the 'modern soul,' but it no longer clothes it, nor satisfies it, nor leads it. Something has gone wrong and so something, in the area of faith and religion, must be supplied without delay on this planet. The questions is, what is it we are looking for?"

—"The God of Evolution"

shadow and exile that I must work. And finally, (3) that in order to sustain me in this effort, your collaboration is for me more valuable than ever. *Thanks* for everything you have been for me during last June and July.[327]

At the beginning of December he wrote to Lucile: "Let us converge, you and me, courageously and happily, toward the new face of God which attracts both of us.—For this fascinating task of discovery I need you,—and I shall always do the utmost for helping you." When he went out walking soon afterward, he suddenly became ill and fell on the sidewalk; he was rushed to his doctor, who immediately telephoned Lucile since the stricken Teilhard had asked to be comforted by her. She came at once to reassure him that she loved him just as much as ever. That is what he needed most at this moment.[328]

New York skyline.

He also felt greatly cheered when his friend Pierre Leroy came just before Christmas to spend a few days with him. But he found Teilhard

> tired, half-hearted, apparently without joy, without that optimism that was so characteristic of him. He said little and was absorbed in his own thinking. He kept repeating, "Forward and Upward," as if he wanted to summarize in these two words what he had taught and practiced all his life.[329]

In years to come Leroy was to describe the loneliness, suffering, and "inner martyrdom" of his friend with much sensitivity and perception, admitting that the deepest insight he gained during this visit was on the occasion of a walk when, amid all the hustle and bustle of the streets of New York, Teilhard suddenly stopped and told him that he finally felt he now lived permanently in the presence of God. This was uttered just about three months before his death, and his friend took it to be the testament of a very spiritual man.

"Everyone is prepared to admit the importance of Christianity i n the past; but what about the present? and still more the future?"
—"The Christian Phenomenon"

227

Christy-Omega

I should like to die on the day of the Resurrection.

The Resurrection of Christ by
Andrew Mantegna.

Going back to France was not a real option any more. When he received an invitation from a professor at the Sorbonne, formerly one of his students, to attend a symposium on paleontology in Paris in the spring, he thought it wiser to decline, and he simply sent a paper. Yet when the authorities in Rome learned about this invitation, he was still explicitly informed that he must under no circumstances attend. It was quite unnecessary, but added to his pain.

As if that were not enough, another rebuke came when the publication of some of his essays was again refused. His friends in Louvain, especially the Jesuit theology professor Paul Henry, had negotiated with the Benzinger publishing house in Switzerland to bring out a German translation of some of Teilhard's articles already published in French. He wrote to his provincial in Lyons, Père Ravier, thinking that it might perhaps not be necessary to speak to Rome about this. It would have been such a joy to see at long last something in print, to make his ideas more widely known. If "by any chance the response were to be 'yes,'" Teilhard wanted to know this as soon as possible so that he could make the necessary arrangements for translation.[330] Alas, it was not to be. Despite Ravier's support and his repeated efforts to obtain the necessary authorization, it was not given: "There is no need to spread these ideas any further," the Jesuit general had categorically replied to Ravier's letter.[331]

Though this was very disappointing news, Teilhard took it in his stride and continued to work on new essays instead. He was growing old, but he could still see his vision with full strength. Death held no fear for him; he saw it as a passage to seeing more, to a fuller vision. As he said about a friend who had died, "Now he can see."[332] So, despite his nervous disposition and growing weakness, he continued to write. On New Year's Day 1955 he completed a short essay, "The Death-Barrier and Co-Reflection," which dealt with "the imminent awakening of human consciousness to the sense of its irreversibility." He argued that a materialistic understanding of the world led to a dead end; only a spiritual view of evolution could do justice to all the phenomena around us. Humanity was reaching a new psychological stage; it was becoming adult and crossing new thresholds. Science needed the stimulation of religion, and the understanding of revelation could only develop more fully if it took into account "the new contributions that scientific research is gradually making to human consciousness."

His science, religion, and mystical spirituality came together in his understanding of Christ in whom all things are made one. What could christology possibly mean today if new horizons "were not opening up for our modern way of understanding and worshiping" Christ?[333] This question exercised him to his last day. Five years earlier he had already so beautifully described this Christic vision in his spiritual autobiography, *The Heart of Matter*, but it was not enough. He felt compelled to present his fundamental vision yet once again, say what he saw, say it once more, but differently.

So he worked away on one of his *clandestins*, secretly drafting and revising a new essay, "The Christic," his last major work and mystic testament. He had been thinking about the theme of this essay for five years. In September 1954 he had written to Mademoiselle Mortier that he was planning "The Christic" as "a kind of quintessence of *The Divine Milieu*, "The Mass on the World," and *The Heart of Matter*."[334] He put his personal *summa* down on paper during the last two months before his death. His nervous disposition certainly shows in the first draft of the text, with many passages crossed out and numerous additions and changes that give it an untypically untidy appearance, so much in contrast with the elegant, neat presentation of earlier works.

He makes his position clear right at the start of the essay:

"So here I am back again, with a new and rather enigmatic year to face. In order to be ready for any eventuality I have begun by making a week's retreat—which will, I hope, have brought me close to Him who every day is 'coming closer' and of whom, if I am to end well, I have every day a greater need. Above all, I have been trying to sharpen my perception, and to intensify in myself the presence of what I call the "Christic.' I shall probably devote one of my next essays to the subject."

—Letter to Marguerite Teillard-Chambon, August 29, 1954

The Assumption of the Virgin by Titian.

A late photograph of Teilhard.
(Georgetown University Library)

It is a long time now since, in "The Mass on the World" and *The Divine Milieu*, I tried to put into words the admiration and wonder I felt as I confronted perspectives as yet hardly formulated within me.

Today, after forty years of constant reflection, it is still exactly the same fundamental vision which I feel the need to set forth and to share, in its mature form, for the last time. With less exuberance and freshness of expression perhaps, than at my first encounter with it, but still with the same wonder and the same passion.[335]

It is a vision of extraordinary brilliance, of great consistence and coherence, a vision that "transfigured" for him "the very depths of the World." The energizing power of this vision centers on the powers of love and hope, made so dynamic by the convergent consummation of the universe by Christ, and of Christ by the universe: "If the World is becoming so dauntingly vast and powerful, it must follow that Christ is very much greater even than we used to think." Rightly understood, it is Christ who is able to "save Man from revolt against Life, justifiably prompted by the mere threat, the mere suspicion, of a total death—but also to give him that most forceful stimulus without which . . . Thought cannot attain the planetary term of its Reflection."[336]

Like many people today, Teilhard felt that the dimensions of "classical Christianity" are not large enough, not sufficiently dynamic to animate the contemporary world and develop human spiritualization in tandem with our advances of knowledge and technology:

We must admit that if the neo-humanisms of the twentieth century de-humanize us under their uninspired skies, yet on the other hand the still-living forms of theism—starting with the Christian—tend to under-humanize us in the rarefied atmosphere of too lofty skies. These religions are still systematically closed to the wide horizons and great winds of Cosmogenesis, and can no longer truly be said to feel with the Earth—an Earth whose internal frictions they can still lubricate like a soothing oil, but whose driving energies they cannot animate as they should.[337]

Well aware of the great spiritual needs of the contemporary world, the deep hunger for a greater vision and zest for life, Teilhard, more than most, was keenly concerned with giving meaning, direction, and purpose to human endeavor. He was looking for a dynamic "neo-Christianity," a "re-born" Christianity, "a Christianity re-incarnated for the second time (Christianity, we might say, squared) in the spiritual energies of Matter," an "ultra-Christianity," the sort of faith the world urgently needs, but has not yet formulated anywhere at all. And yet he believed that a Christianity "resolutely connected" with the world in movement was the only form of worship "that can display the astonishing power of energizing to the full, by 'amorizing' them, both the powers of growth and life and the powers of diminishment and death, at the heart of, and in the process of, the Noogenesis in which we are involved."[338]

Yet Teilhard was not without doubt. Questioning his own position he asked:

> How is it, then, that as I look around me, still dazzled by what I have seen, I find that I am almost the only person of my kind, the only one to have seen? . . .
>
> How, most of all, can it be that "when I come down from the mountain" and in spite of the glorious vision I still retain, I find that I am so little a better man, so little at peace, so incapable of expressing in my actions, and thus adequately communicating to others, the wonderful unity that I feel encompassing me?
>
> > Is there, in fact, a Universal Christ, is there a Divine Milieu?
> >
> > Or am I, after all, simply the dupe of a mirage in my own mind?
> >
> > I often ask myself that question.[339]

"The world-zest
The essence of all energy
The cosmic curve
The heart of God
The issue of cosmogenesis

The tide of cosmic
convergence
The God of evolution
The Universal Jesus . . .

Focus of ultimate and
Universal energy
Center of the cosmic sphere
Of cosmogenesis
Heart of Jesus,
Heart of evolution,
Unite me to yourself."
—*"My Litany"*

"I am going to broadcast the seed and let the wind carry it where it will."

—"How I Believe"

Icon of Christ Pantrocrator.

At the end of his life, this was a courageous and challenging question to ask. Could he faithfully stand by his convictions to the very end? Did the fire still lead him? He was aware of "the ambitious grandeur" of his ideas, his own disturbing imperfections, but he could think of enough reasons why his vision of the "Christic" was not an illusion. He could also feel the "contagious power" of that form of love "in which it becomes possible to love God 'not only with all one's body and all one's soul' but with the whole Universe-in-evolution."

He could find an explanation for his "isolation and apparent idiosyncrasy," but he could not fail to see that his ideas were beginning to become more widely accepted among countless people "ranging from the border-line of unbelief to the depths of the cloister." So in the end it was "heartening to know that I am not a lone discoverer, . . . exhilarating to feel that I am not just myself or all alone, that my name is legion, that I am 'all men.'"[340]

Everywhere in the world, he felt, a new spiritual atmosphere is being created through the idea of evolution—through the coming together of the love of God and the new faith in the world. The fusion of these two faiths would sooner or later occur and provide a new energy that would spread like fire. His vision of "the promised land" was the development of something "Ultra-human" that eventually was to lead to Christ-Omega, the center and summit of the universe, of all creation.

Sometime in March 1955, when Teilhard had finished writing "The Christic," he worked on another short paper, his last, titled "Research, Work, and Worship." It was written for his provincial, Père Ravier, to address the situation of "worker-priests" or those doing research, pointing out "that it is impossible for a priest to be in the laboratory (or the factory) without being obliged to reconcile Christian faith in the supernatural and the new 'humanistic' faith in an ultra-human, so that they form a single energizing force within him," as he wrote to his cousin Marguerite on April

1, 1955.[341] But its message can be applied more generally.

This very last paper deals briefly with science and religion in the modern world, emphasizing that "the very notion of Christian perfection" and its basic orientation has to be revised today:

> We need a new theology . . . and a new approach to perfection, which must gradually be worked out in our houses of study and retreat houses, in order to meet the new needs and aspirations. . . . But what we need perhaps even more . . . is for a new and higher form of worship to be gradually disclosed by Christian thought and prayer, adapted to the needs of all of tomorrow's believers without exception.[342]

What he really meant here are "new and higher forms of adoration" rather than simply worship.

He was thinking, writing, seeing a few friends, making plans for the summer, but he was mostly alone. Lucile still came to see him, and she commented that she had "a wonderful visit" sometime late in March. She wrote to him: "What a wonderful talk we had." He had spoken to her about a new theory that she found thrilling. She saw it as "the key to a real Unity which would lead to the spiritual awakening of which we dream." But she added, "Dearest, it makes me sad if I am partly the cause of your malaise. Don't let me be. You know I have found Peace and it is the thing I long for you more than anything else—the real Peace of God's presence."

He replied to her on March 30:

> Yes, stupidly enough, I am still nervous,—more nervous than I would,—than I should be.
>
> And at the same time, I need definitely your presence, your influence, in my life.
>
> I hope (I am sure) that things will gradually settle, "emotionally" speaking. . . . In any case, we know, both of us, that we "are always here" for each other.[343]

"I can still see Teilhard clearly in my mind's eye: his face with its fine features had a transparent expression, his whole personality seemed to radiate spirituality of the most concentrated sort."
—Helmut de Terra

A medal struck with one of Teilhard's mottos: "Everything that rises must converge." (Fondation Teilhard de Chardin)

"In him, the scientist was doubled by a Christian thinker of great originality and vision—two sides of his character which were facets of a singularly well-knit and integrated spirit, whose philosophy of the Universe developed continuously right up to the time of his death."
—Dorothy Garrod

He was soon to find "the real Peace of God's presence" Lucile had wished for him. In 1955 Easter Sunday fell on April 10. Teilhard had made his confession to his fellow Jesuit, Père de Breuvery, the previous day. After celebrating his Mass on Easter morning, he went to attend High Mass at St. Patrick's Cathedral in Manhattan, and in the afternoon he enjoyed listening to a concert. He felt he had a "magnificent day" and was in excellent spirits. He went to see Rhoda de Terra and her daughter, but suddenly, while standing at the window of their apartment, he fell full length to the floor like a stricken tree. He had suffered a massive heart attack and was unconscious. When he eventually opened his eyes again, he couldn't remember anything, but said "this time I feel it's terrible," as if he knew that this time his attack was fatal.

A doctor was called, but seeing his serious condition, he advised sending for a priest. By the time one of the Jesuits from St. Ignatius arrived, Teilhard was already dead, but he was still given the final rites. Had he not mentioned to one of his nephews the year before that he would like to die on Easter day, the day of Christ's resurrection? His great wish had been granted, and he had obtained "the grace of all graces," to end well without ever being unfaithful to his vision and calling.

His life had been a splendid adventure of the spirit; his death was the seal on a life lived from the depths of the Christian faith, nourished by hope, and transformed by love—warm, human loves, but loves that extended to the end of creation and embraced the Universal, the All. Here was a man whose mind, heart, and spirit were incandescent with the fire of a vision that transfigured his humanity and pointed his fellow human beings to the transforming energy and presence of divine life in the midst of the world, among us here and now.

He had lived almost half his life in exile, and he died there alone and unknown. His body lay for two days in the chapel of the Jesuit house on Park Avenue, and the few who saw him spoke of his face bearing "a striking resemblance to that of his compatriot from Clermont, Pascal: the smooth forehead, the sunken cheeks, the prominent nose and cheek-bones, the tightly drawn lips."[344]

Père de Breuvery officiated at the funeral, in the presence of just a few friends. The cemetery was far away, some sixty miles from New York, at the Jesuit novitiate of St. Andrew-on-Hud-son. Only Père Leroy and another priest accompanied Teilhard on his last journey. The coffin had to be laid in a temporary vault because the earth was still too frozen for a grave. Teilhard now lies among the members of his Order in the cemetery of the Jesuit Fathers of the Province of New York. He is buried under a simple stone, inscribed with his name, still in exile. Today, there is no Jesuit novitiate in the large building nearby, now taken over by another organization.[345]

When Pascal died, in the year 1654, a piece of paper was found sewn in his clothes on which he had left a moving testimony of his spiritual experience. It begins with the words "FIRE—God of Abraham, God of Isaac, God of Jacob, not of the philosophers and scholars. Certitude, certitude, feeling, joy, peace. *God of Jesus Christ.*" When his countryman Pierre Teilhard de Chardin died three hundred years later, he left an equally moving testimony, written on Maundy Thursday, three days before his death, in his journal. It speaks in brief note form of the Christ of St. Paul, the cosmos in evolution, the human phenomenon, Christ as the center of the cosmos, the phenomenon of Christianity, and "neo-Christianity."[346] On his desk stood a picture of the radiant heart of Christ with a litany addressed to the heart of God, the heart of Je-sus, the heart of the world written on its front and back.[347]

These final lines—his supreme testimony as Christian thinker and mystic—point to the transforming vision he lived and died for. If others can also see and follow it, it may give rise to the spiritual awakening and renewal he so much hoped and prayed for. As he said at the end of his last great essay, "The Christic," "Truth has to appear only once, in one single mind, for it to be impossible for anything ever to prevent it from spreading universally and setting everything ablaze."[348]

"It is not easy to convey the deep impression which Pierre Teilhard made on those who came into contact with him; the tall, distinguished figure—'cette silhouette de colonel anglais,' as one of his friends said the other day—and the keenly intelligent face with vivid eyes lit by an inner flame of enthusiasm will not soon be forgotten by those who had the privilege of know-ing him."

—Dorothy Garrod

Grave of Teilhard de Chardin in the Jesuit cemetery at St. Andrew-on-Hudson, near Poughkeepsie, N.Y.

Celebrating Pierre Teilhard de Chardin's Legacy

Bust of Teilhard by Malvina Hoffman.

Pierre Teilhard de Chardin died in New York on Easter Sunday 1955. He was buried in the cemetery of the Jesuit novitiate at St. Andrews on the Hudson in upstate New York, a relatively isolated spot few are likely to visit, especially after the grand building with its extensive grounds was redeveloped into the Culinary Institute of America. Now visitors need a key to the cemetery gate to gain access to the simple grave where this great man is buried, hidden under a small headstone simply inscribed with his name, the date of his birth (May 1, 1881), of his death (April 10, 1955), and that of joining the Jesuits (March 19, 1899). It seems a forlorn place for someone who traveled the world and is said to have influenced the thinking of both the United Nations and the Second Vatican Council. It is almost as though Teilhard were still living in exile, sixty years after his death.

As soon as he had died, his works could be published without any church intervention. Mademoiselle Mortier, appointed by Teilhard as his literary executrix in 1951, had already prepared everything before his death to undertake this task. She had gathered an international committee of distinguished scientists and intellectuals under the royal patronage of the Belgian Queen Marie-José to head the publication of *Le phénomène humain* by the Éditions du Seuil in Paris. This great *summa* of Teilhard's work, with its compelling unitary vision of the evolution of matter, life, and thought, of the world and human destiny, was the first of his works to be published, in 1955, the very year of Teilhard's death. The first English translation, *The Phenomenon of Man*, appeared in 1959 with an introduction by Sir Julian Huxley; it was later, in 1999, more correctly translated as *The Human Phenomenon*. This book soon became a bestseller, leading to a widespread interest in Teilhard's ideas, but not necessarily to a deep knowledge of his thought. For a time he became fashionable, yet without his ideas being really understood or critically debated.

Between 1955 and 1976, Teilhard de Chardin's writings were published in thirteen volumes in their original French version, soon followed by translations into English and other languages. However, these translations are not always accurate and can sometimes be rather misleading. *The Human Phenomenon* is one of Teilhard's more difficult works and not the easiest for gaining access to his ideas, which come across more clearly in some of his shorter essays. To fully capture the spiritual power of his vision it is important to know his earliest work, but the foundational essays in *Écrits du Temps de la Guerre* were only published in 1965, and translated into English as *Writings in Time of War* in 1968.

As for Teilhard's many essays collected in different books, these have been arranged thematically rather than chronologically, so that each volume offers material written during different years of Teilhard's life. These range from 1916-1955, except for *The Human Phenomenon* and *The Divine Milieu*, which were written as independent books. The mixture of essays from different years found in Teilhard's collected works makes the critical, chronological study of his thought a demanding task. Yet only such an analysis can retrace the origin and genetic unfolding of his ideas and grasp their full meaning.

Teilhard's scientific works, published in specialized scientific journals around the world, were collected together in a separate set of eleven volumes. A large number of letters from Teilhard's vast correspondence has also been published by now, yet more letters still remain to appear in print. Since Teilhard's death a large number of studies have been published in different languages; many study groups, lecture courses, conferences, seminars, broadcasts, and now documentary films, have been devoted to Teilhard, the planetary thinker, scientist, seer, and mystic.

Every decade the anniversary of his death leads to special celebrations. Now that it is sixty years since Teilhard passed away, what is left of his work and influence? What is his lasting legacy?

Is he still a seminal thinker, to be studied and taken seriously? Or has his influence passed, and have his key ideas been absorbed by others? Was he really a prophetic voice and a visionary whose works have attracted people from many different walks of life and countries, but whose real influence has been greatly hampered by the uncritical worship of many of his followers, or by the vitriolic attacks of his worst opponents? Or is even more damage being done by the well-meaning, but often misguided efforts of fellow Christians who want to domesticate his revolutionary insights by forcing them into the straightjacket of traditional orthodoxies?

Teilhard's legacy deserves to be rediscovered anew; it must be examined in a far more systematic and critical manner than has happened so far. This is a challenging task, given the unsystematic publication of his works, where little attention has been paid to the precision required for administering a true legacy. Of course, there can be no doubt that Teilhard's ideas are far better known in the twenty-first than in the twentieth century. There are more than half a million entries on Teilhard currently listed on the worldwide web—and the number increases daily. A younger generation is showing a new interest in the breath-taking range of Teilhard's thought, so much engaged with evolutionary becoming, with further cultural and spiritual evolution, with joint human responsibility for creating a sustainable future for all of humanity and planet earth. This raises questions of global governance, global ethics, of the further awakening of the human brain and the growth of consciousness, of transhumanism and the final summit of evolution, but also about the urgent need for a conscious nurturing of universal justice, peace, and love.

Teilhard reflected early in the twentieth century on the meaning of cultural and religious diversity, on global interdependence, and the growing "planetization" of the human community, on the significance of biodiversity, and the fragility of life on the planet. He also asked questions about the vital contribution of China in shaping the future of humanity.

It was amid the killing fields of the First World War that he first perceived the emergence of the "noosphere," of another, additional layer that encircles the planet like the biosphere, and is deeply embedded within it. It was shortly after the Second World War, and after many years of living in Asia, that Teilhard became actively involved in interfaith dialogue in Paris; yet like so many other details of his life, this is generally little known.

Where is Teilhard's legacy debated today, his prophetic voice listened to and taken note of? Where are his ideas experienced as energizing and empowering? Answers to these questions will depend on the respective standpoint and global location of each individual speaker, since it is impossible to provide a global overview. I will mention a few examples to illustrate where Teilhard's ideas have been influential in different areas of human creativity.

Scientists, philosophers, theologians, writers and poets, musicians, painters, sculptors, urban planners and environmentalists, retreat leaders and people from different faiths, broadcasters and filmmakers as well as countless college teachers and students have been inspired by Teilhard's ideas and example. Characters based on the figure of Teilhard have appeared in several novels, of which the earliest example, later followed by others, is probably the figure of Father Jean Telemond created by the Australian writer Morris West in *The Shoes of the Fisherman* (1963), made into a film in 1968. Most recently, Niels de Terra, son of the noted geologist Helmut de Terra, a colleague and friend of Teilhard's, has published a graphic novel called *Overkill: The Vatican Trial of Pierre Teilhard de Chardin, SJ* (2012).

Frank and Mary Frost of Frank Frost Productions LLC have for some time been working on a two-hour television biography, "The Evolution of Teilhard de Chardin," to be shown during the sixtieth anniversary of Teilhard's death in 2015,[349] while earlier documentaries about Teilhard's life were made in England and France.

The Maltese composer Charles Camilleri created a piano piece, "Noospheres," inspired by Teilhard. This was performed during Teilhard's birth centenary in 1981 at the Purcell Room in London, and also at the Centenary Celebration Concert organized by the British Teilhard Association in the concert hall of St. John's Smith Square, Westminster. The British composer Edmund Rubbra called his 1968 Symphony No. 8, "Hommage à Teilhard de Chardin," and he is quoted as having said that Teilhard's writings "opened so many doors, and gave to the history of man a purpose that I always instinctively felt was there . . . that I wished to pay homage to him the best way that I could, through a symphony."[350]

In Scotland, the composer Kenneth Leighton set Teilhard's "Hymn to Matter" to music for baritone solo, choir, strings and percussion, whereas Teilhard's "Hymn to the Universe" is the theme of a large stained glass window in the Martyrs' Church in St. Andrews, Scotland.

Many more examples are found in the visual arts. To list just a few, in 1962, the French painter Alfred Manessier created a brightly colored canvas entitled *L'Offrande de la Terre ou Hommage à Teilhard de Chardin*. The American sculptor Frederick Hart was much influenced by Teilhard's vision of evolution and consciousness in his masterwork "Ex Nihilo," completed after almost twenty years' work in 1990. These dynamic panels on "Creation," for which Hart is justly renowned, decorate the outside of Washington National Cathedral. Teilhard's influence can also be seen in some other works of Hart, especially his acrylic resin sculptures "The Divine Milieu" and "Christ: The Omega."

Another American sculptor and priest, Henry Setter, created a cast aluminium sculpture of the "Omega Point," placed near the entrance of the Roesch library at the University of Dayton.

The Italian American visionary architect Paolo Soleri, a disciple of Frank Lloyd Wright, was strongly influenced by Teilhard's ideas when he created his experimental eco-town Arcosanti in the center of Arizona. This includes a "Pierre Teilhard Cloister," described by Soleri as

a center designed for encounters and retreats for groups belonging to different faiths . . . possibly the first conscious and coherent attempt at gathering in one structure the use of passive solar energy, natural habitat and cultural-religious events traditionally given to temples or other spaces.[351]

The international diffusion of Teilhard's ideas has been much facilitated by conferences, publications, and networks of different national associations devoted to the study of Teilhard's works. In France the Fondation Teilhard de Chardin was set up in 1962 and located at the National Museum of Natural History in Paris. There is also the Association des Amis de Pierre Teilhard de Chardin (www.teilhard.fr) which publishes a regular journal, *Teilhard Aujourd'hui*. The British

Spirit of Fire

Teilhard Association (www.teilhard.org.uk), founded in 1963, published for many years excellent articles in *The Teilhard Review* (1966-1994), still found in many university libraries. The American Teilhard Association (www.teilharddechardin.org), founded in 1967, publishes a bi-annual newsletter, *Teilhard Perspective*. This provides fresh insights for understanding Teilhard's remarkable evolutionary vision, often in ways that directly relate to an ecologically and spiritually sustainable Earth community. It also publishes a regular series of essays, *Teilhard Studies*, which engage in lively debate with different aspects of Teilhard's thought.

By now a large number of academic studies and dissertations on Teilhard's thought have been written, listed in numerous bibliographies in different languages. To give one example, during the period of 1959-1972 when Teilhard's writings became first widely available in North America, over five hundred primary and secondary works were published on them in the United States alone.[352]

The contemporary renewal of interest in Teilhard is perhaps stronger in the United States than elsewhere. This is not only evident from the activities of the American Teilhard Association, but also from several edited collections of essays that have been published in the United States during the last decade. Beginning with *Teilhard in the 21st Century: The Emerging Spirit of Earth* (eds. Arthur Fabel and Donald St. John, 2003), followed by *Rediscovering Teilhard's Fire* (ed. Kathleen Duffy, S.S.J., 2010) and *The Legacy of Pierre Teilhard de Chardin* (eds. James Salmon, SJ, and John Farina, 2011) where special emphasis is given to Teilhard's legacy in science. It has now been further enriched by reflections on how to take Teilhard's major ideas forward, as in Kathleen Duffy's *Teilhard's Mysticism: Seeing the Inner Face of Evolution* (2014) and Ilia Delio's edited collection *From Teilhard to Omega: Co-creating an Unfinished Universe* (2014).

Comparisons can be made between Teilhardian ideas and process thought, especially regarding the shared legacy of Teilhard and Alfred North Whitehead. A Teilhardian influence is also noticeable in some parts of the ecological movement, especially in the works of the great "geologian" Thomas Berry and those of the cosmologist Brian Swimme, who wrote the Foreword to the new translation of *The Human Phenomenon*. Elements of a truly balanced ecological spirituality are present in many of Teilhard's writings, as is evident from the essays in Celia Deane-Drummond's edited book *Pierre Teilhard de Chardin on People and Planet* (2006).[353] Some of the thoughts expressed in the Earth Charter, aimed to ensure the future of the community of life on our planet, would have deeply resonated with Teilhard. How he would have rejoiced seeing this document, created by the most participatory consultation process ever conducted in connection with an international statement.

Another area of great importance is Teilhard's understanding of the mutual embeddedness of the biosphere and noosphere, the continuity between the latter and the former, yet also the specificity of the human sphere of thinking and action which includes aspects of what we today call eco-justice and social justice, animated above all by the transformative and healing powers of love. The relationship between biosphere and noosphere has been researched by some environmental scientists who have shown how the idea of the "noosphere," a word created by Teilhard and his philosopher friend Édouard Le Roy in the early 1920s, caught on with several scientific writers, especially in Russia, and with some users of the Internet, more so than with traditional academics.[354]

For Teilhard, the noosphere has a deeply spiritual dimension which he expressed as the presence of "the divine milieu," a field of divine energy and a central focal point that is both immanent and wholly transcendent at the same time, culminating in the Omega point, the ultimate summit of all evolutionary development.

This brings me finally to the most powerful influence of all, Teilhard's personal experience and example of a vivid love for life, fed by an ardent zest and deep hope, not due to an easy optimism and superficial belief in progress. Teilhard encouraged people again and again to develop a new kind of "seeing," a deep inner vision of

Omega Point. (University of Dayton Marketing and Communications Department, photo by Laurence Burgess)

heightened consciousness drawing us forward into a new future, a realm of new emergence and possibilities.[355] He wanted to share with others what he saw and felt so deeply; he called all fellow human beings to follow "the road of fire" and become passionately involved in the further evolution of the human species.

His was a passionate, practically oriented spirituality and mysticism linked to the dynamism of the modern world, but also firmly anchored and centered in his vision of the cosmic Christ. It is particularly this aspect of a deeply personal Christian faith rooted in the cosmos and related to the vivid dynamism of contemporary secularity that attracts many of his followers.

More than anything else Teilhard praised the spiritual energies available to us, including the energies of suffering, but above all the energies of love, so indispensable for feeding our zest for life, for transforming the world and ourselves, for creating a viable, sustainable future. He suggested that we study these energies in a much more systematic and scientific way than has been done hitherto. He is not alone in thinking this; remarkable parallels can be found in the writings of the sociologist Pitirim A. Sorokin, and to some extent also in the Russian theologian Pavel Florenskij. Other parallels exist between Teilhard's thought and the Hindu thinker Sri Aurobindo, as also the Muslim philosopher, poet, and politician, Sir Muhammad Iqbal.

Pierre Teilhard de Chardin was a truly modern mystic who combined science and mysticism in teaching a mysticism of action and transformation by "communion with God through the world." Throughout the vicissitudes of his life he remained single-mindedly focused on "the only thing needful" to give meaning and direction, unswerving hope, trust, and love: the empowering spark of divine presence that was alive in him until the end. He realized early that the spiritual energy resources available to contemporary humanity have to be drawn from all cultural, philosophical, religious, and spiritual traditions, and not from one faith alone. In contemporary works on spirituality Teilhard is rarely given the careful attention he deserves as a creative thinker in this field, as someone who embodies some of the best Christian spiritual practice combined with an all-embracing, universal vision.

Let us celebrate the unique legacy and singularity of Pierre Teilhard de Chardin. Let us rejoice that the Catholic tradition has brought forth such a man of faith and dynamic vision wherein science, religion, and mysticism are so creatively interrelated. As John Grim and Mary Evelyn Tucker have written:

> Teilhard achieved a radical reconceptualization of the mystical journey as an entry into evolution, discovering there an immanental communion with the Divine . . . Teilhard's mysticism is activated . . . in scientific investigation and social commitment to research as well as in a comprehensive compassion for all life.[356]

Far from being outlived and passé, Teilhard's innovative ideas and powerful spiritual vision will attract further waves of interest during the twenty-first century. His daring thought and probing questions can greatly enrich contemporary discussions and initiatives that seek to shape the future of people and planet. His shining example of courage, endurance, fidelity, and a relentless search for the truth provides a strong witness to the life-giving powers of a deep religious faith combined with brilliant intellectual and personal gifts that were passionately dedicated to the hopes, desires, and strivings of the vast, evolving world we live in.

Select Bibliographical and Electronic Resources

Collected Works in French and English

Le Phénomène Humain	1955	*The Phenomenon of Man*	1959
		The Human Phenomenon (new English translation)	1999
L'Apparition de l'Homme	1956	*The Appearance of Man*	1965
La Vision du Passé	1957	*The Vision of the Past*	1966
Le Milieu Divin	1957	*Le Milieu Divin* (or The Divine Milieu)	1960
L'Avenir de l'Homme	1959	*The Future of Man*	1964
L'Énergie Humaine	1962	*Human Energy*	1969
L'Activation de l'Énergie	1963	*Activation of Energy*	1970
La Place de l'Homme dans la Nature	1963	*Man's Place in Nature*	1966
Science et Christ	1965	*Science and Christ*	1968
Comment Je Crois	1969	*Christianity and Evolution*	1971
Les Directions de l'Avenir	1973	*Toward the Future*	1975
Écrits du Temps de la Guerre	1976	*Writings in Time of War*	1968*
Le Coeur de la Matière	1976	*The Heart of the Matter*	1978

L'Oeuvre Scientifique, 11 vols., eds. N. & K. Schmitz-Moormann, Olten, 1971.
Pierre Teilhard de Chardin, Writings Selected with an Introduction by Ursula King. Modern Spiritual Masters Series, Maryknoll, NY: Orbis Books, 1999.

---

* This translation is based on an earlier French edition of the war essays, published by Éditions Grasset, Paris, 1965.

Select Collections of Letters

The Making of a Mind: Letters from a Soldier-Priest (1914-1919), ed. Marguerite Teillard-Chambon. London: Collins, 1965.
The Letters of Teilhard de Chardin and Lucile Swan, eds Th. M. King, S.J., and M. Wood Gilbert. Foreword by P. Leroy, SJ. Washington, DC: Georgetown University Press, 1993.

Letters from a Traveller (1923-1955), ed. C. Aragonnès. London: Collins, 1962 and 1966.
Letters to Two Friends (1926-1952), ed. R. d'Ouince. London: Collins, 1972.
Letters to Léontine Zanta (1923-1939), eds R. Garric & H. de Lubac. London: Collins, 1969.

Biographies

The foremost Teilhard scholar in France was Claude Cuénot, son of the great biologist Lucien Cuénot, who knew Teilhard well. Claude Cuénot wrote the first biography of Teilhard, published in Paris in 1958. The first biography in English was by the Anglican theologian Charles Raven. The major biographies where more information on Teilhard as a person and thinker can be found, are listed below. Several are now out of print and only available in libraries:

Claude Cuénot. *Teilhard de Chardin: A Biographical Study.* London: Burns & Oates, 1965.

Charles E. Raven. *Teilhard de Chardin Scientist and Seer.* London: Collins, 1962.

Robert Speaight. *Teilhard de Chardin: A Biography.* London: Collins, 1967.

Mary Lukas and Ellen Lukas. *Teilhard: A Biography.* New York: Doubleday, and London: Collins, 1977.

Günther Schiwy. *Teilhard de Chardin: Sein Leben und seine Zeit.* 2 vols. Munich: Kösel Verlag, 1981.

Édith de la Héronniére, *Teilhard de Chardin. Une mystique de la traversée.* Paris: Pygmalion, Gérard Watelet, 1999.

Patrice Boudignon, *Pierre Teilhard de Chardin. Sa vie, son oeuvre, sa réflexion.* Paris: Les Éditions du Cerf, 2008.

Helpful Reference Works

Baudry, G.-H. *Dictionnaire des correspondants de Teilhard de Chardin.* Lille: G.-H. Baudry, 1974. Informative biographical sketches on Teilhard's correspondents for letters published until 1974.

Cowell, Siôn, *The Teilhard Lexicon: Understanding the Language, Terminology and Vision of the Writings of Pierre Teilhard de Chardin.* Brighton and Portland, OR: Sussex Academic Press, 2001. Most helpful for brief explanations of Teilhard's major concepts.

Montavani, F., *Dizinario delle Opere di Teilhard de Chardin.* Verona: Gabrielli editori, 2006. The only survey of all Teilhard's essays and books in strict chronological order, including a brief summary of the main ideas of each work.

Books Relating to Teilhard's Life and Thought

Aczel, A. D. *The Jesuit & the Skull: Teilhard de Chardin, Evolution, and the Search for Peking Man.* New York: Riverhead Books, 2007.

Deane-Drummond, C., ed., *Pierre Teilhard de Chardin on People and Planet.* London and Oakville, CT: Equinox, 2006.

Delio, Ilia, ed., *From Teilhard to Omega.* Co-creating an Unfinished Universe. Maryknoll, NY: Orbis Books, 2014.

Duffy, K., SSJ, ed., *Rediscovering Teilhard's Fire.* Philadelphia: St Joseph's University Press, 2010.

Duffy, K., SSJ, *Teilhard's Mysticism. Seeing the Inner Face of Evolution.* Maryknoll, NY: Orbis Books, 2014.

Fabel, A. and D. St. John, eds, *Teilhard in the 21st Century: The Emerging Spirit of Earth.* Maryknoll, NY: Orbis Books, 2003. See pp. 57-73 for Thomas Berry, "Teilhard in the Ecological Age."

Galleni, L. *Darwin, Teilhard de Chardin e gli alteri . . . Le tre teorie dell'evoluzione.* Ghezzano, PI: Felici Editore, 2010.

Grumett, D. *Teilhard de Chardin. Theology, Humanity and Cosmos.* Leuven (Louvain) and Dudley, MA: Peeters, 2005.

Haught, J. F., *Christianity and Science. Toward a Theology of Nature.* Maryknoll, NY: Orbis Books, 2007; see especially chp. 5, "Teilhard de Chardin and the Promise of Nature."

Haught, J. F., *Making Sense of Evolution. Darwin, God, and the Drama of Life.* Louisville, KY: Westminster John Knox Press, 2010.

King, Th. M. *Teilhard's Mass: Approaches to "Mass on the World."* New York, Mahwah, NJ: Paulist Press, 2005.

King, U. *Teilhard de Chardin and Eastern Religions. Spirituality and Mysticism in an Evolutionary World.* New York/ Mahwah, NJ: Paulist Press, 2011. This book contains an annotated Study Guide (pp. 363-415) dealing with Teilhard's thought and writings. It is divided into six sections: 1. Teilhard's Life and Thought. 2. His China Years, Paleontology, and Peking Man. 3. Science, Evolution, Biosphere, Noosphere, and Ecosphere. 4. Religious Pluralism and Interreligious Dialogue. 5. Spirituality and Mysticism. 6. Teilhard's Legacy.

Lubac, H. de, *The Religion of Teilhard de Chardin.* London: Collins, 1967.

Meynard, Th., ed. T*eilhard and the Future of Humanity.* New York: Fordham University Press, 2006.

Process Studies 35/1 (2006). Special number on *Teilhard de Chardin and Process Thought.*

Salmon, J., SJ, and J. Farina, eds, *The Legacy of Pierre Teilhard de Chardin.* New York/ Mahwah, NJ: Paulist Press, 2011.

Savary, L. M. *Teilhard de Chardin,* The Milieu Divin *Explained: A Spirituality for the 21st Century.* New York / Mahwah, NJ: Paulist Press, 2007.

Skehan, J. W. *Praying with Teilhard de Chardin.* Winona, MN: St. Mary's Press, 2001.

Electronic Resources

International associations:

www.teilhard.fr provides information about the activities of the French Association.

www.teilhard-world.com provides information about their international outreach.

www.teilhard.org.uk is the official website of the British Teilhard Association.

www.teilharddechardin.org is the official website of the American Teilhard Association.

Other helpful sites:

www.teilhardforbeginners.com was established by Lou Savary, author of several books on Teilhard's spirituality.

www.teilhardproject.com provides wide-ranging information linked to "The Teilhard de Chardin Project" and was developed by by Frank Frost Productions and their international advisers in connection with a television biography on "The Evolution of Teilhard de Chardin."

A very helpful, extensive discussion of "Teilhard de Chardin and Transhumanism" by Eric Steinhart is found in the electronic *Journal of Evolution and Technology* 20/1 (December 2008), 1-22; see http://jetpress.org/v20/steinhart.htm

www.onbeing.org/program/teilhard-de-chardins-planetary-mind-and-our-spiritual-evolution/4965/ audio is an NPR program in the series "On Being" hosted by Krista Tippett which can be downloaded. It includes interviews with Andrew Revkin, David Sloan Wilson, and Ursula King.

Several times a year, the University of California San Diego hosts a Burke Lecture on Religion and Society. Several of these relate to Teilhard de Chardin; see http://ucsd.tv/series for Burke Lectureship on Religion and Society. Some may also be found on YouTube: see www.youtube.com.

Many library holdings can be searched electronically for data on Teilhard de Chardin. Most helpful is www.worldcat.org, a composite collection of information from some 71,000 libraries, that can be sorted by date, author and title. Their Teilhard page is: http://worldcat.org/identities/lccn-n79-32934.

Copies of American editions of Teilhard's collected works and letters can be found at the

Internet Archive (www.archive.org) by adding the titles of individual works. For example: http://archive.org/details/TheDivineMilieu or http://archive.org/details/ChristianityAndEvolution or http://archive.org.details/WritingsInTimeOfWar.

Abbreviations

AE   Pierre Teilhard de Chardin. *Activation of Energy*. London: Collins, 1970.

AM   Pierre Teilhard de Chardin. *The Appearance of Man*. London: Collins, 1965.

CATL   *The Teilhard de Chardin Centenary Exhibition Catalogue*. London, 1983.

CE   Pierre Teilhard de Chardin. *Christianity and Evolution*. London: Collins, 1971.

CU   Claude Cuénot. *Teilhard de Chardin: A Biographical Study*. London: Burns & Oates, 1965.

FM   Pierre Teilhard de Chardin. *The Future of Man*. London: Collins, 1965.

HE   Pierre Teilhard de Chardin. *Human Energy*. London: Collins, 1969.

HM   Pierre Teilhard de Chardin. *The Heart of Matter*. London: Collins, 1978.

HPh   Pierre Teilhard de Chardin. *The Human Phenomenon*. A New Edition and Translation of *Le phénomène humain* by Sarah Appleton-Weber with a Foreword by Brian Swimme. Brighton & Portland, OR & Sussex Academic Press, 1999.

HU   Pierre Teilhard de Chardin. *Hymn of the Universe*. London: Collins Fontana Books, 1970.

LAG   Teilhard de Chardin. *Lettres à l'Abbé Gaudefroy et à l'Abbé Breuil*. Monaco: Editions Rocher, 1988.

LF   Pierre Leroy. *Lettres familières de Pierre Teilhard de Chardin mon ami 1948-1955*. Paris: Le Centurion, 1976.

LI   Pierre Teilhard de Chardin. *Lettres intimes à Auguste Valensin, Bruno de Solages, Henri de Lubac 1919-1955*. Paris: Aubier Montaigne, 1976.

LLZ   Pierre Teilhard de Chardin. *Letters to Léontine Zanta*. Introductions by Robert Garric and Henri de Lubac. London: Collins, 1969.

LT   Pierre Teilhard de Chardin. *Letters from a Traveller*. London: Collins, 1962.

LTF   Pierre Teilhard de Chardin. *Letters to Two Friends 1926-1952*. London: Collins Fontana, 1972.

LTLS   Thomas M. King, S.J., and Mary Wood Gilbert, eds., *The Letters of Teilhard de Chardin and Lucile Swan*. Washington, D.C.: Georgetown University Press, 1993.

MD   Pierre Teilhard de Chardin. *Le Milieu Divin: An Essay on the Interior Life*. London: Collins, 1963.

MM   Pierre Teilhard de Chardin. *The Making of a Mind: Letters from a Soldier-Priest*. London: Collins, 1965.

Mortier   Pierre Teilhard de Chardin. *Lettres à Jeanne Mortier*. Paris: Éditions du Seuil, 1984.

OSc   Pierre Teilhard de Chardin. *L'Oeuvre Scientifique*. Olten: Walter Verlag, 1971.

SC   Pierre Teilhard de Chardin. *Science and Christ*. London: Collins, 1968.

TAL   Jeanne Mortier and Marie-Louise Aboux, eds., *Teilhard de Chardin Album*. London: Collins, 1966.

Terra   Helmut de Terra. *Memories of Teilhard de Chardin*. London: Scientific Book Club, 1964.

TF   Pierre Teilhard de Chardin. *Toward the Future*. London: Collins, 1975.

WTW   Pierre Teilhard de Chardin. *Writings in Time of War*. London: Collins, 1968.

Notes

1. Jeanne Mortier and Marie-Louise Aboux, eds., *Teilhard de Chardin Album* (London: Collins, 1966), 15. Hereafter TAL.

2. Quoted in Claude Cuénot, *Teilhard de Chardin: A Biographical Study* (London: Burns & Oates, 1965), 3. Hereafter CU.

3. P. Teilhard de Chardin, *The Heart of Matter* (London: Collins, 1978), 16; my translation. Hereafter HM.

4. CU, 3.

5. HM, 16.

6. HM, 17.

7. Quoted in TAL, 18.

8. Quoted in CU, 5.

9. P. Teilhard de Chardin, *Writings in Time of War* (London: Collins, 1968), 198. Hereafter WTW.

10. Quoted in TAL, 20.

11. Quoted in CU, 6.

12. WTW, 60.

13. P. Teilhard de Chardin, *Journal 26 août 1915-4 janvier 1919* (Paris: Fayard, 1975), 49: entry for March 5, 1915; my translation.

14. HM, 75.

15. HM, 46.

16. Quoted in TAL, 33.

17. CU, 8.

18. Quoted in TAL, 35.

19. A line from *Cosmic Life* quoted in CU, 10.

20. Quoted in TAL, 36.

21. Françoise Teilhard de Chardin, *Lettres et témoignages* (Paris: Éditions Beauchesne, 1975), 176; my translation.

22. Quoted in CU, 13.

23. P. Teilhard de Chardin, Lettres d'Hastings et de Paris 1908-1914 (Paris: Aubier, 1965), 43; my translation.

24. HM, 25f.

25. Quoted in TAL, 42.

26. Quoted in TAL, 44.

27. HM, 25.

28. HM, 25.

29. HM, 26f.

30. HM, 27.

31. HM, 25.

32. I have analyzed Teilhard's fundamental change of perspective in more detail elsewhere: see Ursula King, "A Vision Transformed: Teilhard de Chardin's Evolutionary Awakening at Hastings." *The Heythrop Journal* 54/4 (July 2013), 590-605. The quotations are found in P. Teilhard de Chardin, *The Future of Man* (London: Collins, 1965), 84f. Hereafter FM.

33. CU, 17f.

34. *The Teilhard de Chardin Centenary Exhibition Catalogue* (London, 1983), 57. Hereafter CATL.

35. Quoted in CU, 18. Original text in P. Teilhard de Chardin, *L'Oeuvre Scientifique* (Olten: Walter Verlag, 1971), 1:421f. Hereafter OSc.

36. Quoted in TAL, 48.

37. Quoted in CATL, 58.

38. CATL, 58.

39. Quoted in P. Teilhard de Chardin, *Letters from Paris 1912-1914* (New York: Herder and Herder, 1967). See p. 105, n. 2. Also quoted by Cuénot; see CU, 21. For a detailed discussion of Teilhard's involvement with the discovery of Piltdown Man see Noel Keith Roberts, *From Piltdown Man to Point Omega. The Evolutionary Theory of Teilhard de Chardin* (New York: Peter Lang, 2000), 15-24.

40. P. Teilhard de Chardin, *The Making of a Mind: Letters from a Soldier-Priest* (London: Collins, 1965), 47f. Hereafter MM.

41. MM, 54, 26, 30, 31.

42. MM, 53. Teilhard's cousin Marguerite has provided an excellent essay on Teilhard's experience of the war on which I have drawn in this chapter; see "The Great War 1914-1919," MM, 23-39. For more information on the work of stretcher-bearers see the informative study of Emily Mayhew, *Wounded. The Long Journey Home from the Great War* (London: Vintage Books, 2014)

43. MM, 125.

44. WTW, 93.

45. Signed Douaumont, October 14, 1916, the essay was completed ten days before the French recaptured the fort of Douaumont at Verdun; P. Teilhard de Chardin, *Hymn of the Universe* (London: Collins Fontana Books, 1970), 51. Hereafter HU.

46. TAL, 55.

47. Quoted in TAL, 54. Teilhard's substantial war journal is only available in French. See P. Teilhard de Chardin, *Journal 26 août 1915-4 janvier 1919* (Olten: Walter Verlag, 1971 & Paris: Fayard, 1975).

48. WTW, 32. See Thomas Berry, *The Great Work. Our Way into the Future* (New York: Bell Tower, 1999). See also Thomas Berry: *Selected Writings on the Earth Community*. Selected with an Introduction by Mary Evelyn Tucker and John Grim. Maryknoll, NY: Orbis Books, 2014.

49. Facsimile of the first essay in French found in P. Teilhard de Chardin, *Écrits du temps de la guerre* (Paris: Grasset, 1965); my translation. This passage is not reproduced in WTW.

50. WTW, 14 (partly my translation). 69, 70.

51. HU, 62

52. MM, 267.

53. WTW, 91.

54. HU, 42.

55. HU, 43.

56. HU, 43.

57. HU, 50.

58. HU, 49.

59. WTW, 120, 121.

60. WTW, 124.

61. WTW, 129

62. WTW, 130.

63. WTW, 122.

64. WTW, 137.

65. *"Jesus must be loved as a world,"* see WTW, 148. For Kathleen Duffy's interpretation of "The Mystical Milieu," see her book *Teilhard's Mysticism. Seeing the Inner Face of Evolution* (Maryknoll, NY: Orbis Books, 2014).

66. See Gerard Manley Hopkins's poems "God's Grandeur" and "As Kingfishers Catch Fire, Dragonflies Draw Flame."

67. CU, 42.

68. WTW, 147.

69. Quoted in C. Rivière, *Teilhard, Claudel et Mauriac* (Paris: Éditions Universitaires, 1963), 52f.

70. MM, 155f.

71. Paris: Grasset, 1965. The English *Writings in Time of War*, 1968 (WTW) contain only a selection of thirteen essays; others are found in HU and HM.

72. HM, 175.

73. HM, 177.

74. HM, 179.

75. HM, 179.

76. WTW, 222.

77. WTW, 205, 207.

78. WTW, 218, 219.

79. HU, 59.

80. WTW, 201.

81. MM, 195; my translation.

82. HM, 59.

83. HM, 41.

84. WTW, 198.

85. WTW, 199.

86. HM, 58; my translation.

87. HM, 58.

88. WTW, 193f.; see P. Teilhard de Chardin, "The Eternal Feminine," WTW, 191-202.

89. HM, 59.

90. HM, 59f.

91. WTW, 117f.

92. WTW, 120.

93. MM, 197f.

94. MM, 282f.

95. MM, 248.

96. MM, 251.

97. P. Teilhard de Chardin, *Letters to Léontine Zanta*, introduction by Robert Garric (*"Père Teilhard and Mademoiselle Zanta"*) and Henri de Lubac (*"The Trial of Faith"*), (London: Collins, 1969). Hereafter LLZ.

98. Henri de Lubac in LLZ, 19.

99. Letter of July 4, 1920, quoted in CU, 34. See also the numerous letters written by Teilhard to Abbé Gaudefroy and Abbé Breuil between 1923 and 1955: P. Teilhard de Chardin, *Lettres Inédites. Lettres à l'Abbé Gaudefroy et à l'Abbé Breuil* (Monaco: Éditions du Rocher, 1988). Hereafter LAG.

100. Quoted in CU, 58. In his biography, Cuénot quotes from Teilhard's letters to Le Roy (see CU, 58-59) which are now published: Pierre Teilhard de Chardin, *Lettres à Édouard Le Roy (1921-1946)*. Maturation d'une pensée. Introduction de François Euvé, S.J. Éditions Facultés Jésuites de Paris, 2008. The original French text of these quotations is found in the Teilhard-Le Roy correspondence on pp. 136 and 42.

101. TAL, 64.

102. Quoted in CU, 40.

103. HU, 64f.

104. See his essay "Pantheism and Christianity" (1923), in P. Teilhard de Chardin, *Christianity and Evolution* (London: Collins, 1971), 56. Hereafter CE. See also a later essay of 1944 dealing with the same theme in its conclusion on "Christianity and Pantheism, CE, 171f.

105. CE, 68.

106. CE, 65.

107. CE, 64; written in 1923.

108. Quoted in CU, 38; this is a passage from the essay "The Great Monad" in HM, 182-195.

109. P. Teilhard de Chardin, *The Vision of the Past* (London: Collins, 1966), 78.

110. Quoted in CU, 59.

111. P. Teilhard de Chardin, *Letters from a Traveller* (ed. Claude Arragonnès [his cousin Marguerite Teillard-Chambon's pen-name], London: Collins, 1962) contains letters written between 1923 and 1955 to Marguerite and some other recipients. The letters are preceded by essays on Teilhard, "The Thinker" (Julian Huxley), "The Man" (Pierre Leroy, S.J.), "The Traveller" (Claude Arragonnès). Hereafter referred to as LT. See LT, 74 for the quotation from a letter written on 25 May, 1923 to Abbé Breuil.

112. O. D. Rasmussen, *Tientsin: An Illustrated History* (Tientsin: Tientsin Press, 1925), 254.

113. LT, 73.

114. LAG, 125; my translation.

115. LT, 100.

116. Quoted in CU, 137.

117. CU, 48.

118. Quoted in CU, 52.

119. LT, 81.

120. LT, 83.

121. HM, 47; LT, 88.

122. HM, 47.

123. LT, 89f.

124. LT, 101.

125. LLZ, 52.

126. HM, 119. The "The Mass on the World" is found in Teilhard's book *The Heart of Matter* (HM, 119-134, published in 1978) from which I quote here. An earlier publication appeared in *Hymn of the Universe* (HU, 19-35, published in 1970). The Belgian Scheut missionary and linguist, W. A. Grootaers, who spent many years in China, wrote an illuminating article explaining the setting of this text: "When and Where was the 'Mass on the World' written?" *Teilhard Review* 12/3 (1977), 91-94.

127. HM, 119f.

128. HM, 131f.

129. HM, 133.

130. LT, 86.

131. LLZ, 52

132. Huxley is quoted in HU, 9; for Thomas M. King's spiritual reflections see his book T*eilhard's Mass: Approaches to "Mass on the World."* (Mahwah, NJ: Paulist Press, 2005).

133. LT, 85f.

134. P. Teilhard de Chardin, *Letters to Two Friends 1926-1952* (London: Collins Fontana, 1972). This book is divided into two sections offering a selection rather than the complete set of letters written to these two friends, whose names are not mentioned in the book: Letters I (1926-1952) are known to be addressed to Ida Treat, and Letters II (1938-1950) are addressed to Rhoda de Terra whom Teilhard met later. Quotations from this correspondence are hereafter referred to as LTF. Over the years, more work has been done on both recipients, most recently by John Cowburn, S.J., l who published more details about both Ida Treat and Rhoda de Terra in his book *Pierre Teilhard de Chardin. A Selective Summary of His Life* (Mosaic Press, Preston, Vic. 3072, Australia, 2013). After the Second World War, Dr. Ida Treat (1889-1978) returned from France to the USA where she taught at Vassar College in Poughkeepsie until her retirement in 1954. She continued to live there until her death.

135. LTF, 43f.

136. P. Teilhard de Chardin, *Science and Christ* (London: Collins, 1968), 38. Hereafter SC. For the important essay "My Universe" (1924), see SC, 37-85.

137. See " Note on Some Possible Historical Representations of Original Sin", CE, 45-55. This note is not precisely dated, but described as having been written "Before Easter 1922."

138. Quoted from a note Teilhard had written to sum up his position, cited in Henri de Lubac's essay on "The Trial of Faith" in LLZ, 29.

139. P. Teilhard de Chardin, *Lettres intimes à Auguste Valensin, Bruno de Solages, Henri de Lubac 1919-1955* (Paris: Aubier Montaigne, 1976), 115. Hereafter LI. The quotations from these letters are my translations.

140. Quoted in CATL, 37.

141. LI, 117.

142. LI, 122.

143. In LLZ, 30; see H. de Lubac's excellent essay "The Trial of Faith" which precedes Teilhard's *Letters to Léontine Zanta*, 27-44.

144. René d'Ouince, S.J., in LTF, 5. Père d'Ouince knows the story well. He was Teilhard's Jesuit superior in Paris after the Second World War and wrote the "Prologue" to *Letters to Léontine Zanta* (see 3-19). Even more details can be found in his remarkable study *Un prophète en procès; Teilhard de Chardin dans l'église de son temps* (Paris: Aubier-Montaigne 1970) where Teilhard's great crisis of the mid-1920s is discussed in the two chapters "Sur la liste des suspects" (100-119) and "L'épreuve de l'obéissance" (120-137).

145. See "My Universe," SC, 74.

146. LT, 133f.

147. LTF, 44.

148. P. Teilhard de Chardin, *Le Milieu Divin: An Essay on the Interior Life* (London: Collins, 1963), 121. Hereafter MD. A very helpful introduction and commentary on this spiritual classic has been provided by Louis M. Savary, *Teilhard de Chardin* The Divine Milieu *Explained. A Spirituality for the 21st Century* (New York, Mahwah, NJ: Paulist Press, 2007).

149. MD, 94.

150. SC, 74.

151. MD, 136f.

152. MD, 152f.

153. Quoted in CU, 69.

154. Quoted in CU, 77.

155. LLZ, 80.

156. LLZ, 70, 78f.

157. LTF, 70. Teilhard published two articles anonymously in the Indian journal *The Week* which are not included in his published works. Further information on these can be found in Ursula King, "Teilhard's Attitude towards the Modernization in China—Two Documents from 1927," *The Teilhard Review*, 16, 1-2 (1981), 6-15.

158. SC, 86f.

159. SC, 97.

160. LI, 181; quoted in TAL, 80.

161. Quoted in CU, 93.

162. Quoted in TAL, 81.

163. Quoted in CATL, 38.

164. "The Sense of Man" (1929), in P. Teilhard de Chardin, *Toward the Future* (London: Collins, 1975), 13-39, hereafter TF; see TF, 13 for the quotation.

165. TF, 38f.

166. LT, 165f.

167. CU, 78.

168. OSc 2:868.

169. LT, 154.

170. Quoted in CU, 81.

171. LT, 155.

172. CU, 97.

173. Jia Lanpo and Huang Weiwen, *The Story of Peking Man: From Archaeology to Mystery* (Beijing: Foreign Languages Press, and Hong Kong: Oxford University Press, 1990), 249, 250, 251. See Amir D. Aczel, *The Jesuit and the Skull: Teilhard de Chardin, Evolution, and the Search for Peking Man* (New York: Riverhead Books, Penguin, 2007).

174. P. Teilhard de Chardin, *The Appearance of Man* (London: Collins, 1965), 59f. Hereafter AM. This quotation comes from Teilhard's article "Sinanthropus Pekinensis. An Important Discovery in Human Palaeontology." Written in April 1930, it was published in the French journal *Revue des Questions Scientifiques*, 20 July, 1930; reprinted in AM, 58-67.

175. LAG, 86.

176. George B. Barbour, *In the Field with Teilhard de Chardin* (New York: Herder and Herder, 1965), 23.

177. LT, 170.

178. P. Teilhard de Chardin, *Human Energy* (London: Collins, 1969) Hereafter HE. For "The Spirit of the Earth" (1931), see HE, 19-47. The quotations are from HE, 42, 43, 44.

179. LT, 180.

180. Comment by G. M. Haardt, the expedition leader, quoted in TAL, 114.

181. LT, 189.

182. LT, 190.

183. LT, 192.

184. LT, 192.

185. CU, 131.

186. LT, 177f.

187. He also mentioned the "eastern" and "western" solution in a letter to Léontine Zanta on March 20, 1932 (see LLZ, 108). His essay "The Road of the West: To a New Mysticism" (TF, 40-59) was completed in September 1932. Teilhard's different approaches to eastern and western mysticism are examined in great detail in my book *Teilhard de Chardin and Eastern Religions. Spirituality and Mysticism in an Evolutionary World*. Foreword by Joseph Needham (New York/Mahwah, NJ: Paulist Press, 2011).

188. LTF, 45.

189. CU, 74.

190. Thomas M. King, S.J., and Mary Wood Gilbert, eds., *The Letters of Teilhard de Chardin and Lucile Swan* (Washington, D.C.: Georgetown University Press, 1993), hereafter LTLS. The quotation comes from LTLS, 1. For a commentary, see Ursula King, *The Letters of Teilhard de Chardin and Lucile Swan: A Personal Interpretation*, Teilhard Studies No. 32 (Lewisburg, PA.: American Teilhard Association, Fall 1995).

191. CU, 106, 107.

192. LTLS, 7. The quotations are as written by Teilhard in English.

193. LTLS, 9.

194. LLZ, 34f.

195. LTLS, 17.

196. LTLS, 19.

197. LTLS, 19.

198. LTLS, 20.

199. LTLS, 19.

200. LI, 143.

201. See "The Evolution of Chastity," TF, 60-87; the quotation is from TF, 66.

202. TF, 84f.

203. See TF, 80f., 82, 84, 86f. The last, often quoted passage about harnessing the energies of love provides the background for the inspiring study by Anne Hillman, *Awakening the Energies of Love. Discovering Fire for the Second Time* (Putney, VT: Brambling Books, 2008). See also Ursula King, "Love—A Higher Form of Human Energy in the Work of Teilhard de Chardin and Sorokin," *Zygon Journal of Religion and Science*, 39/1 (2004), 77-102.

204. LTLS, 63. For the essays mentioned see "Christology and Evolution (1933), CE, 76-95; "How I Believe" (1934), CE, 96-132; "Sketch of a Personalistic Universe" (1936), HE, 53-92; "The Phenomenon of Spirituality (1937), HE, 93-112; "Human Energy" (1937), HE, 113-162; "The Mysticism of Science" (1939), HE, 163-181.

205. LTLS, 118.

206. Quoted in TAL, 144.

207. CU, 143.

208. "The Significance and Positive Value of Suffering," HE, 48-52; the quotations are from HE, 48, 51.

209. LT, 206.

210. CE, 94.

211. LT, 206.

212. LTLS, 11.

213. Jia Lanpo and Huang Weiwen, *The Story of Peking Man*, 246.

214. CU, 158.

215. "How I Believe," CE, 96-132; see CE, 97, 129, 131 for the quotations.

216. LTLS, 25.

217. LTLS, 45.

218. Helmut de Terra, *Memories of Teilhard de Chardin* (London: The Scientific Book Club, 1964), 66. Hereafter referred to as Terra.

219. TAL, 135.

220. See LTF, 121-218.

221. TAL, 136.

222. CATL, 43.

223. LTLS, 60.

224. LT, 227.

225. CU, 135f.

226. This was written in a preface to a book about his sister's life, published in 1950. See "The Spiritual Energy of Suffering" in P. Teilhard de Chardin, *Activation of Energy* (London: Collins, 1970), 245-249. Hereafter AE. The quotation is from AE, 249.

227. TAL, 140.

228. For "Some Reflexions on the Conversion of the World" (1936), see SC, 118-127. A note says that "This report was asked for by a member of the Apostolic Delegation in China." HE, 118,

229. Terra, 70.

230. Quoted in CU, 160.

231. "The Phenomenon of Spirituality," HE, 93-112; see HE, 112 for the quotation.

232. HE, 106f.

233. HE, 110.

234. See the essay "Human Energy," HE, 113-162; the quotation is from HE, 135.

235. HE, 139, 137.

236. HE, 147f.

237. Terra, 97.

238. CATL, 44.

239. LTLS, 114, 116.

240. LTLS, 118.

241. LT, 243.

242. LI, 326.

243. P. Teilhard de Chardin, *Lettres à Jeanne Mortier* (Paris: Éditions du Seuil, 1984), hereafter Mortier; see Mortier, 16. Simone Bégouën, the wife of Teilhard's close friend Max Bégouën, typed Teilhard's essays from 1928 onwards. In 1933 she suggested to cyclostyle them for easier distribution. After organizing this for many years the Bégouën couple moved abroad in 1941. Mademoiselle Mortier then took over the reproduction of Teilhard's writings in a much more systematic manner. Details about the exceptionally close friendship between Teilhard and the Bégouëns can be found in P. Teilhard de Chardin, *Le rayonnement d'une amitié. Correspondance avec la famille Bégouën (1922-1955)*, eds. Michel Hermans & Pierre Sauvage (Bruxelles: Éditions Lessius, 2011).

244. LT, 248f.

245. LT, 257.

246. LT, 260, 261.

247. CU, 244f.

248. LT, 263.

249. See Teilhard's letter in French, quoted in P. Teilhard de Chardin, *Le Phénomène Humain* (Paris: Éditions du Seuil, 1955, facsimile of the original letter in Teilhard's handwriting between p. 24 and p. 25); my translation.

250. LTF, 98.

251. P. Teilhard de Chardin, *The Human Phenomenon*. A New Edition and Translation of Le phénomène humain by Sarah Appleton-Weber with a Foreword by Brian Swimme (Brighton & Portland, OR & Sussex Academic

Press, 1999, hereafter HPh. This is an augmented and much improved edition, different from the first translation into English which became known as *The Phenomenon of Man* (London: Collins, 1959). I am using the new translation of 1999 in this book. For the quotation see HPh, 7.

252. CU, 244.

253. CU, 244.

254. "The Mysticism of Science," HE, 163-181; for the quotations see HE, 177, 180.

255. CU, 225.

256. CU, 208.

257. LT, 261.

258. LT, 265.

259. CU, 240.

260. LT, 273, 283.

261. LTLS, 143.

262. LTLS, 148.

263. See Pierre Leroy's description of his friend Teilhard in his detailed essay "The Man," (the French original reads "Teilhard de Chardin tel que je l'ai connu") that opens the correspondence *Letters from a Traveller* (1962), LT 15-47. The quotations are all taken from Leroy's essay: LT 34, 35, 36.

264. LT, 285, 286.

265. LLZ, 112f.

266. Claude Rivière, *En Chine avec Teilhard de Chardin* (Paris: Éditions du Seuil, 1968), 142; my translation.

267. CU, 248.

268. CU, 246f.

269. LTLS, 179.

270. LT, 290, 291. Some of the major essays from 1939 to 1946 are "The Grand Option," (1939), FM, 37-60; "Some Reflections on Progress," (1941), FM, 61-81; "Christ the Evolver," (1942), CE, 138-150; "Reflections on Happiness," (1943), TF 107-129; "Introduction to the Christian Life," (1944), CE, 151-172; "Centrology. An essay in the dialectics of union," (1944), AE, 97-127; "Christianity and Evolution: Suggestion for a New Theology," (1945), CE 173-186; "The Planetization of Mankind," (1945), FM, 124-139. The diaries which Teilhard left in Beijing on his return to France seem to have got lost and have never been found. The fossils of *Sinanthropos* or Peking Man have also disappeared without a trace. Many theories exist about their disappearance and the search continues; see the engagingly told story by Amir D. Aczel, *The Jesuit and the Skull*.

271. "The Spiritual Contribution of the Far East," (1947), TF, 134-147; the quotations are from TF 134,

141, 145. This essay is discussed in detail in Ursula King, *Teilhard de Chardin and Eastern Religions* (see note 187 above).

272. "The Zest for Living," (1950), AE, 229-243; see AE, 238 for the quotation. AE,

273. LTLS, 195, 196.

274. CU, 247.

275. CU, 262.

276. LTLS, 205.

277. LT, 294f.

278. LTLS, 220. Teilhard speaks of "trust in life."

279. CU, 281, 282.

280. Pierre Leroy, *Lettres familières de Pierre Teilhard de Chardin mon ami 1948-1955* (Paris: Le Centurion, 1976), 25. Hereafter LF; all translations are mine.

281. LTLS, 226, 227, 228, 229.

282. CU, 262, n. 3.

283. LT, 297f.

284. "My Fundamental Vision" (1948), TF, 163-147; the quotation is from TF, 164.

285. LF, 39.

286. LT, 299f.

287. See René d'Ouince, vol. I: *Un prophète en procès: Teilhard de Chardin dans l'église de son temps*; vol. II: *Teilhard de Chardin et l'avenir de la pensée chrétienne* (Paris: Aubier-Montaigne, 1970).

288. TAL, 181.

289. LT, 299.

290. London: Collins, 1966.

291. George B. Barbour, *In the Field with Teilhard de Chardin* (New York: Herder & Herder, 1965), 128.

292. LF, 66.

293. Unpublished letter to Fr. Martindale, December 2, 1948.

294. CU, 246.

295. FM, 141-46f. *passim*; partly my translation.

296. FM, 189f.

297. CU, 264f.

298. LTLS, 95.

299. HM, 16.

300. HM, 47, 55, 57f. Teilhard's mystic love of Christ and his life-long veneration of the "ever-greater Christ" is at the center of his ardent faith, expressed for the last time in the essay "The Christic" (HM 80-102) written shortly before his death. See Ursula King, "'Consumed by Fire from Within': Teilhard de Chardin's Pan-Christic Mysticism in Relation to the Catholic Tradition" in *The Heythrop Journal* 40/4 (1999), 456-477.

301. LTLS, 265, 267.

302. CATL, 47.

303. CU, 307.

304. Mortier, 75, 78; my translation.

305. LF, 98

306. LTLS, 272.

307. LTLS, 275, 276.

308. LT, 41, 42, 43, 44.

309. LTLS, 276.

310. Mortier, 82f.

311. CU, 311f.

312. LT, 331.

313. CATL, 76.

314. LT, 329.

315. LTLS, 280, 283.

316. CU, 330.

317. LF, 201.

318. Mortier, 142.

319. LTLS, 285.

320. LTLS, 285.

321. Mortier, 145f. See "The Stuff of the Universe" (1953), AE, 373-383; "The God of Evolution" (1953), CE, 237-243,

322. "The Singularities of the Human Species" (1954), AM, 208-73. This is an excellent summary of Teilhard's ideas about the evolution of humans as individuals and species. It was published in *Annales de Paléontologie*, XII, 1955.

323. CATL, 52.

324. LTLS, 287

325. LTLS, 286f., 288, 290.

326. CU, 366.

327. Mortier, 161.

328. LTLS, 292.

329. LF, 224.

330. LI, 453; my translation.

331. LF, 246.

332. CU, 385.

333. AE, 405. This quotation is from his essay "The Death-Barrier and Co-Reflection" (1955), AE, 395-406.

334. Mortier, 162.

335. "The Christic" (1955), HM, 80-102. The quotation relates to HM, 83. I have followed the different translation given in an editor's note at the end of *The Divine Milieu*: see MD, 153.

336. HM, 83, 93, 92.

337. HM, 98.

338. HM, 96, 99.

339. HM, 99, 100.

340. HM, 101.

341. LT, 363.

342. Teilhard's last paper was "Research, Work and Worship" (1955), SC, 314-320; the quotation is from SC, 220.

343. LTLS, 293f.

344. CU, 388.

345. It belongs to the Culinary Institute of America.

346. For the last page of Teilhard's diary, dated April 7, 1955, see HM, 104.

347. The full text of "My Litany" is found in CE, 244-245.

348. HM, 102.

349. See Frank Frost Productions LLC in conjunction with Oregon Public Broadcasting, and their important website on "The Teilhard Project": www.teilhardproject.com.

350. Quoted in an unpublished paper by the musicologist Lucy Cradduck, Southampton University, April 21, 2012.

351. Quoted from a leaflet by Paolo Soleri, "Pierre Teilhard Cloister." See also his book *Arcosanti. An Urban Laboratory?* (San Diego, CA: Avant Books and Cosanti Foundation, 1984). More information can be found under www.arcosanti.org. See also Soleri's reflections on Arcosanti as an example of an alternative urban landscape (what he calls "arcology," that is a fusion of architecture and ecology) in his essay "Myriad Specks/ Teasing Grace," in Jerome Perlinski, ed. *The Spirit of the Earth. A Teilhard Centennial Celebration* (New York: Seabury Press,1981), 131-144.

352. See Susan Kassman Sack, "Teilhard in America: The 1960s, the Counterculture, and Vatican II." PhD, University of Dayton, 2014.

353. London & Oakville: Equinox Publishing, 2006.

354. See Paul R. Samson and David Pitt, eds, *The Biosphere and Noosphere Reader. Global Environment, Society and Change*. With a Foreword by Mikhail S. Gorbachev (London and New York: Routledge, 1999).

355. See John A. Grim and Mary Evelyn Tucker, "An Overview of Teilhard's Commitment to 'Seeing' as Expressed in his Phenomenology, Metaphysics, and Mysticism," in Celia Deane-Drummond, ed. *Pierre Teilhard de Chardin on People and Planet* (London and Oakville: Equinox Publishing Ltd., 2006), 55-73.

356. John A. Grim and Mary Evelyn Tucker, "Introduction," in Arthur Fabel and Donald St. John, eds., *Teilhard in the 21st Century. The Emerging Spirit of the Earth* (Maryknoll, NY: Orbis Books, 2003), 8, 9.

Index